Lynne Harne is a lesbian feminist and has [been active in the Women's] Liberation Movement since the early 1970s. She has been a member of Lesbians in Education and the Lesbian History Group and has campaigned, researched and written extensively on issues concerning lesbian mothers and their children. She has a grown-up feminist daughter. She is a policy group member of Rights of Women, and currently works part-time as a women's studies and social policy lecturer at the University of Westminster, and as a freelance researcher and writer.

Elaine Miller is a lesbian and a resilient revolutionary feminist. She was born in 1939 into a mining family in the South Yorkshire coalfield, and graduated in Literature from University College, London, in 1961. A life-long feminist, she discovered lesbian feminism through the Women's Liberation Movement. She was formerly on the London Lesbian Archive collective and was active in the planning and organisation of the Lesbian History Group from 1986 until its dissolution in 1995, contributing to the group's book *Not a Passing Phase: Reclaiming Lesbians in History 1840–1985* (The Women's Press, 1989). She has a chapter in *Volcanoes and Pearl Divers: Essays in Lesbian Feminist Studies* (1995), and has written reviews for several international feminist journals. She is a founder member of RADS, a London-based radical lesbian-feminist group set up in 1995. She has taught on women's studies and literature programmes in further and adult education, and in the University of London Extra-Mural Department. She sees teaching and writing as important forms of feminist activism and is at present researching a biography of Mary Taylor, a Victorian radical feminist.

GENERAL EDITORS
Gloria Bowles
Renate Klein
Janice Raymond

CONSULTING EDITOR
Dale Spender

The **Athene Series** assumes that those who formulate explanations of the way the world works need to know and appreciate the significance of basic feminist principles.

The growth of feminist research internationally has called into question almost all aspects of social organization in our culture. The **Athene Series** focuses on the construction of knowledge and the exclusion of women from the process—both as theorists and subjects of study—and offers innovative studies that challenge established theories and research.

ATHENE, the Olympian goddess of wisdom, was honored by the ancient Greeks as the patron of arts and sciences and guardian of cities. She represented both peace and war, the latter in its cognitive aspect. Her mother, Metis, was a Titan and presided over all knowledge. While pregnant with Athene, Metis was swallowed whole by Zeus. Some say this was his attempt to embody her supreme wisdom. The original Athene is thus twice born: once of her strong mother, Metis, and once more out of the head of Zeus. According to feminist myth, there is a "third birth" of Athene when she stops being an agent and mouthpiece of Zeus and male dominance, and returns to her original source: the wisdom of womankind.

All the Rage

Reasserting Radical Lesbian Feminism

**Lynne Harne and
Elaine Miller, Editors**

Teachers College Press
Teachers College, Columbia University
New York and London

Published in the United States of America by Teachers College Press
1234 Amsterdam Avenue, New York, NY 10027

First published by The Women's Press Ltd, 1996
A member of the Namara Group
34 Great Sutton Street, London EC1V 0DX

ISBN 0-8077-6284-9 (paper)
ISBN 0-8077-6285-7 (cloth)

Typeset in Great Britain by Intype London Ltd
Printed and bound in Great Britain by BPC Paperbacks Ltd

00 99 98 97 96 1 2 3 4 5

contents

SECTION FIVE:

PREFACE

Queer, sado–masochism, lipstick lesbianism together with post–modernism – the system of thought that gives them respectability – have become the highly visible faces of lesbianism in the mainstream today and are all the rage in lesbian communities. *All the Rage* explores the undermining of feminism (the political movement to end the oppression of women) through the currently fashionable representations and practices of lesbianism that urge us to join with the gay boys in playing with gender, embracing the penis and adopting exploitative and objectifying sexual practices towards other women, rather than dismantling the power bases of male supremacy. It looks at how queer theory, therapism, lifestylism and the reconstruction of lesbianism as merely a sexual identity or preference have also served to undermine the original challenge of political lesbianism. This highlighted the importance of valuing women and of solidarity between women, and identified the institution of heterosexuality as key to the maintenance of patriarchal systems.

At the same time this book shows how a new generation of radical lesbian feminists are continuing to connect lesbianism with feminism and are working in coalitions with other feminists to re–assert a radical feminist agenda.

WHERE WE ARE NOW

Radical feminists have struggled down the years against patriarchal control over ourselves and our children, against the use of male violence and sexual abuse in the subordination of women and against patriarchal control over our bodies and minds. Some gains have been made. Radical feminism has put sexual violence and abuse of women and children on the mainstream political agenda. (Alderson 1993)

Domestic violence, for example, is now generally regarded as unacceptable and has become the stuff of which soap operas are made. A number of feminist support services have also been created, such as Women's Aid, Women's Health Information, Rape Crisis Centres, Lesbian Advice Lines and Feminist Legal Services. Feminists have struggled to set up women's centres, housing co-ops, feminist publishing houses and women's bookshops, as well as women's studies and more recently lesbian studies courses. The impact of black feminism and the demand that differences between women be recognised during the 1970s and 1980s has broadened the basis of radical feminism and resulted in numerous feminist campaigns on specific issues among black and white women, and across nationalities, which operate at local and international levels.

Yet any small gains made have always been precarious, and have been continually resisted by male interests and power. (Radford this volume) At a local level autonomous feminist services to women have a constant struggle to survive; there has been very little progress since the 1970s towards actually treating domestic violence as a serious crime. Single and lesbian mothers are under constant attack from the policies of the new right. The abuse and exploitation of women's bodies through sanctioned, militarised rape (such as took place in the wars in former Yugoslavia) prostitution and pornography have become normalised throughout the world.

Such developments make it appear even more bizarre that within western cultures some lesbians are now claiming that the lesbian 'right' to objectify and abuse other women's bodies is radical, transgressive and exciting. Queer cultural theorist Cherry Smyth, (1992) for example, has written that queer enabled her to: 'celebrate the pleasure in objectifying another body . . . to admit that I also love men' and in 1994 she described as 'sheer visual magic' a film in which 'women delight in the romance of cruelty and take pleasure in humiliation'. (Humberstone this volume)

Sarah Schulman, the US queer activist who has a cameo part in the first lesbian slasher movie, recently stated in a popular lesbian life-style magazine that:

I get to slash in the shower and it gets covered in blood. I get to

kill a baby. It's really disgusting . . . It was really, really fun. (!)
(Schulman *Diva* Feb/March 1995)

What these so-called 'bad girl' assertions disguise is that there has
been a continuous struggle between feminist definitions of lesbianism
and those which primarily support the interests of patriarchy, within
both the first- and second-wave feminist movements. (Jeffreys 1993,
Miriam 1993, Miller this volume) While a number of articles in this
collection critique different aspects of queer, one of its most lethal
aspects for lesbians is the notion that the imitation of male sexual
violence (gay or heterosexual) represents a new freedom for lesbians
– the freedom of personal choice. (Reeves and Wingfield, Harne and
Parnarby this volume) In reality the opposite is the case. As the
radical feminist Somer Brodribb has written in her critique of post-
modernism, of which Queer Theory claims to be a part:

What we are permitted, encouraged, coerced into, and rewarded
for, is loving the male sex and male sex: the (real) bad girls are the
ones who don't and who thereby risk men's rage and women's fear.
(Brodribb 1992 p xix)

As with queer, Lesbian Chic is a version of lesbianism that specifically
seeks male approval and that remains unthreatening because it is
based on the idea that women will always want to return to men for
the real thing. (Wilkinson, Humberstone and Hutton this volume) It
is mirrored in a revamped liberal version of heterosexual feminism
that is desperately trying to sell itself as feminine and sexy.

The British magazine *Everywoman* hailed with enthusiasm:

the advent a couple of years ago of a band of lipstick-sporting
young feminists from across the Atlantic . . . most breathed a hearty
sigh of relief and the Establishment rushed to embrace these comely
figures, though with many a whinge that Britain had no feminists
of its own (meaning none whose faces would do justice to the
cover of a Sunday supplement). (*Everywoman* March 1995 p 5)

Everywoman does not despair of Britain, however, since:

Feminism is slowly reinventing itself in a brand new guise and nudging its way into the mainstream. (Ibid)

It is difficult to see what is 'brand new' about lipstick and admiration for youthfulness and cover-girl comeliness. As Nawal el Sa'adawi (1994) has stated:

... lipstick is just another version of the post-modern veil.

As a number of chapters in this book show, radical lesbian feminists who have objected to such regressive moves have been dismissed or attacked and their arguments distorted. Such attacks frequently take the form of accusations that radical lesbian feminists are anti-sex or sexually repressed, or they are described as, 'the new feminist agents of sexual repression'. (Assitor and Carol 1993 p 2) It is hard to see how this differs from attacks made on feminists throughout history; attacks such as those on spinster teachers in the 1920s and 1930s who were arguing for equal pay and equal promotion prospects with men. In an illuminating article on this issue, Alison Oram (1989) records a Dr Williams who, speaking at an education conference in 1935, felt free to express the view that:

The women who teach these girls are, many of them, embittered, sexless or homosexual hoydens who try to mould the girls into their own pattern. And far too often they succeed. (*Daily Herald*, 5 September 1935)

As Mary Taylor, an English Victorian radical feminist, had noted much earlier:

The thick-headed opposition that has made bluestocking and strong-minded woman into terms of abuse, shows that pressure has been applied and that some people do not like it. (Taylor 1870 p 276)

Far from being anti-sex, radical lesbian feminists have put the politics back into sex and forcibly restated that sexual practice and sexual relationships are political, and are not merely a matter of style or sexual preference. Radical lesbian feminism has argued that sexual practice takes place within particular social and historical contexts which are structured by the dominant institutions and controlled by the most powerful forces within our society. The development of lesbian feminism signified a challenge to the patriarchal institution of heterosexuality, to constructions of sexuality as eroticised dominance and submission, to male sexual violence as a means of controlling women, and to the idea that women enjoy being sexually abused. We have stated that sexual desire and pleasure is socially constructed, that it is not some innate or unconscious mechanism that cannot be changed or needs to be fulfilled. We have posed the realities and possibilities of equality in sexual relationships without violence or objectification.

Radical lesbian feminists spent a great deal of time collectively discussing and deconstructing (in a feminist rather than post-modern sense) our own sado–masochistic fantasies and the trappings of sado-masochism and phallocentric culture and analysing and researching how and why this has come to be constituted as sex within western European societies. (For example, Rhodes and McNeill 1985) But, for many lesbians, critically questioning what is represented as sex in our society has ceased. It appears that if lesbians do get together to talk about sexual practice and what constitutes sexual desire it is to reinforce and justify the models provided by heterosexual and gay male culture rather than to challenge them. (For example Smyth 1992) This lack of what was once called collective consciousness-raising among lesbians makes it extremely difficult to challenge such dominant constructions.

The success with which such representations of sexual practices have been received as new, radical and transgressive can be explained partially by the ubiquitous generation gap which Audre Lorde has characterised as 'an important tool for any repressive society'. (Lorde 1984) It is a gap which cuts young women off from history, from understandings and gains already made, dividing the generations rather than strengthening political struggle across them.

Yet this is only one part of the story. The revisionist version of 1970s lesbian feminism as 'the restrictive mother' of lesbian sex has also been put forward by older lesbians who never embraced political lesbianism; just as another version of the myth is that all young lesbians today support and practice sado-masochism. As chapters in this book show, many young lesbians reject it.

Radical lesbian feminists have also been accused of being nostalgic, looking back to the golden decade of the 1970s. According to this version, radical feminist politics are mistakenly perceived as belonging to a particular style or era that is no longer relevant today. On the contrary, while retaining our anger and radical feminist analysis, we recognise only too well that the political context and conditions are very different from the idealistic optimism of the early women's liberation movement, when lesbianism was defined as the 'rage of all women condensed to the point of explosion.' (Radicalesbians 1970)

As a number of these chapters will show, our politics, while holding fast to radical feminist values, are both critically self-reflexive and adaptable to changing conditions. This committed pursuit of long-standing feminist goals together with a receptiveness to new insights that can inform new theories and new strategies for achieving them has been precisely described by Audre Lorde in *Poetry is not a Luxury*. (Lorde 1984) It exactly reflects our own position throughout this anthology because:

> there are no new ideas waiting in the wings to save us as women, as human. There are only old and forgotten ones, new combinations, extrapolations and recognitions from within ourselves – along with the renewal of courage to try them out.

Acknowledgement

We would like to thank Kathy Miriam for the idea for the title of this book.

Lynne Harne and Elaine Miller
June 1995

References

Alderson, L, 'The Failure of the Sensible Agenda', in *Trouble & Strife* No 27, Winter, 1993.

Assiter, A, and Carol, A, *Bad Girls and Dirty Pictures: The challenge to reclaim feminism* Pluto Press, London, 1993.

Brodribb, S, *Nothing Mat(t)ers: A Feminist Critique of Post-modernism*, Spinifex, Melbourne, 1992.

Jeffreys, S, *The Lesbian Heresy: A feminist perspective on the lesbian sexual revolution*, The Women's Press, London, 1994.

Lorde, Audre, 'Age, Race, Class and Sex: Women Re-defining Difference', and 'Poetry is Not a Luxury', in *Sister Outsider*, Crossing Press, Freedom CA, 1984.

Miriam, K, 'From Rage to all the Rage: Lesbian Feminism, Sado-masochism and the Politics of Memory', in I Reti (ed), *Unleashing Feminism*, Herbooks, Santa Cruz CA, 1993.

Oram, Alison, 'Embittered, Sexless or Homosexual: Attacks on Spinster Teachers 1918–1939', in Lesbian History Group (ed), *Not a Passing Phase*, The Women's Press, London 1989.

Radicalesbians, 'The Woman-Identified Woman', in S L Hoagland and J Penelope (eds), *For Lesbians Only – A Separatist Anthology*, Onlywomen Press, London, 1988.

Sa'adawi, Nawal el, 'Thinking and Acting: The Challenge of Global Feminism', Keynote speech, Women's Studies Network UK Annual conference, University of Portsmouth, 1994.

Smyth, C, *Lesbians Talk Queer Notions*, Scarlet Press, London, 1992.

Smyth, C, 'Beyond Queer Cinema: It's in her kiss', in L Gibbs (ed), *Daring to Dissent*, Cassell, London 1994.

Taylor, M, *Miss Miles: A Tale of Yorkshire Life Sixty Years Ago*, Remington & Co., London, 1890, and OUP, 1990.

section one

INDIVIDUALISM, IDENTITY AND THE NEW LESBIANANDGAY CONSERVATISM

This section critiques the conservatism of the gay movement and the gay male politique as the primary model for lesbian activism and identity. It challenges the individualisation that has taken place within the lesbian community in the adoption of therapeutic and psychological models of 'freedom', and critically examines how identity politics within the women's liberation movement have also served to undermine a radical-feminist agenda.

Julia Parnaby's chapter looks particularly at the politics of queer. She demonstrates that the 'in your face radicalism' of the queer movement is in fact no different from old-fashioned liberalism. Queer's main concern is that lesbians and gay men become included in straight society rather than construct a challenge to its patriarchal nature. She points out that queer politics is based solely on a male agenda and critiques the basic anti-feminism of Cherry Smyth's book *Queer Notions*. She expresses the view that the ultimate goal of queer politics is a reversion to heterosexuality and, as such, is a clearly identifiable part of the backlash against lesbian feminism.

Lynne Harne addresses the struggle between lesbians and gay men over the political agenda from the early 1970s in the gay liberation movement, to the present. She emphasises the ongoing differences between an agenda for 'gay' liberation and sexual libertarianism, and a radical lesbian-feminist agenda, located within a movement for the liberation of all women. She traces the history of some aspects of this struggle over the last twenty-five years in Britain, and argues against alliances between lesbians and gay men because, as we learn from history, lesbian feminists lose out and patriarchal power is reinforced.

Celia Kitzinger and *Rachel Perkins* argue that therapy has been a key factor in undermining lesbian-feminist community. They state that the therapeutic framework is antithetical to lesbian feminism because it individualises and psychologises the oppression of women. In particular they demonstrate how therapy has taken over and subverted the language of oppression with the result that the real, material inequality that women experience in their daily lives has become redefined as an individual problem of personal power. Therapy, they argue, has undermined lesbian friendships and allowed lesbians to avoid the responsibility of making moral and political judgements. Finally they suggest that there is a need for the development of a lesbian-feminist politics of madness and an inclusion of 'distressed' lesbians who are currently marginalised.

Sandra McNeill looks at how radical feminism, which set out to address the oppression of all women in its diverse forms, has been undermined by the rise of identity politics. She argues that radical feminism struggled to name male power as a system of oppression, and its main means of control, as male violence and sexuality. She states that while radical feminism attempted to address the way women were differently oppressed by the systems of race and class, this became subverted by identity politics which constructed hierarchies of oppression, 'stifled debate', and meant the end of a broad-based women's liberation movement. She argues that while radical feminists continue to be politically active mainly in single-issue campaigns, there is still a need for a broad-based movement for women's liberation.

JULIA PARNABY

> It has been a long haul back to reclaiming the right to call my cunt, my cunt, to celebrating the pleasure in objectifying another body, to fucking other women and to admitting I also love men and need their support. That is what queer is. (Smyth 1992)

Queer, as a political theory and practice, has been viewed as the 'radical' face of the lesbian and gay movement. Yet in a surprisingly short time, it has become respectable. The popular media has lapped up the language and imagery of queer. Queer cultural theory now abounds in academic books and courses. Queer claims to be a more 'inclusive' politics, but inclusive of whom and of what?

In one of the first British books to address the relevance of queer politics to lesbians, *Lesbians Talk Queer Notions* (1992), Cherry Smyth argued that the new 'radical' queer movement had brought about a transformation in lesbian politics, and provided an alternative to feminism. This chapter focuses specifically on some of the ideas about queer discussed in that book, and looks at the implications these have for lesbians and feminists.

Smyth argues that queer has grown out of AIDS activism in the United States, and from a dissatisfaction with the way lesbians and gay men have previously worked around issues of sexuality and homophobia. Not surprisingly, queer has been quick to take hold in Britain where the agenda is so often set by what goes on in the US. Queer activism is centred around actions which make gays (and supposedly lesbians) more visible in straight society. Outrage is such an activist group, and has employed a number of 'shocking' tactics such as staging a mass lesbian and gay wedding, 'Wink-Ins' and 'Kiss-Ins', designed to highlight the ways in which lesbians and gays are excluded by the British legal system. It is argued that other aspects of queer activism are rather more threatening to both the gay and straight 'mainstream'; in Britain the Manchester group Homocult, who have achieved more than an ounce of notoriety through their 'upfront' poster campaigns and sloganeering, including their infamous 'Paki Poof' images. Even the FROCS 'outing' hoax, which turned queer activism on its head by tempting the homophobic press with its promised revelation of closeted lesbians and gays, only to leave the press foaming at the mouth with a statement about homophobia, and none of the promised star names, was hailed as a triumph for queer tactics. What is clear from reading *Queer Notions* is that the 'in your face radicalism' which is claimed to be the most important signifier of queer, is, in the end, hard to distinguish from plain old liberalism; queer's 'shocking' tactics constitute little more than a plea to be included in straight society, rather than a demand that we change it. Queer demands that lesbians and gays should be allowed to get married *too*, but doesn't question the validity of that institution. It seems clear that in the wake of the backlash around feminism (and indeed socialism), queer as a lifestyle has found its audience.

So why the term 'queer'? Queer – that old-style homophobic insult – has been 'reclaimed', we are told, as a way to remind ourselves of how we are seen in heterosexist society. Smyth quotes Joan Nestle, proponent of butch-femme who says:

> I need to remember what it was like to fight for sexual territory in the time of McCarthy . . . to keep alive the memory that in the 1940s doctors measured the clitorises and nipples of Lesbians to prove our biological strangeness . . . (pp 14–15)

Using terms of hatred is a tool feminists have used in the past for our own purposes, and to help illustrate our arguments; *Trouble and Strife* is one example. However, we do not have the belief that in doing so we have the power to redefine the term's meaning in a wider context, or indeed remove from it its misogynist associations. Neither would feminists wish to advocate that men should continue to use such terms. Reclaiming 'queer' as a name is based on the assumption that doing so strips it of its homophobic power, that it turns the word against the queer-basher, rather than the bashed. It is a direct consequence of post-structuralist arguments around language which claim that the meaning of words are constantly redefined each time they are used by the individuals who use them, and that we can therefore make words mean what we want them to mean. Clearly such arguments remove language from both its historical and social context; in heterosexist society 'queer' cannot be other than abusive, just as in white supremacist society racist insults are statements of hatred, and words like 'bitch' reflect patriarchy's misogyny.

'Queer' is a very specific word; it is not only a term of abuse, but also a term of abuse for *men*. Queer betrays its origins in male politics even as it names itself, and despite Smyth's attempts to claim otherwise her book fails to convince that 'queer' ever did or could include women or could address their concerns. Queer, just like other attempts at mixed movements, has been plagued with accusations of sexism. Attempts to form a lesbian wing of Outrage – LABIA (Lesbians Answer Back in Anger) – failed; indeed, the few lesbian members left in Outrage have consistently had to shout to make themselves heard, and have also been obliged on several occasions to prove their existence in the gay (sic) press, after reports that, exhausted by the misogyny in Outrage, all the women had left.

Radical feminism has long recognised the contradictions of working in mixed movements. Queer, however, tries to make lesbians believe that it is in their interests to ally with gay men. What this fails to comprehend is the way in which patriarchy functions to oppress lesbians. By falsely assuming that lesbians and gay men have shared interests, queer aims to provide an arena where women and men work together to fight men's battles. One of the major demands of Outrage, for example, has been a change in the age of consent laws. Clearly this is an issue which does not affect lesbians, yet queer tries to convince women to join a movement based almost solely on a male agenda. Queer is not an attempt to challenge the very basis of the hetero-patriarchal society in which we live, but rather a campaign for liberal reform to increase the 'rights' of the vocal few. For lesbians to be really free from oppression it is crucial that we engage in struggle for much more fundamental change.

None the less, *Queer Notions* tries hard to present queer as an attractive alternative to feminism in a post-feminist age. Feminism, with its emphasis on fighting patriarchy and heterosexuality as institutions, has – Smyth argues – failed. It has failed because it has not addressed the fact that some women *like* dominant/subordinate relationships; some women *want* to be objectified; and hey – and here she really gets to the point – some women *want to objectify other women*. What can a woman do, if she wants to call herself a feminist, and yet she wants the right to do sexually to women what men have always done? Where can she go? Cherry has the answer – queer:

> The attraction of queer for some lesbians is flavoured by a rebellion against a prescriptive feminism that had led them to feel disenfranchised by the lesbian feminist movement. (p 26)

Lesbian feminism, it seems, has disenfranchised some lesbians through its very analysis of heterosexuality as an institution and men as a class as oppressors of women. What about women who also want to be fucked by men? What about women who want to act like men? Well, queer provides a place for them too: by arguing that it is possible to have sexual relationships with men, yet still call yourself a lesbian. The most integral point seems to be naming oneself (in true post-modern fashion):

> there are times when queers may choose to call themselves heterosexual, bisexual, lesbian or gay, or none of the above. If queer develops into an anti-straight polemic, it will have betrayed its potential for radical pluralism. (p 25)

One can be queer whatever one does and if that's what one chooses to be known as. The concept actually has very little at all to do with lesbian or gay sexuality. As Smyth clearly shows, queer is about breaking down the

> strict binary homo–hetero opposition which still tyrannises notions of sexual orientation (p 12)

One of the most bizarre aspects of queer politics – and one which enables those disenfranchised lesbians who want to do what men do, without feeling guilty – is its emphasis on the importance of 'gender-fuck', a concept most vocally coined by pornographer Della Grace. Gender-fuck means to 'play' with gender, and has resulted in 'lesbian boys' and 'daddy–dykes' – a direct imitation by women of gay male sexuality. Thus lesbianism becomes the poor copycat cousin of male homosexuality:

> In the past two years more lesbians have been discussing their erotic responses to gay male pornography and incorporating gay male sexual iconography into their fantasies, sex play and cultural representations. (p 42)

Here there is no desire for the female, but rather a worship of the penis, second only to that of many gay men. 'Chick with a dick' is the slogan and reality most likely to be adored. For Smyth and her ilk this is the height of queerness.

> Della Grace's photograph, 'Lesbian Cock', presents two lesbians dressed in leather and biker caps, both sporting moustaches and one holding a life-like dildo protruding from her crotch. *In this delicious parody of phallic power, laced with an envy few feminists feel able to admit*, these women are strong enough to show they're women. (my emphasis) (p 43)

The theory buys straight into the age-old Freudian and homophobic arguments that all women are frantic with penis envy, and that lesbian sexuality cannot possibly exist without a penis substitute. This, of course, is a lie.

Perhaps unsurprisingly the logical conclusion of queer politics is a reversion to heterosexuality. The deification of gay men has reached such a peak that the ultimate experience for queers has been sex between 'lesbians' and 'gay men'. This is yet more gender-fuck, dabbling in what is seen to be naughty and unconventional, but really what could be more boring than men and women sleeping together!

The play around butch-femme and gender roles, however, is not a flippant bit of fun. Smyth attempts to pay dues to her 'feminism' by pointing out that:

when lesbians take on behaviour perceived as macho and beat up their femme or lesbian-boy identified lovers in the name of transgression, then it's plain old reactionary chickenshit. (p 44)

However, it is not 'reactionary chickenshit', Smyth believes, if the partner 'consents' to this abuse. Consent is one of the major focuses of queer's position, but there is no understanding of the way such a concept may or may not operate in a hetero-patriarchal society. Consent is not something which is freely given, solely based on an individual's desires. If a person pressurises her or his partner then it may well be the case that she or he gives her 'consent'. It may also be the case that an individual is threatened into a situation; the coercive partner can easily claim that she or he agreed to being tied up or beaten, and she or he will be the one who has the loudest voice. Smyth cannot say that some scenes of abuse are okay if both partners 'agreed' and that others are abusive. It is clear that *all* situations of power inequality are oppressive and must be challenged, not celebrated as some part of queer liberation. We must ask ourselves, liberation for whom?

Queer represents a violent and forceful attack on women who have spoken out about abuse and degradation. Here sexuality is explicitly about power games. Whereas lesbian feminists have questioned the notion that sex is necessarily about dominance and subordination, queer chooses to celebrate and deify such forms of behaviour. It is a reversion to the old libertarian argument that what consenting adults do in private is fine – indeed it is even better if they do it in public shouting 'fuck you!'. Queer politics is the apotheosis of teen rebellion – it's as naughty as we want to be and you can't stop us.

The widespread hysteria around the so-called tyranny of political correctness is a large part of what Smyth has swallowed. Queer claims to be challenging the alleged rampant feminist censorship of the individual right to do just what one likes, as and when one feels like it. Anyone who has been active in radical feminist politics will be painfully aware that radical feminism has *never* had a stranglehold over any part of our hetero-patriarchal society; and to claim that we are the powerful majority denying the libertarians their chance to fuck who and how they like is astounding! Queer, however, is providing a powerful voice for the libertarian community, a voice which says

'Leave us alone – we do what we like without your permission'. In the 'new' lesbian and gay politics if you're not queer then you might as well not exist, and you're certainly not credible or worth listening to.

Queer is a deeply conservative movement. It says nothing can change – we've got to stop believing that it can – we've got to accept the inevitability of our situation, and not try to pretend that the world can change. For Smyth, the most we can aspire to is minor parliamentary reform. For her, the burning issue is:

> With its anti-assimilationist stance, can the queer agenda help to achieve constitutional reform in Britain? (p 56)

In the queer world we learn that power exists and that is all there is to it. Individuals should just choose which side of the power-divide they are on and then get on with acting on it. This, queer argues, is what lesbians and gay men have wanted all along, not the idea that fighting heterosexism ought also to mean fighting the way we oppress people in our own lives. The longstanding feminist position that the personal is political is nothing but an oppressive slogan denying people's right to choose how they have sex, and indeed making them feel guilty about their desires.

In choosing its name, 'queer' gives its politics away: it fails to recognise the reality of the material world we live in and the fact that neither lesbians or gay men can or do live in a vacuum. 'Queer' remains a term of abuse for an oppressed group, and as such cannot form the basis for political action to end homophobia. What queer seems to forget is that we *know* that there has always been hatred and oppression of lesbians and gay men, and we *know* that this continues to this day, and is no less vigorous. We do not need to 'remind' ourselves by using the language of our oppressors. Such language cannot be made to mean something nice simply by re-using the word in a different context. Revolution requires more than this.

Queer has certainly found a niche for itself, and the movement is in the ascendant, but lesbian feminists should be very wary indeed of a system which fails to acknowledge the role that patriarchy plays in oppressing us and which seems almost totally to have rejected feminist arguments. Queer fails seriously to address the ways in which men oppress women, and as long as it continues to be a male-led movement there will never be any serious considerations of issues relating specifically to women.[1]

Cherry Smyth tries her hardest to show that queer *can* appeal to women, but she fails to convince. Queer is far from the revolutionary movement it would like itself to be, it is little more than a liberal/libertarian alliance – neither of which is noted for its commitment to feminist politics. It represents the logical conclusion of 'post- ism'. Post-structuralism means that there are no longer clear gender categories – girls will be boys and boys will be girls – and post-feminism means there's no contradiction in 'feminists' working in a male-led movement for male-defined goals. We know, however, that this is not the case: queer offers us nothing. It is yet one more face of the backlash, trying to pass itself off as something new – we will not be fooled!

This chapter is substantially based on the article of the same name, first published in *Trouble and Strife*, No 26, Summer 1993.

References
Smyth, C, *Lesbians Talk Queer Notions*, Scarlet Press, London, 1992.

[1] Hence the emphasis on AIDS, for example, while breast cancer, which is reaching enormous proportions among lesbians, is never mentioned.

DANGEROUS LIAISONS: REASSERTING MALE POWER THROUGH GAY MOVEMENTS

LYNNE HARNE

This time has been dubbed 'the gay moment' . . . Significantly the unmarried mother and the juvenile delinquent, but not the homosexual have returned as 'social problems' and scapegoats. (Angela Mason, *Stonewall News* Autumn 1993)

This chapter looks at some of the history of lesbians and gay men organising politically together in the last 25 years and contends that far from advancing the interests of lesbians, gay movements have increased male power and misogyny, and the institution of patriarchy has been reinforced. This is in many ways not a new analysis; lesbians and some gay men developed such an analysis in the 1970s. What is significant, however, is what happened to such radical conceptions and how they became undermined so that what exists today is an unthreatening conservative gay movement and gay political agenda that has been effectively assimilated into the existing capitalist and patriarchal order. Instead of accepting this assimilation, I propose that there is a need for the reconstruction of a lesbian political identity and movement which sees and allies itself integrally with radical feminism and in opposition to capitalist patriarchy.

WHERE WE ARE NOW

In the present day, there *appears* to have been a considerable shift in the political position of many lesbians. Once, in Britain and the US, many lesbians joined the women's liberation movement and a political perspective was developed where feminism and lesbianism were seen as inseparable. Today, lesbian and gay interests are represented as inseparable in the lesbianandgay movement, or in more current jargon, the queer movement. The merging of lesbian identity with gay male identity is such that lesbians, if we are to believe all we read and see, have indeed become constructed as 'gay men of smaller growth'. (Jeffreys 1994)

However, many lesbians have not thrown in their lot with gay men but exist in a political wilderness, euphemistically called political diversity. In this political wilderness, the cultural hegemony, i.e. the dominant control by white gay men over the representation of political ideas – is so strong that we are led to believe that the vast majority of lesbians see their interests as the same as those of gay men's.

While this control of representation by the largely white gay male establishment is discussed elsewhere in this volume, I want to emphasise that representation is not reality, even though it undoubtedly has an important influence and effect on political practice. Radical lesbian feminists do still exist, young and old, in small towns, as well as in larger cities. We do still develop theory, and initiate political action, albeit often on single-issue campaigns, and in a fragmented way. However, our ideas, campaigns, and actions are given little space or credence in popular gay culture or within the hegemony of gay academia. It is therefore not surprising that there is no longer a fairly visible radical lesbian-feminist movement. A political movement that cannot positively voice its ideas is unlikely to spread. Of course, the hegemony of gay politics and culture has not participated in this process alone, but has made a contribution to it.

Moreover, radical lesbian-feminism has had a precarious existence during second wave feminism. The strong, activist radical lesbian-feminist movement which developed in the 1970s was not embraced by all lesbians. Some saw being a lesbian as having a particular sexual orientation, one which you were born with. Others saw it as a matter of individual choice and equal opportunity, a choice equal to that of choosing heterosexuality. Both these perspectives have been linked to sexual and life-style constructions of lesbian identity, rather than a feminist construction of lesbianism which recognises the importance of being for women and opposing patriarchal values. (Raymond 1985)

Lesbian identity, as Kathy Miriam (1993) has argued, has always been a contested one, and the current political suppression of lesbian feminism is therefore not an accident. It can be seen as part of the *ongoing* patriarchal resistance to the wider feminist project to eliminate male supremacy, racism and capitalism. The reconstruction of lesbian political identities today, to one of being merely members of a sexual 'minority' movement (along with gay men, bisexuals, paedophiles, and other sexual '*transgressors*') has to be seen within this context. The main political demand of this movement is for freedom to practice and represent the practice of sexualised dominance and submission; in other words, to reflect and reinforce the hierarchical power relations within the dominant culture. As such it can hardly be described as a radical oppositional movement, since its main aim is to be accepted within the dominant culture rather than to change it.

LEARNING FROM HISTORY

The historical reality of an ongoing struggle between a lesbian-feminist political identity and an assimilationist gay or queer identity can be seen in the last quarter-century history of lesbians and gay men attempting to organise politically together. This struggle operates not only at the level of ideology but also reflects the real unequal power differences between lesbians and gay men. Of course this struggle has also gone on at another level between lesbians themselves. Some lesbians have benefited materially from taking on an assimilationist queer identity, either economically or from sexually objectifying and 'doing over' other women. It has also gone on between radical lesbian feminists and heterosexual feminists. These aspects are focused on in other chapters of this book in particular chapter 5.

GAY LIBERATION: 'RADICAL RHETORIC'

It is not inevitable that gay men ally themselves with heterosexual men in the hetero-patriarchy. The gay liberation movement of the early 1970s has been represented by Jeffrey Weeks (1977) as a radical movement which identified 'the roots of gay oppression in the concept of sexism' (p 191). In his account of the Gay Liberation Front in London, Weeks writes how the movement set out not only to assert a gay identity as 'out and proud' and to reject previous constructions of the 'homosexual' as sick and sorry, but also to reject the objectification of people, and the 'meat market' of the commercial gay scene. The cottage was seen as a 'coffin', not as something to be celebrated as part of queer outlawry, as it is today.

> The meat market smells! Drink up and leave the racketeering bars. Pull the flush in the cottage. Have a revolution in your life. (*Come Together* No 6 p 4)

An edition of the GLF newspaper *Come Together* had argued that:

> Women and gay people are both victims of the cultural and ideological phenomenon known as sexism. This is manifested in our own culture as male supremacy and heterosexual chauvinism. (No 2 p 4)

Weeks argues that gay liberation was seen as 'the first step in the cultural de-manning of man'. He also writes about how the GLF Manifesto written by a collective of men and women in 1971 identified the patriarchal heterosexual family, and 'the gender role system of society' as being the basis of gay oppression.

But within two years, the women in the London GLF had left to put all their energies into the women's liberation movement. Some gay men eventually formed Gay Left, others entered into more commercial ventures such as founding *Gay News*, and others joined the less militant and more formally organised Campaign for Homosexual Equality (CHE). (Brackx 1980)

The seemingly radical analysis of GLF, and its perception of an alliance with feminism, appeared to have dissipated, but gay men's and lesbian accounts differed as to why this happened.

Male accounts such as those of Weeks, while recognising the sexism in GLF, suggest that its goals were utopian and idealistic. They emphasise what they call 'the moralism' of GLF in its insistence on the possibility of the voluntary change of gay male life-styles towards the 'cultural demanning of manhood'. (Weeks 1977)

What is missing from these accounts are specifically lesbian experiences and any analysis that what actually happened in the gay movement of the early seventies was a collective refusal by gay men to confront their own sexism and phallocentrism in practice.

Janet Dixon (1988) writing of her experience in London GLF, comments that women were frequently struggling against a 'thinly disguised misogyny'. She states that the key difference which led to lesbians breaking away and joining the women's movement was the issue of sexuality, underlined by the fact that 'lesbians did not want to pick up women in public toilets' as many gay men did. Further, the few men in GLF who did not simply ignore the lesbians, as many did, expected them to raise their consciousness for them. Dixon states that 'once again women were serving men.' Her conclusion is that lesbians like herself abandoned GLF because it ended up as being merely a movement around the freedom to choose and practice your own sexuality.

Anny Brackx writes particularly of the misogyny embodied in the camp and 'radical drag' image that many GLF men had adopted at the time:

> Ceremoniously we went into the crammed hall, declared we'd had enough of their hypocrisy, their youth cult, their camp and their drag – parodies of female oppression, and that we felt that the women's liberation movement was where we belonged. Amidst moans of 'Don't leave us sisters, what will we do without you' we walked out. (Brackx 1980 p 167)

These same themes of misogyny, women servicing men, and differences over sexuality, are echoed by Liz Stanley's detailed account of working in gay movements in the north of England in the 1970s. She in particular emphasises gay men's resistance to feminist challenges to change their sexual behaviour. She challenges the male accounts of gay liberation which represented some men as less sexist than others, and argues that gay men in both GLF and in CHE displayed the same behaviour in resisting the feminist challenge to change their sexual objectification of other men and of women, and in refusing to take any responsibility for this.

Working in CHE as the women's organiser and as part of the CHE women's campaign, and in other gay groups, she describes how male resistance to the feminist challenge took two main but related forms. The first and most obvious form was that of misogyny. This took place as the women's campaign organised to get more women in to CHE and to have autonomous women's groups within the organisation:

> Persistently I and other women in the WCC received complaints that the women in the local groups smelled. This was a feature of all women who literally stank. Women's cunts were suppurating sores, full of crawling worms. They should not be permitted in the same room as men. Lesbians didn't want to have sex with men: this meant they hated men, all men including gay men, and wanted to castrate them. Attempting to get women involved in CHE was an attack on the gay movement, which belonged to men. (Stanley 1982 p 199)

At the same time as women were being vilified for being in CHE at all, they were also attacked for and at times prevented from organising in autonomous groups. Stanley states that what was so threatening to these men was that women were identifying as women, not just as gay, and they were concerning themselves with their own interests rather than those of gay men within the organisation.

The second form of male resistance was to the challenge lesbian feminists were making against men's sexual objectification of other men and of women, and its phallocentric emphasis. She describes how the feminists set out to confront the sexism of gay men in local groups, who would use 'befriending' (a process where a new member was introduced to a gay group) as a means to sexually exploit the new member by having sex with him, even though this was against the stated policy of the group.

Another example she gives of sexual objectification and phallocentrism is how both gay and straight men got off on accounts of obscene phone calls made to lesbians on gay help-lines. She writes:

> what they found arousing was the phallic imagery, the violence and the insistence on 'doing' sex to other people. It was nothing, or only peripherally to do with anything about women in the calls – instead it was the cock, the almighty penis they all reacted to. (Stanley 1982 pp 202–3)

Finally she talks about the double life some gay men in CHE and GLF – who described themselves as feminists – were leading. Overtly these men were supporting the alternative gay social scene and rejecting the meat-market of the commercial clubs. She describes how the lesbians involved in this alternative scene discovered that these 'feminist' men were going to the commercial gay clubs after socialising with the women. When challenged, the men reacted in two ways. Firstly, they suggested that women should challenge the discrimination of gay male clubs so that they too could go to such places. Stanley states that the men deliberately failed to understand that the women did not want to go to them, because of their sexually exploitative practices, and that they did not want the men to go to them. One of the arguments the gay men used when challenged by the lesbian members, was 'that come the revolution, you too sister will be liberated enough to do this'. (This so-called revolution has now taken place!)

Secondly, those men who did realise that it was a contradiction in their politics, avoided taking any responsibility by defining it as a male need – the male need for the 'company' of other men. She quotes a statement from one gay man:

> What may be true, is that, however well individual men get on with individual women, we become misogynists at the point we begin to acknowledge and express our needs as men. It may also be that gay men are no exception to this. Why we are no exception is that our needs as gay men are conditioned by our maleness. (p 208 quoted from Shiers 1979 p 5)

Stanley argues that the male needs that gay men claim they cannot control or take responsibility for, are purely and simply sex, and sex of a particularly phallocentric and objectifying kind. Their resistance to feminism, then, is resistance to a movement which would:

> provide less opportunity for them to fuck each other, and fuck each other over . . . The reaction of all phallo–centric and sexist men to women, who, they fear do not need them as they define themselves – as phalluses on legs.' (Stanley 1982 p 212)

She points out that even though these gay men had the analysis that their 'male needs' were not biological but socially constructed, they argued that they could not take responsibility to change them, since the answer lay outside 'everyday action', and could only be effected by structural change; structural change itself being perceived as something that lay 'outside the behaviours and relationships of everyday life'. (p 208)

She concludes that:

> The use of lesbians in the gay movement is to salvage men from the consequences of their sexism, but to do this in a way that nothing is disturbed and nothing changes. (Stanley 1982 p 212)

Because of experiences like these, many lesbians left the gay movements in the 1970s, and struggled within the women's liberation movement and with other feminists to assert a lesbian identity integrally connected to feminism. The strength of this radical lesbian-feminist movement, as it became in the late seventies and early eighties, enabled it to reject an essentially patriarchal phallocentric and sexually objectifying vision of lesbian identity, and to construct a vision which incorporated feminist values.

> A feminist society . . . would be one in which the essentials of phallocentrism are dismantled. Its achievement would entail the end of the lifestyle of the average, sexist phallocentric gay man. (Stanley 1982 p 212)

No wonder so many gay men resisted such a challenge – it would be far easier and far less threatening to convince lesbians that they too should fight for the equal opportunity to embrace phallocentric culture and the opportunity to do over other women.

EMBRACING THE (MEAT) MARKET

Shiers (1988) writes about how many gay men began in the mid-seventies to develop a new style. This style embraced the expanded commercialisation of the gay scene, which began first in the US and in cities like Amsterdam and Berlin. This commercialisation reflected the economic differences between lesbians and gay men with gay men having higher earning power as men and access to economic resources to set up their own businesses and to support them.

The expanded commercialised gay scene also embraced a new affirmation and worship of masculinity.

Homosexuality had previously been characterised as effeminate. Now the use of leather, military or police uniforms, and increasingly open interest shown in various forms of sado–masochistic sexual practics and in body-building symbolised a big break with past images and concepts . . . . What in essence began to happen was the appropriation of heterosexual male symbolism, and its sexualisation into gay male style. (Shiers 1988 pp 238–9)

He also writes about the increase in casual sex among gay men. This opportunity for increased 'recreational sex', as he describes it, was created by the gay scene newly expanded to pubs and clubs, and an increasingly liberal ideology towards sex in general (what feminists would describe as sexploitation) and more liberal attitudes towards pornography.

Lesbian feminists who attempted to challenge gay men's sexist behaviour during this period, often at gay clubs, frequently experienced threats and physical violence; as well as being forcibly ejected from the clubs themselves.[1]

---

[1]During the 1970s there were few places lesbians could go to socialise separately from men. While lesbian feminists often organised their own social and cultural events and set up their own discos in pubs, these were frequently closed down by misogynist landlords.

Thus gay men had, by the end of the 1970s, become quite easily assimilated into the hetero-patriarchy. Theirs was no longer the politics of opposition, if in practice it ever had been, as Weeks describes it:

First [there was] the gradual merging of the gay movement and the commercial homosexual culture into a new, more open diverse culture – 'the ghetto is coming out'; secondly, the gradual, conditional integration of homosexuality into the mainstream heterosexual culture. (Weeks 1977 p 222)

MUNICIPAL GAYNESS AND ASSIMILATION OF LESBIAN FEMINISM

The early and mid 1980s saw the setting up of local authority women's units, equal opportunities units and a very small number of lesbian and gay units (perhaps not surprisingly there were no lesbian-only units). This municipal context signified an important political moment where the radical agenda of lesbian-feminism was undermined in the promotion of gay rights. As Susan Hemmings writes, of lesbians working with gay men in local authorities:

Lesbians especially did not want to drift into a ready alliance with gay men without careful thought. We were for the most part uneasy: years of experience had shown us that gay men had been largely uninfluenced by feminism. (Hemmings 1988 p 10)

This erosion did not take place without a struggle between lesbian feminists and gay men, and those heterosexual municipal socialists who found the gay agenda less threatening than a radical lesbian feminist one.

My own experience in working for the Greater London Council (GLC) was of fighting a losing battle; we were constrained in our arguments by continual attacks on GLC policies by central government, and we were also up against a powerful (male) gay mafia within the higher echelons of the Council itself, and working with politicians who had little understanding of feminism as a politics. For these politicians everything was conceived as a series of issues, which reinforced notions of distinct separate areas of oppression. There were women's issues, black people's and ethnic minority issues, disability issues, and lesbians were frequently lumped together with gay men so that there were lesbianandgay issues. Thus the GLC was both influenced by, and in its turn influenced and reinforced the growth of, identity politics, in which feminism as a political force began to get lost. (Bindel this volume)

One example was over the development and use of the concept of heterosexism. In the GLC the term heterosexism became used to describe discrimination against lesbians and gay men equally, and was enlisted to support civil rights arguments. It lost its original radical meaning, which had been developed by radical lesbian feminists in the US and taken up elsewhere to describe 'the institution of compulsory heterosexuality' as a key means of male supremacy. (Bunch 1976, Rich 1980)

In writing about the connection between lesbian-feminism and heterosexism in 1976 Bunch stated:

> Lesbian feminism, however, is far more than civil rights for queers or lesbian communities and culture. It is a political perspective on a crucial aspect of male supremacy – heterosexism, the ideological and institutional domination of heterosexuality. (p 436)

A further problem was that gay men within the authority were arguing that homosexuality was natural, whilst the lesbian-feminists stated that all sexuality was socially constructed; a difference that was to resurface in the struggle over Clause 28.

'CLAUSE 28' – PROMOTION VERSUS TOLERANCE

The introduction of legislation in Britain to prevent the 'promotion of homosexuality' by local authorities, has been represented in gay accounts as a reaction to the AIDS crisis, and as an attack on gay (male) rights which were being addressed by some left-wing authorities. (Mason 1994) Some accounts go even further than this and argue that Clause 28 was just an excuse to reduce the powers of left-wing local authorities. (Healey and Mason 1994)

These accounts 'disappear' the challenge that radical lesbian feminism was making to male power within the family. This challenge included lesbian mothers' campaigns which asserted that children did not need fathers, and campaigns against male sexual abuse of children. They also 'disappear' the fact that lesbian feminists were promoting lesbianism as a positive choice for women. (Alderson and Wistrich 1988)

While the GLC was busy trying to reassure liberals that their support for lesbian and gay rights was no more than the support for an individual sexual preference, not surprisingly the Tories didn't see it that way. Not surprisingly, it was the way the GLC Women's Committee had taken up lesbianism that appeared most threatening.

The *Daily Mail* reported:

Militant GLC feminists are said by the Tories to be launching a £700,000 campaign dedicated to proving to women that heterosexuality can chain, fetter and oppress our lives . . .

Describing GLC feminists as 'woman haters' and using the headline HATE it went on:

Because they concentrate their energy and venom trying to abolish everything that is enriching, (sic!) entrancing, fun and innocently frivolous in our lives.

They've already worked themselves into hate over pretty models in bras and suspenders on the Underground, tried to get beauty contests banned and want to install women watch-dogs in factories to censor and preferably sack any man who dares to wink at a female colleague. (The Linda Lee Potter page, *Daily Mail*, 7 Nov. 1984)

Was this the beginning of the derogatory use of the term 'political correctness' in Britain? It was certainly a reaction against many of the feminist achievements of the GLC Women's Committee, such as getting pornographic advertising banned on the underground and trying to tackle sexual harassment in the workplace. It was the GLC's Women's Committee support for black lesbians, lesbians with disabilities and lesbian mothers, black and white, which was particularly vilified by the gutter press. After the abolition of the GLC it was lesbian-feminist groups such as Lesbians in Education and the Rights of Women Lesbian Custody Project that continued to push for positive representation of lesbian households with children in schools.[2] It appeared to be specifically lesbian mothers who were under attack in Section B of the Clause (now section 2A.1.b. Local Government Act, 1988) which stated that:

> A local authority shall not . . . promote the teaching in any maintained school of the acceptability of homosexuality as a pretended family relationship.

As Lynn Alderson has pointed out, the campaign against the Clause probably saw the biggest coalition of lesbians and gay men ever in this country; but the dominant perspective of the campaign was not to see it as a hostile reaction by the New Right to the limited gains that radical feminism had made in challenging male power within the family.

Rather, the main focus was on the attack made on individual lesbian and gay civil rights and many of the arguments used to combat them were essentialist ones. Echoing gay men in the GLC, points were made by MPs and public figures in the campaign which emphasised 'the naturalness of homosexuality'.

> We are as we are, we can't help it, you must accept and tolerate it on this basis, i.e. we are not a threat to you. (Alderson 1988 p 5)

The result was an obscuring of radical feminist analysis which sees lesbianism as '*a positive choice* for women' and 'carries with it a devastating critique of male power and its manifestation in heterosexual relations and society.' (Alderson p 5)

Those lesbian–feminist groups which organised separately from

---

[2]These campaigns were initially targeted at the Inner London Education Authority (ILEA) which had set up a 'sexuality' project to address the issue of 'homosexuality' for young people. Again, however, this project operated within a sexual preference perspective, rather than a feminist one. This perspective was challenged by lesbian-feminist youth workers in particular.

Gay accounts often suggest that it was the book *Jenny Lives with Eric and Martin* which was put on a resource list by ILEA, that caused the focus of the Clause on 'pretended families'. This was only one example in a series of events, that highlighted the New Right's concern with the undermining of patriarchal power within the heterosexual family.

mixed Clause groups, did not use essentialist rationales. In some parts of Britain, where there had been a strong lesbian-feminist presence for many years, the anti-clause campaign was led by lesbian feminists.

But many of the lesbian-feminist groups toned down their arguments, adopting an identity politics approach, and focusing on arguing against discrimination for specific groups of lesbians. Few of the leaflets produced at the time emphasised lesbianism as a positive choice or identified the Clause as part of an anti-feminist backlash specifically.[3]

While those of us involved as lesbian feminists in this coalition believed we were being tactical, in retrospect this was a serious mistake. Taking a more liberal approach did not stop the Government from passing the Clause; all it did was to reinforce an idea of lesbianism as a purely sexual identity unthreatening to the hetero-patriarchy.

Ultimately, the coalition promoted a sense of false unity between lesbians and gay men, and only served to reinforce an agenda based on gay-male interests. It also encouraged many lesbians who had never taken political action before to see the way forward as organising with gay men.

SERVICE AND SUBORDINATION – GAY AIDS ACTIVISM AND THE GAY AIDS INDUSTRY

The issue of AIDS has also had the effect of drawing in lesbians to work with gay men. Since the mid 1980s in Britain the AIDS crisis has been the impetus for increased political activism by gay men and some lesbians; initially through left gay politics, and more recently through groups like ACT UP and within queer politics. Significantly a whole gay AIDS industry has also been created, connected with the new ideology of safe sex.

At first glance, it is surprising that some lesbians have regarded gay AIDS activism as unproblematic. Undoubtedly lesbians experienced increased violence, hostility and discrimination as a result of AIDS

---

[3]In researching this chapter I ploughed through hundreds of leaflets on the Clause, held at the Lesbian Archive. I found only one (unattributed) which specifically mentioned the Clause as an attack on feminism

being represented as the 'gay plague' in the early and mid 1980s. But the extent to which some lesbians have been prepared to service gay men and take part in gay AIDS activism has meant that lesbian interests have been increasingly sacrificed. Gay AIDS activism has unleashed new forms of male power and of male control of lesbians.

While gay men have appeared to be happy to have lesbians acting in a servicing role and promoting AIDS as a gay issue, their misogyny towards lesbians seems to be largely unchallenged. Many gay men regard lesbians working within gay AIDS activism as having 'virus envy'. In other words these lesbians are viewed as wishing they were gay men and could get AIDS too! Nor does there appear to have been reciprocal support from gay men for health issues which affect us most as women in Britain. Women's lives are not as important as men's, it seems.

A radical feminist perspective sees the AIDS issue in a global feminist context, linked to women's struggles against compulsory heterosexuality internationally. In this perspective the struggle against AIDS is also about women's resistance to the spread of AIDS through the exportation of sex tourism and prostitution by western imperialist patriarchal powers, and support for women from the so-called third world who are the fastest growing victims of the disease.

The AIDS crisis offered particular opportunities for gay men to critique and change their own phallocentric and sado-masochistic sexual practices; to develop a different gay identity not solely constructed on sex and the worship of masculine values. However, the reverse appears to have happened. The construction of 'safe sex' has promoted even more bizarre forms of phallus worship and sado-masochism; a trend which began in the US, and was later exported elsewhere.

While some people have opted for monogomy or chastity, the signs are that new forms of recreational sex which are safe but still raunchy are emerging. Sex over the phone has become a major gay American pastime. Jack-off parties, where groups of men meet to explore fantasies with each other, are replacing the dark backrooms and potentially risky bathhouse sex scenes. (Shiers 1988 p 243)

EQUAL OPPORTUNITIES AND SAFE SEX

The construction of safe sex created a new marketable pornographic product for gay men but it also created an opportunity to market 'safe sex' to lesbians. Firstly, lesbians had to be persuaded in true marketing fashion that lesbian sexual practices were 'unsafe', and that they needed to protect themselves. This spawned a whole industry of dental dams and 'female condoms'. How many lesbians were taken in by this marketing ploy is not clear; certainly no one I know rushed out and bought these products.

Secondly, as Sheila Jeffreys has pointed out, it also created an opportunity to promote a mirror image of gay male sex to lesbians. Objectifying, phallic, sado-masochistic practices could be represented as 'safe sex' and provide pornographic representations of what lesbians do as sex; at the same time promoting this as adventurous and exciting.

The gay 'safe sex' industry provided a golden moment to promote the 'equal opportunities' approach to sexual practice for lesbians; an approach that some gay men had wanted lesbians to adopt years earlier.

COME THE REVOLUTION, SISTER, YOU TOO WILL BE LIBERATED ENOUGH TO DO THIS

Some lesbians have benefited materially from the 'safe sex' industry; from the promotion of lesbian pornography; from selling sex to lesbians; from objectifying and doing over other women. But the invention of 'lesbian safe sex' has also reversed the meaning of lesbian sexuality as constructed within a lesbian–feminist context. Lesbian feminists have long argued that lesbian–feminist sexual practice *is* safe sex. Practised within a context of equality, it does not involve violence or abuse; nor does it carry the health risks of heterosexual sex for women, such as increased risks of cervical cancer, having to use risky contraception such as the pill, or risks from unwanted pregnancies.

The new 'safe sex' is in *reality* what is harmful to lesbians, because it encourages them to *actually* abuse (not in fantasy, or in play) their own bodies; to despise themselves as women; to feel that in order to create desire between women, they have to reconstruct themselves as pseudo gay men, as 'phalluses on legs'. The adoption of this 'equal opportunities approach' to lesbian identity, equal to that of gay men, is a deeply reactionary strategy. It smacks of the 'if you can't defeat them, join them' philosophy that has been the downfall of so many political movements.

The queer movement has gone one step further than this, by advocating that lesbians have sex with men. This is, after all, the logical step in phallus worship and completes the final assimilation of lesbians into the hetero-patriarchy.

QUEER VERSUS WOMEN'S LIBERATION

Frankly my dears, I couldn't care less if men choose to nail their dicks to a plank, I only wish they'd all do it. But SM dykes, posing as sexual outlaws and claiming to be radical, are merely a big yawn. What hasn't changed since the sixties is that lesbian politics mean nothing if they are not seen in the context of the liberation of all women . . . (Langford 1993)

Today in Britain we are left with two highly visible conservative male-dominated gay organisations, both with very similar political agendas. Stonewall was created as a professional lobbying group in the aftermath of the anti-Clause campaign. Its mission is:

to bring about legal equality for lesbians and gay men by putting our arguments in terms that parliament and policy makers understand. (!) (*Stonewall News* 1993)

The agenda of Outrage, which likes to present itself as the 'radical tendency', because it advocates non-violent direct action, also goes no further than a liberal framework for lesbian and gay civil rights, as can be seen from its aims, which are to:

- assert the dignity, pride and human rights of lesbians and gay men

- fight homophobia, discrimination and violence against lesbians and gay men
- affirm the rights of lesbians and gay men to sexual freedom, choice and self-determination. (quoted in Smyth 1992 p 17)

At the time of writing one of the most recent 'radical' actions of Outrage was to demonstrate against a ban on nude sunbathing for men on Hampstead Heath!

But in practice it is far worse than this, because both organisations have proved themselves to be deeply anti-feminist and as a consequence have taken actions and supported legislation which have increased male power over women. An example of this has been support for the legalisation of buggery within heterosexual relationships. Such legislation only serves to legitimise further the sexual abuse of women.

Stonewall has to date concentrated almost exclusively on gay male rights; focusing most of its energy on trying to equalise the age of consent law for gay men to that of heterosexuals. On the other hand its support for lesbian rights has been conspicuous by its absence. This was evidenced in the lack of any visible support, either in terms of cash or in public statements, for a lesbian-feminist headteacher, who was victimised by a local authority for her school-based anti-heterosexist equal opportunities policies.

Outrage recently proposed an age of consent campaign for lesbians. Such a proposal fails to acknowledge that such an age of consent for lesbians, equal to that of heterosexuals, already exists. But in any case this kind of campaign would not only worsen the situation for lesbians, but would only serve to reinforce a construction of lesbian identity in the image of gay men.

These examples highlight how problematic civil liberties strategies are for feminists. As Marilyn Frye (1983) has pointed out, civil liberties arguments within the current patriarchal context are based on ideas of male citizenship. Male standards and values define what the concepts of citzenship are, and most importantly male rights that are at stake. When these male rights are threatened by the assertion of women's rights (for example the rights of women not to be sexually exploited in pornography and prostitution) then it is male rights which are asserted and defined as civil liberties.

At the time of writing, a number of lesbians in Britain are once again breaking away from male-dominated gay organisations. Following the example of lesbians in the US, some lesbians have set up Lesbian Avengers groups. Lesbian Avengers define themselves as 'a non-violent direct action group committed to raising lesbian visibility and fighting for lesbian rights.' (*Everywoman*, Nov. 1994) It remains to be seen whether British Lesbian Avengers will ultimately reject the queer agenda and adopt a more feminist perspective.

But queer politics is not only conservative in its mimicry of heterosexual culture and its male defined agenda; like other libertarian movements before it, it equates liberation with the endless pursuit of sexual pleasure and tells us – this is all there is. This is an escape from radical politics. Lesbian feminists spent a lot of time in the early 1970s talking about and pursuing 'sexual fulfilment', but have fairly quickly moved beyond this: we realised it was a dead end. Having better orgasms wasn't going to change the world: changing the world involves fighting for the liberation of all women. This is a very long-term project, and not a 'fashionable' one. While the queer agenda will soon cease to be fashionable, radical lesbian-feminist politics will continue. The key issue now is not just about how lesbian feminism has been disappeared by the queer agenda, but how in these pessimistic times we can continue to contribute to the reconstruction of a broad, radical autonomous women's liberation movement; a movement that actively challenges the material poverty, racism and violence that is the reality of the majority of women's lives globally.

References

Alderson, L, In L Alderson and H Wistrich, 'Clause 29: Radical feminist perspectives', *Trouble and Strife* No 13, 1988.

Brackx, A, 'Prejudice and Pride', in Feminist Anthology Collective (eds), *No Turning Back. Writings from the Women's Liberation Movement 1975–80*, The Women's Press, London, 1980.

Bunch, C, 'Learning from Lesbian Separatism', *Ms Magazine* Vol 5, No. 5. Nov 1976, reprinted with additional material in Karla Jay and Allen Young (eds), *Lavender Culture*, Harcourt, Brace, Janovitz, New York, 1978.

Dixon, J, 'Separatism: a look back at anger', in B Cant and S Hemmings (eds), *Radical Records. Thirty Years of Lesbian and Gay History*, Routledge, London, 1988.

Everywoman November 1994 'Lesbian Avengers fight for equality'.

Frye, M, *The Politics of Reality: Essays in Feminist Theory*, Crossing Press, New York, 1983.

Greater London Council and GLC Women's Committee *Tackling Heterosexism. A Handbook of Lesbian Rights*, 1986.

Healey, E, and Mason, A, *Stonewall 25*, Virago, London, 1994.

Hemmings, S, Introduction in B Cant and S Hemmings (eds), *Radical Records*, Ibid.

Jeffreys, S, *The Lesbian Heresy. A feminist perspective on the lesbian sexual revolution*, The Women's Press, London, 1994.

Langford, D, 'For a lost warrior', in *Shebang*, Issue 6 Oct/Nov 1993, Gay Community Press, London.

Mason, A, 'From the Director's Desk', in *Stonewall News* Autumn 1993, Stonewall, London.

Miriam, K, 'From Rage to all Rage: Lesbian Feminism, Sado-masochism, and the Politics of Memory', in I Reti (ed), *Unleashing Feminism: critiquing Lesbian Sadomasochism in the Gay Nineties*, Herbooks, Santa Cruz, 1993.

Rich, A, 'Compulsory Heterosexuality and Lesbian Existence', in *Signs. Journal of Women in Culture and Society*. Vol 5, No 4, 1980, reprinted by Onlywomen Press, London, 1980 reprinted 1981.

Smyth, C, *Lesbians talk Queer Notions*, Scarlet Press, London, 1992.

Shiers, J, 'One step to heaven?', in B Cant and S Hemmings (eds), *Radical Records*, Ibid.

Stanley, E, 'Male needs. The problems and Problems of Working with Gay Men', in S Friedman and E Sarah (eds), *On the Problems of Men: two feminist conferences* The Women's Press, London, 1982.

Weeks, J, *Coming Out. Homosexual Politics in Britain, from the nineteenth century to the present*, Quartet, London, 1977.

SHRINKING LESBIAN FEMINISM: THE DANGERS OF PSYCHOLOGY FOR LESBIAN-FEMINIST POLITICS

RACHEL PERKINS AND CELIA KITZINGER

At the beginning of second-wave feminism it was common for feminists and lesbians strenuously to oppose psychology and therapy as instruments of hetero–patriarchal control. Back in 1970, Barbara Leon of Redstockings described how 'the field of psychology has always been used to substitute personal explanations of problems for political ones, and to disguise real material oppression as emotional disturbance'. Other feminists characterised psychology as 'a pseudo scientific buttress for patriarchal ideology and patriarchal social organisation' (Weisstein 1970), and as 'a myth to keep women in their place' (Hanisch 1971). In her groundbreaking book *Women and Madness* Phyllis Chesler (1972) documented the extent of women's oppression at the hands of psychology.

Despite these criticisms, the last twenty years have seen the development of what have been described as 'lesbian' and 'feminist' psychologies and therapies. Now many feminists enthusiastically embrace psychological models of understanding and feminist writers, who once spoke in very different terms, increasingly employ psychological explanations of political phenomena. External structures of male supremacy are ignored when feminists argue that responsibility for our oppression lies, in the words of Ros Coward's book title, with 'our treacherous hearts'. She argues that 'women have enough opportunity, experience, and dare I say it, power to demand great changes. But they have not done so . . . The reasons for this passivity lie . . . in aspects of the male and female psyche'. (Coward, 1992, p 13) Similarly, it is now 'Revolution From Within' which preoccupies Gloria Steinem (1992) – her book of this title was number one on *The New York Times Book Review*'s best-seller list and sold nearly 17,000 copies in hardback within the first three months of publication.

Once feminists and lesbians set ourselves up in clear opposition to psychology. Now, all too often, psychology and therapy are part of what passes for feminism. And so invidiously have they insinuated themselves into feminist thinking, that many now speak in psychological or therapeutic terms without any awareness that they are doing so. Self improvement goals like feeling better about oneself, surviving one's toxic family, raising one's self-esteem and loving one's inner child, have taken over from the political goals of radical lesbian and feminist politics. As Diane Hamer (1990), an Australian lesbian feminist living in London, points out 'more and more of us are going into therapy and it is almost becoming unfashionable not to be in it'. In the United States three out of four lesbians have been 'in therapy' at some point in their lives (Lyn 1991), and an increasing number of lesbian/feminist authored psychology and therapy books are to be found in women's bookshops and many lesbians' bookshelves. Psychology's influence extends beyond those in therapy and self-help groups: many feminists now think about themselves in purely *psychological* terms. Psychology is rapidly replacing feminism as a way of understanding the world.

We are both lesbians, both feminists, and both fully qualified psychologists, but we do not call ourselves 'lesbian–feminist psychologists' because we do not believe that it is possible to practice a psychology compatible with our lesbian–feminist goals. In this chapter we argue that psychology and therapy are destructive of the lesbian-feminist enterprise. Our critique is not primarily of hetero-patriarchal psychology – many feminists have documented the oppressive nature of the psychology done by men. Nor is it primarily a critique of *heterosexual* feminist psychology. Although some of the feminist psychologists we quote are (as far as we know) heterosexual, we have included reference to their theories and therapies only when we see their work as having been influential for lesbians, for example with the work of the London Women's Therapy Centre. On the whole, our focus is on that psychology and therapy which describes itself as both feminist and lesbian: we use the descriptor 'lesbian/feminist psychology' to mean psychology that claims to be, or is widely accepted as, lesbian, or feminist, or both, and which appears to us to have been influential upon lesbian/feminist communities.

Much so-called feminist psychology is obviously flawed by overt anti-lesbianism or unexamined heterocentricity. Likewise, much so-called lesbian/feminist psychology is easily criticised for its commitment to a white, middle-class Anglo-American vision of the world, its trite platitudes presented as revealed truths; it dilutes and misinterprets feminism in the service of establishment goals. But the problem is more than that of a few bad lesbian-feminist psychologists: rather psychology itself seems profoundly antithetical to lesbian feminism.

Our concern is not with those erudite forms of psychology that stay within the confines of academe; those elitist games and postmodern obfuscations that are largely meaningless outside the university setting. We are concerned about the psychology that is infiltrating lesbian/feminist communities and politics, the psychology that is today becoming what passes for feminism.

We are not concerned with how to make lesbian/feminist psychology *better*, nor with demarcating the differences between 'good' and 'bad' lesbian psychologists, or distinguishing between the 'real' lesbian/feminist therapists and the charlatans. We acknowledge that in criticising the very idea of lesbian/feminist psychology we have lumped together people who would probably rather not be bracketed together – many of them have expressed misgivings about each other. For example, Laura Brown (1990) criticises co-dependency groups (but promotes individual psychotherapy) and Luise Eichenbaum (1987) criticises self-help guides but writes her own best-selling psychology books from an object relations perspective. Of course it matters *how* therapy is done – the perspective and approach taken – but it also matters *whether* therapy is done. We are concerned with therapy as a cultural phenomenon, not as a set of clinical techniques. We address a fundamental question about the compatibility between lesbian/feminist psychology and lesbian/feminist politics.

Much of the work that we cite is of North American origin. This is because most of the world's psychologists and therapists inhabit that small portion of the globe. North America is the capital of psychology, with more professional therapists than librarians, fire fighters or mail carriers, and twice as many therapists as dentists or pharmacists. Although psychology is a rampantly North American product the rest of the world is catching up. Opening a recent issue of *Lesbian London* we found seventeen advertisements for lesbian therapy – more entries than for any other category including housing, services, holidays, courses, contacts, and even 'love and lust'!

We are not denying that lesbian/feminists suffer. Neither are we saying that therapists or those who seek therapy are bad people. We know that many lesbians experience terrible emotional pain, but we are very concerned that labelling it 'merger', or 'codependency', or 'internalised homophobia' or 'erotophobia' (or whatever other label is currently fashionable) simply makes the underlying problems more difficult to address. As lesbian feminists we want to acknowledge the existence of personal problems that need to be addressed here and now (they are not simply going to disappear 'after the revolution'), but to do so from a political rather than from a psychological or therapeutic framework. It is possible to argue that not all of those we cite are lesbians, feminists, or properly qualified therapists. None the less their work passes for lesbian/feminist psychology in the English-speaking world. It may not be 'really' lesbian, 'really' feminist or 'really' therapy, but its effects on our lives are real enough.

PSYCHOBABBLE OR LESBIAN-FEMINIST POLITICS

Psychological language and concepts are steadily invading lesbian/feminism. Words and phrases like 'codependent', 'self-parenting', 'merger', 'processing', 'being centred' and 'being in recovery' are now part of many lesbians' vocabularies. Lesbians speak to each other about 'healing', 'getting in touch with our needs', 'discovering our erotic archetypes' or 'dealing with our own stuff so as not to dump it on others'. Instead of having opinions, we now 'have energy around some issues', instead of agreeing with another's views we 'feel comfortable' with them, and instead of disagreeing we 'can't relate to that'. Unlike words such as 'sexism' or 'sexual harrassment' which were new words invented by lesbians and feminists to describe our experience of the world, this new language is borrowed directly from male-led cults of humanistic and existential psychology via lesbian/feminist psychologists.

Language does more than provide a convenient label for the world. The words that we use to talk about our experience reflect and constitute our politics. The phrase 'father–daughter rape' carries a set of political implications quite different from phrases like 'intergenerational sex'. To call us 'lesbians' is to make one kind of political statement, to call us 'gay women' is to make quite another. Language is important. As Mary Daly (1978) has shown, the power of naming is to define the quality and value of that which is named and to deny the reality of that which is not named.

Lesbian/feminist psychology has influenced language in three ways. First, psychology has redefined existing political words like 'power', 'choice', 'revolution' and 'liberation' in psychological terms. Second, psychology has invented new words like 'merger', 'codependency' and 'homophobia' to give us psychological explanations for our lives. Third, psychology has banned some words altogether. Words like 'should', 'ought', 'right' and 'wrong' are seen as evidence of coercive authoritarianism to be replaced with psychological relativism.

This new psychologised language is incompatible with the *political* language of lesbian/feminism. Take, for example, the word 'power'. As lesbian/feminists we want power. By 'power' we mean economic power, the power to prevent male violence against women, the power to speak and be heard, the power to define our experience of the world. As lesbian/feminists we know that, even under male domination, we are not completely powerless. We have power over those weaker than us (children, for example); we can exercise power, of a sort, over men when we use 'feminine wiles' to get our own way. As a group, we have the power to protest, to picket, to march, the power of sabotage. We have the power to withdraw consent, refuse male definitions of us and our realities, separate ourselves and construct our own alternative versions. These are real powers; but we do not have the kind of power men have to the same extent that men have it. The power of women and lesbians exists within the framework of male–domination and the institution of compulsory heterosexuality. The rules are made by white ruling-class men – women and lesbians sometimes have the power to break, evade or protest against those rules. Those powers are not symmetrical.

Psychology claims to offer women and lesbians power. Real power, power as good as men's, but a special 'female' version – equal but different. This power lies not in laws or governments or institutions, but within us. 'Power' within this psychological reformulation means getting in touch with our authentic, natural female self, the inner child, a free spirit supposedly untouched by social oppression, which can spontaneously generate its own actions and free choices. Power, according to this psychological definition, means reclaiming an elemental inner self. We already have 'power': what psychology does is to help us recognise it and claim it as our own. As lesbian therapist Laura Brown, says:

> part of what I do with the people I work with in therapy is to point out to them that they are already powerful in ways that the culture does not define as being powerful. (quoted in Malina 1987)

Or in the words of Louise Hay (1984a), author of the best-selling *Heal Your Body*:

> No person, no place and no thing has any power over you, for you are the only thinker in your own mind. You are the creative power, and you are the authority in your life.

All that is necessary is to get in touch with this inner power by pursuing psychological programmes which enable us to 'feel more comfortable about being powerful'. (Chaplin & Noack 1988 p 226)

This psychological redefinition of power as a sense of personal agency quite unrelated to the objective and material facts of our lives results in a great deal of victim–blaming. At its most extreme, psychology claims that we have total power over our own lives because we create our own reality.

Louise Hay (1984b) argues 'It is my belief that we are each one hundred percent responsible for every experience in our lives – the best and the worst.' If women are so powerful then it is our own fault if, for example, we get raped or attacked. Morris (1990), writing in *New Woman* magazine, describes psychological research which shows that women who get raped have projected the wrong image – 'a victim look' – because they have the wrong kind of beliefs about power. Power, she argues, is internal – a belief in yourself, not something that you exert on the world outside: 'a victim is someone who feels she doesn't have power.' Women who 'attract' rapists lack the proper mental set.

These victim–blaming accounts are permitted and encouraged when lesbian/feminist psychologies focus on 'empowerment'. In much lesbian/feminist psychology the word 'empowerment' is a great deal more common than the word 'power': empowerment means 'acting as agents or advocates to the process of redefining, experiencing and realizing one's own power.' (Hawxhurst and Rodekohr, cited in Kramarae and Treichler 1985 p 137) Empowerment means redefining the word power in such a way that we feel we've already got some of it. It attempts to create in women a state of feeling powerful *while leaving structural conditions unchanged*.

We need to be clear that women and lesbians do *not* have the powers of psychologists' fantasies. When thinking about the meaning of the word 'power' in relation to rape and sexual assault we need to recognise for the fantasy it is any notion that we brought it on ourselves by not saying 'no' confidently enough (see Kitzinger 1990) or by projecting a 'victim look'. We are victims of male sexual violence and this happens to us against our will and despite the choices we make (Fritz 1979; Spender 1984; Jo, Strega and Ruston 1990). Women's powerlessness is a *reality* that psychologists attempt to obscure and deny by focusing on 'empowerment' and representing power as an internal individual possession.

Lesbians and feminists say that we want power – economic power, power to prevent male violence against women, power to define our own experience of the world in our own terms. But 'power' in its psychological manifestation is already ours – a sense of personal agency just waiting to be tapped. Psychology has redefined power in privatised and individualised terms that are antithetical to radical lesbian politics.

Unlike 'power', *homophobia* was never a lesbian/feminist term, although it is now widely used in lesbian/feminist communities. It is a term that was invented by a psychotherapist (Weinberg 1973) and defined as 'an irrational persistent fear or dread of homosexuals'

(MacDonald 1976). Fear of lesbians is considered as irrational a fear as that of spiders. Lesbians are essentially harmless. This translation of anti-lesbianism into an irrational fear is completely at odds with radical feminist theory. What happened to the belief that lesbians are a radical challenge to hetero-patriarchy, a threat to male supremacy?

Moreover, while it may be convenient to label one's political enemies as mentally ill – homophobic – to do so removes the argument from the political arena and relocates it in the domain of psychology. This reinforces psychology's power to label people as 'sick' or 'mentally healthy' at will. It also depoliticises oppression by suggesting that the oppression of lesbians comes from the personal inadequacy of particular individuals who supposedly deviate from the rest of society in being prejudiced against lesbians. The political goal of overthrowing hetero-patriarchy is translated into a call for the mass treatment of homophobia'. (For a more detailed analysis see Kitzinger 1987a&b; Kitzinger 1993; Kitzinger and Perkins 1993.)

The invention of the term 'homophobia' also laid the groundwork for the invention of two further terms: 'heterophobia' and '*internalised* homophobia'. 'Heterophobia' is an illness suffered almost exclusively by lesbian separatists who do not like men and who have political objections to heterosexuality. 'Heterophobia' is defined as 'fear of and resistance to heterosexuals which sometimes surfaces in women's movements around the world. It relies on a sexual-fundamentalist reduction of curiosity and desire.' (Robin Morgan 1982 p 145) (Kramarae and Treichler 1985 pp 190–91) This translation of political objections to heterosexuality into a sickness, an irrational fear, both defines lesbian separatists as sick and precludes political engagement with the issues. The psychological reformulation of political critique as personal pathology prevents that political debate that is the cornerstone of the development of lesbian/feminist politics.

'Internalised homophobia' is a diagnosis which translates lesbian distress under hetero-patriarchy into poor psychological health. Instead of oppression being understood as a political issue requiring social change, our oppression becomes a private issue requiring individual adjustment. Much lesbian/feminist therapy is directed towards the reduction of 'internalised homophobia'. We no longer go to heterosexual therapists to be cured of our lesbianism. Instead we go to lesbian therapists to be cured of our 'internalised homophobia'.

These therapists have had to educate women and lesbians about what is wrong with us in order to ensure a market for their services. Yet still they are forced to admit that 'clients rarely seek therapy to deal with self-labeled internalized homophobia'. (Margolies *et al* 1987 p 234) Many clients who seek out help with *other* problems find that they are diagnosed instead (or additionally) as suffering from 'internalised homophobia'. Kristine Falco advises therapists:

> Always plan to spend a period of time assessing with your client the effects of possible internalized homophobia. (Falco 1991 p 69)

Words like 'moralistic', 'prescriptive' or 'politically correct' are frowned upon in psychology and have become insults used to dismiss the opinions of those who speak from principled positions. Making moral judgements is called 'being judgemental'. 'Shoulds' and 'shouldnt's' are described as 'pressures which have alienated us from our feelings'. (Ernst and Goodison 1981 p 53) The question 'is this right or wrong?' becomes 'is this going to work for me?'. Whatever is right is what turns you on. Different strokes for different folks. This is not feminism. Feminism is a set of moral judgements about the world. Of course, as lesbians and feminists, we have been critical of the moral frameworks available to us. In recent calls for 'moral rearmament' and a return to 'Victorian values' morality has functioned as a euphemism for banning abortion, hounding lesbians and gay men, and keeping women locked into marriages via the romanticising of the sanctity of 'family life'. But morality is not the exclusive preserve of the political right. Lesbians and feminists have also developed moral frameworks about our lives. We say, for example, that violence against women is 'wrong' and 'should' be stopped, and in doing so we are making moral judgements. There have been at least two lesbian journals – *Lesbian Ethics* in the US and *Gossip: A Journal of Lesbian Feminist Ethics* in Britain – devoted to articulating radical lesbian concepts of what is 'right' and 'wrong' for us, and lesbian ethics and morality have been discussed by numerous other writers (see Cartledge 1983; Berson 1984; Hoagland 1988; Card 1990). As lesbian feminists we need to develop and extend our concepts of right and wrong. 'Gut feelings' are not adequate criteria for ethical choice, nor is each lesbian a free spirit whose only duty is to discover her 'true self' and act accordingly. 'Gut feelings' and 'true selves' are constructed in the context of hetero–patriarchal society.

Psychology treats each 'self' as an independent moral universe. This means that the 'right' act in any situation is simply the one which yields the individual the most good feelings about herself, and we abandon the possibility of developing a collective sense of lesbian/feminist ethics and lesbian/feminist values. Politics degenerates into a struggle not for *social change* but for *self-realisation*.

Psychology can only hinder our efforts to develop a strong and radical lesbian politics. In order clearly to articulate our political goals and strategies we need to be able to tell the difference between political language and psychobabble. We need to speak *politically* not *psychologically*.

THERAPY AND THE PRIVATISING OF PAIN

Lesbian/feminist therapy is a booming industry. Therapy pervades our lesbian/feminist communities: more and more lesbians in individual therapy, therapy workshops, reading DIY therapy manuals, know others who are in therapy or are training to be therapists. The kinds of problems that prompt most lesbians to enter therapy are the ordinary everyday miseries of life. Many lesbians enter therapy when they experience problems in their relationships (Anthony 1982) or experience anxiety (especially about coming out). One lesbian-health group recommends therapy if you feel lonely, isolated, alienated or overburdened with responsibilities, if you experience ongoing unhappiness, feel constantly exhausted or anxious, want to become more assertive or to show gentleness and softness, or if you feel out of touch with feelings (O'Donnell *et al* 1979). Basically, they sat that you need therapy when you want to make a change in your life and would like someone to be there with you and act as a guide.

Emotions like despair, anger, grief and frustration have become 'psychological' problems in need of psychological treatment in the form of therapy. Within a psychological framework, emotions like these have been made to appear not only undesirable, but unnecessary – curable – and therapy has become a way of life. Suffering is increasingly equated with poor mental health and we seem to have given up the right to be both mentally healthy and desperately unhappy at the same time.

We have heard enough lesbians say 'it saved my life' to feel almost guilty about challenging lesbian/feminist therapy. The undivided attention of a sympathetic lesbian/feminist therapist can be valuable in providing us with ways of understanding our distress, in helping us to feel better, stronger, more able to cope and fight to change an oppressive world. Anything that can do this must be a good thing, mustn't it? Well, no. The embracing of therapy – lesbian/feminist therapy – has costs for our politics and our communities. Thinking about the costs of something that may make us feel better is not easy, but it is essential. As lesbian/feminists we must move beyond how therapy makes us feel and examine the price we pay for our acceptance of it.

One of the major insights of second-wave feminism is that 'the personal is political' (Hanisch 1971) – that the personal, day to day details of our lives have political meaning, are shaped by, and influential upon, their broader social context. A feminist understanding of politics means challenging the male definition of politics as something exclusively external – to do with governments, banner waving, protest marches – and moving towards an understanding of politics as central to our very beings: our thoughts, emotions, and the apparently trivial choices we make about how to live.

Much of what passes for feminist therapy quite explicitly replaces political explanations with personal ones. Many lesbian/feminist therapists argue that, while we must acknowledge the strength and pervasiveness of anti-lesbianism within society, 'the major source of distress is usually the individual's internalised homophobia'. (Sophie 1987) Sometimes lesbian therapy attempts to promote political explanations for personal distress. Laura Brown, for example, often explicitly encourages her clients to understand their difficulties in political terms – 'day in day out I ask her how she might see her individual predicament as part of a broader social and political phenomenon of misogyny and devaluation and oppression of women' (Brown 1992 p 242) – and describes her lesbian/feminist therapy as 'a potentially powerful means for *un*adjusting ourselves to patriarchal realities'. (Brown 1992 p 252)

Therapy could be seen as a means of helping a lesbian to understand her difficulties in political terms – as one lesbian persuading another that her own perspective is the correct one. There is nothing wrong with lesbians trying to persuade each other of different points of view. But this should be an *open political debate of what is right and what is wrong* – of different values, perspectives and ways of construing experience. Therapy is *not* political debate.

The therapeutic relationship is a special, privileged, asymmetrical one.

> Lesbian therapists occupy a special position in the social structure of lesbian communities . . . We are leaders, teachers, oracles. In much the same way that the clergy, who healed the wounds in the Black community, are leaders there, so we, the perceived healers of the wounds of sexism, misogyny, and homophobia, have become leaders among white lesbians. The power available to any therapist is potentially magnified for lesbian therapists because of this special position in our culture. Consequently, our power to do harm is magnified as well. (Brown 1989 p 15)

Within therapy, a powerful lesbian – the therapist – helps another in distress – the client – to understand her experience in the therapist's 'expert' terms. Therapists are 'practitioners of a healing art that is neither intuitive nor naturally present in all women.' (Brown 1985 p 298)

Therapists are accorded specialist knowledge and expertise; as Janice Raymond (1986 p 155) says:

> women have come to believe that what really counts in their life is their 'psychology'. And since they don't know what their psychology means, they submit to another who purports to know – a psychiatrist, counselor, or analyst.

Yet what is it that therapists know – what is their 'healing art'? Therapists – even lesbian/feminist ones – have no special training or expertise in lesbian/feminist politics. They have training in how to interpret experience within the specific theoretical frameworks of psychology: they are experts in reframing and reinterpreting our beliefs, thoughts and feelings *not* in political terms of reference but within the psychological terms their profession has invented. Under the guise of helping clients to explore their feelings, therapy interprets and is aimed at helping the client to understand her problems within the therapist's framework. Therapy is essentially a form of covert political re-education.

Nobody enters therapy to have their politics changed. Yet therapy is *always* a form of political re-education whether it takes the form of replacing political explanations with psychological ones (as with concepts like homophobia), or reframing personal distress in political terms. Regardless of whether we approve of the politics dispensed, therapy is an underhand method of political conversion that makes open political analysis impossible.

Therapy also deprives our lesbian friendships and communities. We are rapidly approaching a situation where all the bad things that happen to us, all our distress and our negative experiences, are taken out of our communities and in to therapy. Even if we consider lesbian therapists to be part of our communities it is still the case that lesbian distress becomes the special preserve of only a few of us – experts with the proper training.

In embracing therapy we run the risk of destroying our capacity for genuine lesbian friendships. With the institutionalising of therapy we cease to expect to deal with each others' distress: the pain of those we love and care about is simply not safe in our untrained hands – we should leave it to the experts. This deprives our communities of a whole realm of experience, deprives us of the strength and ability to support each other, and deprives us of understanding the context and meaning of our distress. Ordinary feelings of despair, anger, grief – painful reactions to the vicissitudes of life – have become individual problems in need of therapy. Therapy privatises pain and severs connections between us, replacing friendship in community with the private therapist–client relationship.

This leads to a vicious circle. The more we see our distress as a private specialist affair, the more we see ourselves and our friends as unable to cope with our distress. Our friendships and communities become arid places to which we dare not bring our anguish and our pain, in which we cannot rely on other lesbians to accept our suffering and help us to survive it. As Anna Lee says:

> We bring the most intimate parts of ourselves to paid friends [therapists], while offering the most superficial parts of ourselves to our nonpaid friends. The excuse is that burdening our friends with our pain or anger or sorrow is unacceptable. But if we can only bring our joy to our friends how can we value them? When we exclude our most intimate selves from our friends, we weaken the bonds between wimmin that are necessary to fuel a social movement. (Lee 1986)

As lesbians we should be looking for ways of supporting and helping each other, of dealing with our distress collectively and politically. This does not mean the mass education of lesbians in therapeutic methods. All too often the drive for more supportive, accommodating communities has led to the wholesale translation of feminist goals into psychological goals – what Janice Raymond (1986) calls the 'therapeutising of friendship'.

We do not need psychological training in how to be friends with each other. Friendship between lesbians is not a psychological technique and the relationship between therapist and client is not a good model for our lesbian relationships. Instead, lesbian communities should become able to accept and include misery, distress and anguish (as well as joy, delight and happiness) as normal ordinary experience – part of the rich fabric of our lesbian lives. Dealing with those emotions in ourselves and others should be part of going about our normal everyday lives: we do not need specialist psychological skills to do that.

Our communities must also become able to include those who we currently marginalise. One of us spent several months as an inpatient in a psychiatric hospital following a suicide attempt related to the traumas of coming out as a lesbian at the age of seventeen. One of us has recently experienced a serious depression which rendered her unable to work, read, drive, go out, think properly or look after herself for almost six months. Most of us can think of lesbians whose behaviour is distressing or incomprehensible to us: lesbians who abuse drugs or alcohol, starve themselves, cut their bodies with knives, are severely depressed or suicidal. Too often, lesbians who have experienced problems such as these find themselves marginalised and excluded from lesbian and feminist communities:

Women in the women's movement, in the lesbian movement, women I had known for a long time and worked with, started treating me differently after I had been in hospital . . . They had been my friends, but now they would look at me as if I was crazy. (Nancy, quoted in Chamberlin 1977 p 75)

women pretend that my depression doesn't exist. So they never ask me about it and somehow communicate that it's not the sort of thing they're interested in talking about . . .' (Ruth Elizabeth 1982 pp 15–16)

The women's movement has not been terribly receptive to ex-patients; there are an awful lot of therapists in the women's movement. (Jenny, quoted in O'Hagan 1991 p 40)

Severely distressed and disabled women and lesbians do not need a psychiatry, or a lesbian/feminist therapy that individualises and privatises their problems and attempts to enable them to 'fit in' to an able-minded world. We need to explore ways in which our communities can be rendered accessible and accommodate such lesbians (see Perkins 1992; Kitzinger and Perkins 1993; Perkins and Kitzinger 1993). For example, admission to psychiatric hospital for one of us was only prevented because friends organised a rota to ensure that there was someone with her to look after her at home. In the words of psychiatric-system survivor Judi Chamberlin, (1977) 'we must begin to turn toward the people we now isolate – the troubled (and troubling) relatives and friends we both love and fear.' We need a politics of madness to parallel that which we have begun to construct around physical disability: 'a radical analysis of what is called madness has to be a major cornerstone of lesbian theory.' (*Dykewomon* 1988)

Of course our communities and our friendships are not perfect – we let each other down, are not always there when we need each other. The fact that lesbians in distress have nowhere but therapy to turn for a consistent source of support is an indictment of our lesbian and feminist communities. But then therapists let us down as well – and by recourse to therapy we actively mitigate against the development of our lesbian communities as places that can accommodate us all.

There is a high price to be paid by all of us, including those who have never been in therapy, for our acceptance of therapy and individualistic psychological ways of thinking. Therapy will always be destructive of the lesbian-feminist enterprise.

THE PERSONAL IS POLITICAL, NOT PSYCHOLOGICAL

There was a time when feminists were clear that 'the personal is political'. The 'personal' details of our lives – things like housework, sex, relationships – were topics of political discussion and debate. Now it seems that the situation has been reversed: national and international politics, as well as major social, ecological and economic issues, are now reduced to individual psychological matters. The wholesale translation of the political into the personal is not simply a characteristic of lesbian-feminist psychology, but of psychology in general.

In the US a group of 22 professionals spent the dollar equivalent of £448,000 in coming to the conclusion that lack of self-esteem is the root cause of 'many of the major social ills that plague us today' (*The Guardian* 13 April, 1990). Similarly, Gloria Steinem (1992) argues that low self-esteem affects not only her, but also Hitler, Saddam Hussein, Ronald Reagan and George Bush as well as whole nations (Haiti and Argentina). Sexual violence against women is addressed by setting up social-skills training and anger management training for rapists (*The Guardian* 21 May 1991), and racism has become something to get off your chest in a counselling workshop (Green 1987). Environmental disasters, such as the Exxon Valdez oil spill, have become psychological problems requiring 'disaster psychologists' who have an 'expertise in attending to the special needs of communities struck by tragedy' (*The Guardian* April 15 1989). Almost all activities of life have been translated into some form of therapy: reading books has become 'bibliotherapy', and writing (Wenz 1988), journalkeeping (Hagan 1988), photography (Spence 1990), and art (Chaplin, 1988 p 17) are all ascribed therapeutic functions.

Lesbian/feminist psychologists often state explicitly their belief that 'the personal is political', when in fact what they are doing is insisting that not only is the 'personal' personal, but much of the 'political' is personal as well. One argument used is that the supposedly 'personal' activity of therapy is in fact political because raising our self-esteem and learning to feel better about ourselves are political acts. It is supposedly revolutionary to love and accept ourselves to overcome self-oppression, and if everyone loved and accepted themselves then they would no longer need to project their repressed self-hatred on others and there would be real social change. Most lesbian-feminist psychology talks of discovering and nurturing one's 'inner self', peeling away the layers of patriarchal conditioning. (Brown, 1992) This 'inner self' is invariably seen as a beautiful, spontaneous little girl and getting in touch with her is a first step to creating social change. It is 'revolution from within' (Steinem 1992) – an offshoot of the 'growth' and 'human potential' movements of the 1960s.

The absurdity of taking such arguments to their logical conclusion can be seen in one project, the offspring of a popular therapeutic programme, which proposed to end starvation. Instead of distributing food, cancelling national debt, or sponsoring farming co-operatives, this project offered the simple expedient of getting individuals to sign cards saying that they are 'willing to be responsible for making the end of starvation an idea whose time has come'. When an unspecified number of people have signed such cards a 'context' will have been created in which hunger will somehow end (cited in Zilbergeld 1983, p 5–6). Although many lesbian/feminist therapists would join us in challenging the obscenity of this project, the logic of many of their own positions permits precisely this kind of interpretation.

Lesbian/feminist psychology tells us that only after healing yourself can you begin to heal the world. We disagree. People do not have to be perfectly functioning beings in order to create social change. The vast majority of those who work and go on struggling for social change do so because of their ethical and political commitments and in spite of their own fears, and self-doubts. Political action is an option for us all, whatever our state of personal well-being.

Another psychologised version of 'the personal is political' relies on the notion of 'empowerment': therapy empowers us to act politically. Through therapy we can gain both the feminist consciousness and the self-confidence to engage in political action. Raising one's personal awareness through therapy enables individuals to release their psychic energies towards creative social change. Again this does not reflect our understanding of 'the personal is political'. The personal, within this perspective, consists of 'psychic energies' (never clearly defined) that operate according to a type of hydraulic model: there is a fixed amount of 'energy' that can be released, blocked or redirected. The 'political' is simply one of the ways in which 'energy' can be directed.

Far from embodying the notion that 'the personal is political', this type of argument relies on a radical separation of the 'personal' and the 'political'. The 'political' business of campaigning, going on marches, is distinguished from the 'personal' business of therapy and psychic energy, and then the two are inspected for degree of correlation. Therapy is then credited with enabling a woman or a lesbian to become more active. This 'empowerment' argument completely ignores the political and ethical implications of therapy itself. The fact that some political activists are also in therapy does not render lesbian/feminist politics and therapy politically or ethically compatible: after all, health campaigners sometimes smoke cigarettes and pacifists sometimes hit their children.

If the 'personal is political' then the very process of doing therapy is political and this process (not simply its outcomes) must be critically evaluated in political terms – as we have done in this chapter.

PSYCHOLOGY AS BACKLASH

There are many reasons why so many lesbian/feminists have embraced psychological versions of the world. In part, the psychologising of lesbian/feminism is simply an outcome of the growth of psychology more generally in western cultures. We have *learned* to frame our problems in psychological terms because it is one of the dominant culturally available frameworks for thinking about experience. On top of this, women have historically been excluded from the public world and have always been expected to be more concerned with 'personal' issues. We generally get more support and sympathy if we frame our problems in psychological rather than political terms. It also seems likely that feminist interest in psychology is an attempt to meet perceived deficits in lesbian/feminist communities. It provides prosthetic friendship from a therapist for lonely, unhappy lesbians when real friendship and community are lacking. Certainly, lesbian feminists can feel isolated and overwhelmed with problems, and psychology appears to offer answers – at a price.

Most importantly, in a right-wing political climate where it has become clear that feminist revolution is a long way off, women turn instead to 'personal' cures and private solutions – redefining feminist goals such as 'power' and 'revolution' in terms that seem attainable: revolution from within and a sense of inner power. Old moral and political questions are increasingly supplanted with a new question; 'what makes me feel better right now?'

As lesbians and feminists we must make ethical judgements about our lives. We must reclaim those 'personal' aspects of our lives (our thoughts, feelings and apparently trivial everyday choices) that are now seen as the individualised province of psychology and therapy, and address them collectively and politically. Most of us are adequate human beings most of the time, and on those occasions when we are not able to cope on our own we can care for each other. We do not need a psychology – lesbian/feminist or otherwise – that individualises and privatises distress. Psychology is destructive of lesbian/feminist politics and community.

This article is based on ideas first published in Kitzinger, Celia, and Perkins, Rachel, *Changing Our Minds: Lesbian Feminism and Psychology*, Onlywomen Press, London, 1993.

References

Anthony, B D, 'Lesbian client – lesbian therapist: Opportunities and challenges in working together', in J C Gonsiorek (ed), *Homosexuality and Psychotherapy*, Haworth Press, New York, 1982.

Berson, N, 'On lesbian morality', *Common Lives/Lesbian Lives*, 1984, 13, pp 47–9.

Brown, L S, 'Ethics and business practice in feminist therapy', in L B Rosewater and L E A Walker (eds), *Handbook of Feminist Therapy: Women's Issues in Psychotherapy*, Springer, New York, 1985.

Brown, L S 'Beyond thou shalt not: Thinking about ethics in the lesbian therapy community', *Women & Therapy*, 1989, 8, pp 13–25.

Brown, L S 'What's addiction got to do with it? A feminist critique of codependence', *Psychology of Women: Newsletter of Division 35, APA*, 1990, 17(1), pp 1–4.

Brown, L S, 'While waiting for the revolution: The case for a lesbian-feminist psychotherapy', *Feminism & Psychology*, 1992, 2(2), 239–53.

Card, C, 'Pluralist lesbian separatism', in J Allen (ed), *Lesbian Philosophies and Cultures*, State University of New York Press, 1990.

Cartledge, S, 'Duty and desire: Creating a feminist morality', in S Cartledge and J Ryan (eds), *Sex and Love: New Thoughts on Old Contradictions*, The Women's Press, London, 1983.

Chamberlin, J, *On Our Own*, MIND Publications, London (1988 edition).

Chaplin, J, *Feminist Counselling in Action*, Sage Publications, London, 1988.

Chaplin, J and Noack, A, 'Leadership and self help groups', in S Krzowski and P Land (eds), *In Our Experience: Workshops at the Women's Therapy Centre*, The Women's Press, London, 1988.

Chesler, P, *Women and Madness*, Avon Books, New York, 1972.

Coward, R, *Our Treacherous Hearts: Why Women Let Men get Their Way*, Faber & Faber, London, 1992.

Daly, M, *Gyn/Ecology: The Metaethics of Radical Feminism*, The Women's Press, London, 1978.

Dykewomon, E, 'On surviving psychiatric assault and creating emotional well-being in communities', *Sinister Wisdom*, 1988, 36.

Eichenbaum, L, 'Separate sisters', interviewed by Helen Birch, *City Limits*, 1987 August 6, pp 47–8.

Elizabeth, R, 'Deprivatising pain', *Catcall*, 1982,14, pp 15–16, reprinted and extended in S O'Sullivan (ed), *Women's Health*, Pandora, London, 1987.

Ernst, S, and Goodison, L, *In Our Own Hands*, The Women's Press, London, 1981.

Falco, K L, *Psychotherapy with Lesbian Clients: Theory into Practice*, Brunner Mazel, New York, 1991.

Fritz, L, *Dreamers & Dealers: An Intimate Appraisal of the Women's Movement*, Beacon Press, Boston, 1979.

Hagan, K L, *Internal Affairs: A Journalkeeping Workbook for Self Intimacy*, Harper Row, San Francisco, 1988.

Hanisch, C, 'The personal is political', in J Agel (ed), *The Radical Therapist*, Ballantine Books, New York, 1971.

Hay, L, *Heal Your Body: The Mental Causes for Physical Illness and Metaphysical Way to Overcome Them*, Eden Grove Publications, London, 1984a.

Hay, L, *Cancer: Discovering Your Healing Power* (audiotape), Hay House Inc., Santa Monica, CA, 1984b.

Heriot, J, 'The double bind: Healing the split', in J H Robbins and R J Seigel (eds), *Women Changing Therapy: New Assessment, New Values and Strategies in Feminist Therapy*, Harrington Park Press, New York, 1985.

Hoagland, S L, *Lesbian Ethics: Toward New Value*, Institute of Lesbian Studies, Palo Alto, 1988.

Jo, B, Strega, L and Ruston *Dykes-Loving-Dykes: Dyke Separatist Politics for Lesbians Only*, Battleaxe Oakland, CA, 1990.

Kitzinger, C, *The Social Construction of Lesbianism*, Sage Publications, London, 1987a.

Kitzinger, C, 'Heteropatriarchal language: The case against homophobia', *Gossip: A Journal of Lesbian Feminist Ethics*, 1987b, 5, pp 15–20.

Kitzinger, C and Perkins, R, *Changing Our Minds: Lesbian Feminism and Psychology*, Onlywomen Press, London and New York University Press, 1993.

Kitzinger, J, 'Who are you kidding? Children, power and the struggles against child sexual abuse', in A James and A Prout (eds), *Constructing and Reconstructing Childhood: Contemporary Issues in the Sociological Study of Children*, The Falmer Press, London, 1990.

Kramarae, C, and Treichler, P A, *A Feminist Dictionary*, Pandora Press, London, 1985.

Lee, A, 'Therapy: The evil within', *Trivia*, 1986, 9, pp 34–44.

Leon, B, 'Brainwashing and women: The psychological attack', *It Ain't Me Babe*, August 1970, pp 10–12, reprinted in Redstockings (ed), *Feminist Revolution*, Random House, New York, 1978.

Lyn, L, 'It's a small world: Lesbian and bisexual women therapists' social interactions'. Paper presented at the Association for Women in Psychology Conference, March 1991, Connecticut, US.

MacDonald, A P, 'Homophobia: Its roots and meanings', *Homosexual Counseling Journal*, 1976, 3, pp 23–33.

Malina, D, 'On integrity and integration: Toward a feminist vision of psychology', *Women of Power: A Magazine of Feminism, Spiritualism & Politics*, 1987, 5, 14–17.

Margolies, L, Becker, M and Jackson-Brewer, K, 'Iternalised homophobia: Identifying and treating the oppressor within', in Boston Lesbian Psychologies Collective (ed), *Lesbian Psychologies*, University of Illinois Press, Urbana, 1987.

Morris, M, 'Is it within your power?', *New Woman* July 1990, pp 58–60.

O'Connell, M, Leoffler, V, Kater, P and Saunders, Z, *Lesbian Health Matters*, Santa Cruz Women's Health Collective, 1979.

O'Hagan, M, *Stopovers on My Way Home from Mars*, New Moon Productions, Auckland, New Zealand, 1991.

Perkins, R, 'Working with socially disabled clients: A feminist perspective', in J Ussher and P Nicholson (eds), *Gender Issues in Clinical Psychology*, Routledge, London, 1992.

Perkins, R and Kitzinger, C, 'Madness, social disability and access', *Lesbian Ethics*, 1993, 96–107.

Raymond, J, *A Passion for Friends: Toward a Philosophy of Female Affection*, The Women's Press, London, 1986.

Spence, J, 'Sharing the wounds: Interview with J Z Grover', *Women's Review of Books*, VII, July 1990, pp 38–9.

Spender, D, Untitled, in R Rowland (ed), *Women Who Do and Women Who Don't Join the Women's Movement*, RKP, London, 1984.

Steinem, G, *Revolution From Within: A Book of Self-Esteem*, Bloomsbury, London, 1992.

Weinberg, G, *Society and the Healthy Homosexual*, Anchor, New York, 1973.

Weisstein, N, 'Psychology constructs the female', in R Morgan (ed), *Sisterhood is Powerful*, Vintage Books, New York, 1970, reprinted in C Kitzinger (ed), ' "Psychology constructs the female": A reappraisal', *Feminism & Psychology*, 3(2), June 1993.

Wenz, K, 'Women's peace of mind: Possibilities in using the writing process in counseling', Association of Women in Psychology – Arizona Chapter, 1988 Regional Conference, Arizona State University.

Zilbergeld, B, *The Shrinking of America*, Little, Brown & Co., Boston, 1983.

IDENTITY POLITICS

SANDRA McNEILL

This chapter fills in some background on the Women's Liberation Movement before the rise of Identity Politics. I examine that rise and offer some explanations for it, and look at its effects on the women's liberation movement. I shall argue that once Identity Politics became the currency, feminism became devalued.

UNITY IN DIVERSITY IS OUR STRENGTH

Once upon a time I was a liberal and worked with Amnesty International. This led indirectly to my getting involved with the International Tribunal of Crimes Against Women. Women I met through that tribunal, women from different countries who identified themselves as feminist, changed my life. Through exchanging experiences and discussing ideas with them, I came to see that male control of women was world wide, and had extended through known history. The degree of control differed from country to country and over time: in some countries women were under almost total control, in others we had an illusion of freedom – but the same system of male control operated. However, women were resisting. In different places in different ways, women were fighting back.

This was for me a coming together of the personal and the political. Before then my main political work had been for Amnesty prisoners in other countries. Meanwhile I was suffering blatant discrimination at work, sexual harassment both at work and outside, and I had been sexually assaulted when walking home. I still walked home late, but in fear. I hadn't been able to talk about this with anyone. None of it was acknowledged by the world at large as a serious problem, let alone as oppression. Even my Union had told me I should be tough and ignore the harassment. Now I was going to join a movement to fight my own and others' oppression.

When I joined the Women's Liberation Movement I thought I would meet lots of like-minded women and we would work together learning as we went. This eventually happened but not when I first joined in 1976. I found Marxist feminists who thought the answer lay in the writings of Marx, Lenin, Trotsky (some did), and later in Althuser. I found Anarchist feminists who thought we must abolish the state and all rules. Self-defined radical feminists seemed to be absent from conferences and debates.

So hundreds of us struggled in our socialist or socialist feminist groups. Some of us wanted to talk about the system of male power which was operating. We said it operated through capitalism and the state but existed in pre-capitalist societies. It would continue to exist unless we named it and fought it. We were called ahistorical and biological determinist but we struggled on. Following Sheila Jeffreys' paper 'The Need for Revolutionary Feminism' (1977), we formed groups to share experience, develop theories and take action.

We called ourselves revolutionary feminist or radical feminist, largely but not entirely according to where we happened to live. We were still socialist. The difference between us and socialist feminists was that we named men and their system of control – male supremacy – as the enemy. We analysed the forms of male control and found they lay in male violence in all its guises and in the construction of sexuality. At one point there were 'Women Against Violence Against Women' groups in every town.

This is the time younger women look back to as the golden age, sometimes called the age of sisterhood. That is ironic because our debates were heated, angry, painful, as all debates probably are when you feel you are creating a revolution. But we were able to come together on key issues and campaigns; sometimes we said 'Unity in Diversity is our Strength'.

The women's liberation movement of the 1970s was not perfect; nor was any other political movement. But it was our movement and there were issues within it we had to address. Much that was said and written in the movement was racist and classist. I personally came across the worst classism from self-identified socialist feminists who, while talking about how the real oppressed were women out there, from council estates, managed to make us sound like some kind of monkey. There were very few black women in the WLM at that time, probably because the movement, though very much involved in fighting racism, fascism and imperialism (issuing statements and joining marches), was inadvertently racist and classist. The first groups to organise in the UK specifically to challenge the WLM were working-class women's groups challenging classism. This was very necessary as some working-class women had felt excluded by the movement, and others had felt oppressed within it.

This kind of challenge became a pattern within the WLM. Black women's groups, formed on the same basis, became vocal. Groups were set up to address the anti-lesbianism of the movement. Many of us who had worked against male violence, setting up refuges or rape crisis centres, had been advised not to mention we were lesbians and of course never to talk about our specific oppression. Other groups began to emerge: disabled women pointed out how often we used inaccessible venues, and that we ignored their particular oppression.

All this was positive – and in many places is still necessary. So how did we get from there to Identity Politics? I don't have *the* answer, perhaps no one woman does, but I offer this as a contribution to a debate.

SPEAKING AS A . . .

When I was approached to write this chapter, I was asked to say what was positive about Identity Politics. Absolutely nothing. This does not mean that those of us who organised together around our specific oppressions contributed nothing to the WLM – our contribution was enormous. But Identity Politics as such stifled debate and contributed only to the dissolution of the WLM in the UK.

By 1980 we felt as feminists that it was important to look at our specific oppressions and articulate them. But our attempts to recognise different oppressions very quickly developed into a hierarchy of oppression. We moved away from looking at the complexity of women's lives to a points–count system, where the oppressions were added up. She with the greatest or most oppression was right – about whatever topic was being discussed.

It happened first in London. A friend wrote to me about a meeting she had attended where one discussion was settled when a woman said 'Speaking as an Irish woman I think X'. Her opponent in this discussion had replied 'speaking as an incest survivor, I think Y'. Naturally, Y was the course of action decided upon. My friend commented, 'The sad thing is that the Irish woman is also an incest survivor, but she is not ready to acknowledge that in public – if she had, she would have won the argument.'

The points–count system developed further after a conference on Child Sexual Abuse in 1985. Numbers were limited, the conference was full, and some (white) women were turned away. Then a group of black women arrived and insisted white women leave so they could participate. From then on places were left at conferences for black or other additionally oppressed women. The reservation of places later extended to social events.

A 1990 cartoon illustrates this.

The cartoon may be funny, but it is exactly what was happening. Note also that simply being working class no longer counted.

Then there was the other side of the coin. At the Lesbian Summer

School in 1988, I disagreed with a black woman and a white woman in a debate on pornography. A socialist-feminist journal reporting on the conference mentioned me by name, and accused me of racism as I had argued with a black woman and an Irish woman. This was what was liable to happen if a woman did not at once concede she was wrong, and the woman with more oppression was right. This pressure resulted in a great deal of silencing.

How then to articulate your views in this climate? Clearly, you had to have an identity to speak from. You had to be able to say 'Speaking as a . . .' to even enter a debate. What had been part of your oppression became your identity. We had had papers and discussions on fat women's liberation, but for some fat women this became an identity. This construction of identities was criticised in *Revolutionary and Radical Feminist Newsletter* ('An ism of one's own', October 1989). But it carried on unabated. In a pub in London at that time I was accosted by a dyke, who, perhaps because I am fat, assumed I identified as a fat woman. 'It is all right for you, but I am oppressed as a thin woman, and that is not recognised.' I opened my mouth to ask if she found that clothes turned to nasty viscous when they got to her size, then I realised this was not what it was about. She was trying to establish an identity so she could say 'Speaking as a thin woman . . .'.

It was not only women opposed to radical and revolutionary feminist politics who adopted the shorthand of identity politics; we did, also. And as I have said, once identity politics becomes the currency feminism is devalued, as the following example shows.

At the social event of the Lesbian Sex and Sexuality Conference in London 1990 (reported in *Revolutionary and Radical Feminist Newsletter*, Spring 1990), s-m dykes, including women who were pornographers, were wearing eroticised fascist imagery. Several women complained to the organisers, explaining why, as feminists, they found this offensive. One of the organisers asked the s-m dykes to leave because 'A Jewish woman had been offended'. The organiser was being expedient. She knew she would get an argument if she put feminist objections, so she used the 'unarguable' to be effective. Of course feminists object to s-m because it is particularly offensive to Jewish people and Black people in its use of master/slave routines and Nazi regalia. But we also object to all s-m because it is a mockery of violence against women. The adoption of s-m says violence against women is okay as long as we can get off on it. But once we go down the identity-politics route such feminist objections start to sound hollow in our ears. Not real arguments, not as serious. Just as, before the WLM, whatever happened to women as women was not real oppression.

The effect of Identity Politics has been to stifle debate. Debate still goes on in academia – there the name of the game is debate. For these of us outside, debate has more or less ceased. Identity Politics finished off most of our newsletters (see the case of the London WLM Newsletter in Julie Bindel's chapter). Identity Politics inhibited discussion at conferences until many of us ceased going to them, and finally no one was willing to organise any. Without debate the WLM cannot function.

So why did it happen? I think we underestimated the force of the anger between women due to differences of race, class, and so on. Women organising together around our common interests as women is empowering, but such action has nothing else in the world to validate it or back it up. And much deriding it. Many of us were guilt tripped, or punished into silence. In defence we began also to use the language of Identity Politics – a fatal trap.

CARRYING ON

Now that many of the main exponents of Identity Politics have moved on to post-modernism (where you cannot speak as an anything!) how have we been picking up the pieces? While broad-based women's liberation groups died in the climate of the 1980s, single-issue campaigns have carried on; Justice for Women is one example.

Inspired by Southall Black Sister's Campaign for Kiranjit Ahluw-alia, the Leeds Campaign for Justice for Women was set up to work for Kiranjit's freedom. Shortly afterwards the Leeds Campaign for Justice was contacted by Sara Thornton and began to campaign for her. Because of our involvement in past campaigns such as Free the Maw Sisters we were clear that we wanted more than reduced sentences for some women who have killed abusive partners. More men kill women than women kill men, and most men who kill have previously beaten their partners. Most women kill men who have been abusing them. Yet a disproportionate number of men were going free, while women were given long jail sentences. We wanted a total change in public perception which would affect juries' verdicts. We wanted to change the law and, who knows, one day even judges.

We have yet to change the law but the press and public do now realise that there is an issue about women who fight back against abusive men being punished severely. In campaigning around this we have found many allies. On the issue of men who abuse and eventually kill going virtually unpunished, liberals are not with us and feminists are on their own. But if French feminists can get *rid* of the category 'Crimes of Passion' from French law – and they did – then we can make changes here so that men cannot kill women with impunity.

Another important campaign without which we in Justice for Women could not have existed, is Women Against Fundamentalism. This campaign raises important issues for women in this country and internationally.

A new campaign which is worldwide and potentially a landmark for women, is the campaign to identify the rape of women in war as a war crime.

As well as the campaigns, we also have service providers from Women's Aid and Black Women's Refuges to women's training projects. Such campaigns and projects could not have existed before the WLM and are part of its legacy. But there is another legacy broader than that. We have a legacy of ideas; ideas that were new to us all in the early 1970s. In particular, the idea that women are oppressed as women and that men might have something to do with this has gone beyond the WLM into common currency. And not only has that idea become common currency – it has also become understood that this is not natural and inevitable, but wrong.

section two
LESBIAN SEXUALITY AND SEXUAL PRACTICE

The contributors to this section expose the claims of the so-called lesbian sexual radicals as, in reality, merely the old patriarchal models of sexual oppression, dressed up to satisfy a male agenda and fundamentally hostile to the interests of women.

In 'Serious Porn, Serious Protest' *Carole Reeves and Rachel Wingfield* look at the rise of the pro-pornography lobby among lesbians, highlighting the key struggle that took place at the London Lesbian and Gay Centre in the early 1980s between lesbian-feminists and lesbian sado-masochists/pornographers, which the latter won with the support of gay men on a gay male agenda. They trace the rise of Lesbians Against Sado-Masochism (LASM) and Feminists Against Censorship (FAC). They argue that FAC is motivated by vested interests in money-making, heterosexuality and therefore patriarchy. They describe the activities of the Campaign Against Pornography, in which many radical feminists are active, and make links between the backlash against feminism and the call in Britain for a 'new realism' by the current Labour party.

Sue Wilkinson sees bisexuality as depoliticising sex and turning it into a market-able commodity, a fashion accessory for heterosexual women who buy into it as 'fun', 'safe sex' and 'the glamorous affair'. She argues that those 'lesbians' who have sex with men, far from being transgressive, are re-inforcing essentialist notions of homosexuality and heterosexuality. All variations of bisexuality are analysed as actively hostile to feminism, in that they attempt to mask both the oppression of women within heterosexuality and women's resistance to it.

Sheila Jeffreys detects, in the 'biologism' of the present day, a worrying return to the Victorian values invented by male sexologists a century ago. She points to the political usefulness of this for gay men who are given a 'scientific' basis for the 'we can't help it' approach, which they use in struggles for their civil rights, but highlights the dangers for women of adopting these theories.

SERIOUS PORN, SERIOUS PROTEST

CAROLE REEVES AND RACHEL WINGFIELD

Relatively few lesbians practice s-m (sado-masochism) or use pornography. However, regardless of the numbers involved, during the late 1980s this began to be presented as the dominant form of lesbian sexual practice. Given the wider heterosexual culture this is perhaps not surprising: eroticising power difference is presented to us as sex in western society. The fear seems to have grown that without porn and s-m, lesbian sexuality would not exist.

During the 1970s and 1980s, radical lesbian feminists in Britain developed an analysis of male supremacy, which saw men's oppression of women as central to a systematic structure of power relations, namely patriarchy. They identified heterosexuality as a key institution at the root of this system, and argued that having sex with, and loving the enemy divided women and gave them a perceived stake in individual men and the patriarchal system, making women less able to fight the system. So, for example, many heterosexual women – including those identifying themselves as feminists – refuse to accept the radical feminist perceptions of the extent of male violence against women and children. They don't want to believe that 'their man' is like that, and they don't want to give up on sexual relations with men. This makes it extremely difficult for women to challenge male power. In addition, given that lesbianism is so marginalised and surrounded by fear and loathing in our society, it follows that women don't feel they can step out of heterosexuality without terrible consequences – hence their desire to uphold it.

Within a radical lesbian-feminist analysis the pornography industry is seen as an institution with a key role in legitimising both hetero-sexuality, and violence against women, and so represents an important target in our struggle against patriarchy. It is an industry which pumps out mass propaganda for the institution of heterosexuality. As a consequence, lesbians have always been central to the feminist anti-pornography movement.

In the 1980s British lesbian feminists in Angry Women, and Women Against Violence Against Women (WAVAW) initiated a number of important feminist strategies for fighting the pornography industry – with Angry Women attacking sex shops and literally damaging the industry's profits, and WAVAW developing British anti-pornography slides in order to raise consciousness among women about what pornography actually is and the lies it tells about our sexuality. During the latter part of the decade the backlash set in, and lesbian feminists mobilised against the growth of a pro-porn and s-m movement in the lesbian community; this manifested itself early on in the struggle at the London Lesbian and Gay Centre.

LIFE AT THE LONDON LESBIAN AND GAY CENTRE

In 1985 the London Lesbian and Gay Centre (LLGC) opened in a blaze of publicity. It was the largest centre in Europe of its kind, providing a wealth of resources, and seemed to hold the possibility of a place where politics and social activities could be successfully merged within a mixed-sex environment. There was great optimism there within the lesbian community; given what happened this was absolute naivety.

With the benefit of hindsight, those feminists who were involved with the Centre should have been alerted to the problems which followed. The Centre provided no real stimulus for change, lacking as it did any politics or sense of direction. There was no recognition of the different needs of lesbians and gay men and certainly no awareness of the politics of the women's movement. So it should have come as no great shock that when the s-m issue was raised, the management committee panicked and failed to take a decision: it was left to the workers to sort out the farrago.

The first group to apply for meeting space was the s-m group. As the workers had agreed to work collectively, this had to be agreed by everyone. From the 11 workers, only one – a lesbian feminist – objected. This resulted in an impasse. The worker, Carole Reeves was badgered to change her mind and when she wouldn't she was ostracised. There was no support from within the Centre and so she sought outside assistance.

A meeting for lesbians opposed to the s-m group being at the Centre was advertised in the London Women's Newsletter. This was held at A Woman's Place and was attended by over fifty women. It was from this meeting that LASM (Lesbians Against Sado-Masochism) was created. Lesbian feminists had decided to fight back. Weekly meetings were held at the Centre. Letters were written to the management committee expressing opposition and objections to the s-m group. It was pointed out that nice though it would be to have a centre where all lesbians and gay men could meet, the inclusion of the s-m group meant that women who objected to the woman-hating and fascism symbolised and expressed in s-m dress and practice were, by its very nature, excluded. The management committee prevaricated on making a decision. Meanwhile support grew for LASM, as did hostility from the s-m lobby. This manifested itself, for example, when a number of leather-clad gay men invaded the Centre using bully-boy tactics, refused to leave when asked, and ran amok. On another occasion, the official opening night of the Centre, two lesbians, well known within the community, arrived wearing black leather trousers and jackets complete with nazi-styled caps and riding crops and some male workers were sporting para-military regalia.

This state of affairs continued with both sides deadlocked. An extraordinary general meeting was called at which the members of the Centre were to vote on the issue. The Centre was packed with several hundred people, 40 per cent of whom were women. The s-m dykes sat in the front rows of the hall, completely surrounded by gay men, while the feminists clustered in the middle. The s-m contingent said nothing. They didn't have to given that at every opportunity liberal apologists and gay men sprang to their defence, to roars of approval. Whenever a lesbian feminist managed to get a word in she was met with jeers and verbal abuse. After the vote was taken, the men and s-m dykes had won, even though the majority of the women present voted against the motion. It was devastating. The Centre ended up as a men's club, to which women were admitted if they toed the line.

LASM continued to meet for some while afterwards, and involved itself in several other protests, including being called upon by the women bar staff at a local pub, who were opposed to a lesbian s–m group meeting there on 'women's night'. This resulted in a LASM picket of the pub and subsequently LASM succeeded in having the meetings moved to another night. Lesbian feminists continued to boycott the LLGC for many years and the Centre became increasingly dominated by men. The Centre eventually went into receivership.

What had become clear to feminist activists opposed to porn and s–m during this period, was the extent to which gay male culture was dominating the community, and also the extent to which the backlash against feminism was beginning to set in – not only within straight society, but also within the gay and lesbian scene. Opposition to a feminist analysis of sexuality was then at its peak, and there was a growing monopolisation of the media and lesbian space by a 'postmodern', pro–s–m, pro–porn movement which has become most easily identifiable in the 1990s as 'Queer Nation' politics. It was at this point – with the backlash at its height – that the pro–porn group calling itself 'Feminists Against Censorship' – FAC – was formed. Originally many women gave their support to FAC, without knowing the history or real motivation behind it. However, over the years, FAC has become so publicly pro–porn that the support it once attracted has significantly reduced.

FEMINISTS AGAINST CENSORSHIP

During the late 1980s, political developments in the lesbian community took a familiar form – following a pattern which had previously been seen in the United States.

The debate over s–m was intricately linked with that around pornography, and when 1987 saw the setting up of the first national anti-pornography campaign in this country (CAP), lesbians who had been active in the pro–s–m lobby joined forces with heterosexual academic feminists to form Feminists Against Censorship (FAC) – specifically created to fight feminist campaigns around pornography within the lesbian and women's movements.

FAC first became visible in the political arena after a struggle taking place within Liberty – the National Council for Civil Liberties (NCCL). Many of the well-known FAC members were long-term activists in NCCL, and when anti-porn civil rights campaigners managed to get a motion passed at the 1989 AGM, FAC formed a lobby specifically with the intention of overturning the motion. They achieved this aim the following year. This was not that surprising, since historically liberal organisations formed to protect the rights of individuals have never had much of a material interest in fighting the distribution of power in society. What is interesting, however, is the fact that some liberal and libertarian activists, such as those who joined FAC, were keen to put so much time and resources into defending pornography.

There is clearly an immense amount at stake for women in FAC and other pro-porn lobbies. It is certainly true that 'hell hath no fury like a vested interest', but what exactly is the vested interest for those who describe themselves as feminists and defend porn, and what do some lesbians have invested in porn?

Academic and writer Lynne Segal is one of the most prominent heterosexual women associated with FAC's ideas. Many of FAC's most prominent members are heterosexual but, none the less, the organisation likes to present itself as intricately entwined with the lesbian community. Looking at Lynne Segal's writing on porn and sado-masochism, it becomes very clear how central the pro-pornography position is, in a defence of heterosexuality.

Lynne Segal's first attack on a lesbian radical feminist analysis of sexuality appeared in 1983 in *Sex and Love: New Thoughts on Old Contradictions*. (Cartledge and Ryan eds.) In her article she launches an attack on the radical feminist critique of intercourse, and defends the idea of vaginal orgasm. She seems particularly concerned at the idea that female orgasm may be independent of penetration.

In a later book *Slow Motions: Changing Masculinities, Changing Men* (1990) Segal tells us that radical feminist arguments that all men oppress women, and that heterosexuality plays a crucial role in maintaining this oppression, are extreme and puritanical ideas.

Slow Motions tries to individualise power. Masculinity rather than male power and men's behaviour becomes the issue to be discussed. She argues that since there are so many 'differences between men' (where have we heard that one before?) and masculinity is so shifting – constantly reconstructing itself – then we cannot really even talk about heterosexuality, or men's behaviour in relationships, or men's use of pornography, without losing the complexity of the issue. The implication of this argument is that male sexuality and heterosexuality cannot be addressed as political issues.

Segal's vested interest in believing men are 'really okay' – her vested interest in not questioning heterosexuality – is powerful. She even goes so far as to cite a lesbian s-m proponent, Pat Califia (Califia 1990 pp 217–31), to 'prove' that lesbian sexuality isn't about equality, and that lesbians too get turned on by being sexually violent towards their lovers. As a result of this, she can then go on to argue that heterosexuality isn't the problem. Her most recent book, *Straight Sex* (1994) is a defence of heterosexuality, and in particular heterosexual feminism. *Straight Sex* comes out with what really is at the root of this agenda; defending pornography is about challenging the feminist insight that the personal is political – which straight feminists seem to feel it is increasingly necessary to do.

Despite their association with these ideas, FAC continue to represent themselves as the defenders of lesbianism. Anti-pornography feminists, lesbians or not, are constantly accused by them of homophobia, and of wanting to censor lesbian and gay materials. Yet, in *Bad Girls and Dirty Pictures* (1993), Tuppy Owens writes:

> On the whole, though, I've found women haven't made the best friends for me . . . Women just don't seem to be self-propelled. I've never tried fucking a woman; I think I'd be disappointed they didn't have a nice, juicy propeller. Yes, I'm sure I would. Sex without a dick would be pretty much a waste of time for me . . . Dicks are delectable, incredible, biological structures. The whole apparatus, the size, the way it fits inside, and the precariousness of it all, makes me wonder why people bother to take an interest in anything else in life at all. That so many cocks go unloved and uncherished by women these days is an unbelievable waste of resources and also senseless human cruelty. (p 125)

This is deeply anti-lesbian.

Bad Girls and Dirty Pictures as a whole represents an attack on the fundamental ideas of lesbian feminism. In an attempt to defend pornography, and ultimately heterosexuality, the contributors to that book come out in support of adults having sex with children and child porn (as long as it's 'consensual'), and bestiality (although they don't say whether this must be consensual!). They also argue that child sexual abuse has been hysterically exaggerated in recent years, that it does not exist on the scale radical feminists claim, and that ritual abuse does not exist at all. In the traditional way of patriarchy, they call those women *liars*, who speak out about their experience of abuse.

It is interesting that FAC feels the need to go to these lengths to defend pornography. In order to feel okay about porn, or in order to convince the reader to feel okay, it seems it is necessary to undermine the reality of the events which take place within it, not only in the production of porn, but in society in general. The pornography industry does not exist in isolation from other institutions of male power and, as Andrea Dworkin points out, links male orgasm to the subordination and abuse of women. This is not only a way of legitimising violence against women, it also props up institutionalised heterosexuality. Therefore, pornography necessarily also represents an attack on lesbianism: a massive amount of porn for men involves 'lesbian' scenes of women having sex for the male voyeur, making do with a woman, but desperate for 'the real thing' – the man – to come along and finish it off. The women are forced to employ surrogate penises in the absence of the 'real thing' – dildoes, cucumbers, bottles, anything. The Tuppy Owens' quote reiterates the message of pornography: the penis is everything, heterosexuality is the ultimate experience for women, all lesbians need is a good fuck.

Unsurprisingly, the little pornography there has been produced by and for lesbians in this country has all revolved around traditional 'lesbian' pornographic scenarios of women desperate to act out intercourse, of women with dildoes, of women in s-m scenarios. The first issue of *Quim* contained a story about a nun sexually abusing little boys; the following issue contained a story about a lesbian who breaks into women's houses at night and rapes them (and surprise, surprise they loved it). It seems that the *Quim* collective found very quickly that pornography without inequality was impossible to make, and just wouldn't have 'worked'. Not surprisingly, *Quim* has only produced four issues to date (less than one a year) and has not proved to be a best seller in the lesbian community. Even the publishing house Sheba's attempt to produce a collection of lesbian 'erotica' was an endless repetition of fistfucking, dildoes and s–m. In fact, Sheba and *Quim* shared a joint collective member.

There is, in fact, no discernable difference between the pseudo-lesbian scenarios in mainstream porn, and so-called lesbian–feminist erotica, as the following examples illustrate.

'Get up and bend over that basin.'
I tie each of her wrists to the taps, then ease her skirt up
gently and pull her pants down.
'Spread your legs wider.'
. . . . I whip her round the buttocks. They quiver in slow motion
and ripple to the sound of each smack. I rub them firmly. The
juices from her pussy trickle down her full plump thighs.

I dive into her cunt.
Her folded walls hug me.
I resurface
Then dive into her juices again.
'Please do it harder' she begs.
Fuck me
Harder.

First two fingers, then three, then four. Now my whole hand. She wants them all. We are rocking slowly at first. Slowly my fist pushes inside her. Then faster and faster. She gyrates her hips around my hand. Harder and harder. We are rocking, bucking, fucking together.

'FUCK ME YOU BASTARD'

Her hand was sliding slowly up my thigh, and my pussy felt so hot I was sure I would come as soon as she touched me there. It seemed to take hours before her fingertips brushed the damp crotch of my knickers, and I shivered with pleasure as she pulled my panties round my ankles, right there in front of everyone, so she could slide her fingers into my cunt. I came almost at once, but she kept pumping her fingers in and out, keeping up the pressure on my clitty, until I'd orgasmed another couple of times.

The last of these extracts is from *Penthouse*, a mainstream porn magazine for men, the others from *Serious Pleasure*, a book of short stories published by Sheba (1989), which described itself as a lesbian feminist collective. These extracts are not unrepresentative of the stories in the book: we could have selected from virtually any of them. All of them contain themes common in pornography, ranging from fistfucking, dildoes, sado-masochism and voyeurism. Common to all is the sexual objectification of women and the message that women enjoy being dominated. Pick up any porn magazine, view any porn video, and you will be bombarded with similar violent imagery and language. The language of pornography is not being 'rewritten' or 'reclaimed' in the extract from *Serious Pleasure* – it is simply being repeated.

In their introduction to *Serious Pleasure* the Sheba collective state that they do not label their approach as 'liberal, the differences within *Serious Pleasure* are framed by a feminist perspective'. They also blithely state that 'We are well aware of the ongoing and many-levelled discussions and arguments' around porn and erotica, and they acknowledge that the question being asked by some women is 'What, if anything, is the difference between lesbian erotica or pornography and that written by heterosexuals or gay men?'. What indeed? They avoid answering this. Instead they ask us to forget our differences and to concentrate on being nice to each other. Challenging any woman on her sexual behaviour is tantamount to censorship.

The groundwork for the growing pro-s-m and porn lobby among lesbians had already been laid by the influence of post-modernism and Thatcherite ideology during the 1980s. The influence of these ideologies has made it possible for a group calling itself 'lesbian feminist publishers' to print material which is indistinguishable from *Penthouse*, and feel it is no contradiction.

Given that defending pornography is ultimately about defending male power and institutionalised heterosexuality, we need to ask why those lesbians who are promoting porn, and who are either involved in or are supportive of FAC, actually want to do so? What is their stake in it?

Firstly, there is basic material interest. Lesbian sexuality has become commoditised in recent years, as the market has moved in and developed a sex industry specifically for lesbians. Sex toys, fetish clothes, escorts, and porn have all been marketed at lesbians – in the way capitalism, co-opts what once was dissent, and turns it into a profit. Some women in FAC are themselves involved in making money from porn. It will always be in some women's interests to accept the status quo. Women in management in the porn industry – FAC member Isobel Kaprowski (editor of *Penthouse*) for example – who have succeeded in being one of the boys, and have made personal gains out of the industry, clearly have a vested interest in helping the industry survive, and in helping it to sell itself as 'post-feminist'.

However, what women – both heterosexual and lesbian – in FAC and other pro-porn lobbies often have is a material interest rather than a financial one. For some heterosexual women who define themselves as feminists, no matter what their politics may be in other areas, their personal/political stake in heterosexuality as an institution means that they are willing to employ the most circular and reactionary of arguments in order to attack any feminist analysis which might lead them to question what is one of the most central bases of their lives and identities. For some lesbians, sexualising inequality is also critically central to their identities. For them, there is just as strong a need not to question pornography, or sado-masochism, or even heterosexuality. A woman who wants to treat women in the same sexually abusive way as men have always done, clearly has a material interest in not questioning such practices, as does, for very different reasons, a woman whose sexuality is bound up with forgetting the pain and denying the abuse she has herself experienced.

As lesbian feminists we need to understand why we are being attacked by those we thought of as part of our community. Issues of sadism, masochism, pornography and sexual violence are for most women fraught with fear and a desire to forget, and are often central to the way we see ourselves. For many women who have experienced sexual abuse and violence, eroticising that abuse through porn and s-m involves continuing to believe the lies of the abuser: that the women are worthless, and that they deserve it. In a recent lesbian feminist collection on s–m, *Unleashing Feminism*, (1993) Miriam argues against the idea put forward by some s–m dykes, that s–m is a way of working through past abuse. Instead she argues that s–m is a reaction against the power of the memory of this abuse:

> I suggest that sm took hold in the lesbian community in a moment that was roughly parallel with the eruption of memories within that same community, of childhood sexual violence. This most recent explosion of memory – a memory of rape – was precipitated by feminist activist opposition to male sexual violence, making the latter public and intolerable; it exemplified in a particularly profound way the politics of memory for an oppressed group. (1993 p 242)

In other words, for some women – heterosexual or lesbian – s–m and porn are about a collective refusal to face the pain of memory, the extent of sexual violence, and the reality of the abuse involved in both porn and s–m. Dissociating from abuse is one of the most effective ways of enduring it. Survivors of the sex industry often tell us that they thought all they were there for was to service the sexual demands of others, and that after a time they could dissociate their minds from their bodies so effectively that they couldn't even feel the pain. It is important to understand how the sex industry feeds off other forms of sexual violence, and sets out to target women who have already been made vulnerable by the system.

FIGHTING THE PORN INDUSTRY

Increasingly, lesbian/radical feminists have come to recognise the need to fight pornography both as an industry, and as part of the wider sex industry. Our opposition to pornography as lesbians and as feminists is an objection not only to the products of the industry, but also to how the industry operates globally and locally. Lesbians and survivors are central to campaigns against the sex industry as has always been the case in the anti–pornography feminist movement, for obvious reasons. The testimonies of women who have been harmed by the sex industry give a very clear picture of how the sex industry both recruits and uses women.

In order to understand the sex industry it is crucial that we understand the relationship between pornography and prostitution. In the United States, WHISPER (Women Hurt in Systems of Prostitution Engaged in Revolt) is a collective of former prostitutes who have escaped systems of pornography and prostitution. It has done considerable work in highlighting the ways in which these systems operate: it explains that prostitution is the system on which pornography is built, and that the same women are used in both – the difference being that in pornography there is a permanent record of the abuse.

The pornography industry globally, therefore, is reliant on prostitution and trafficking in women in order to exist. Most women in pornography are prostitutes and their participation is brought about by a number of key mechanisms, a central one of which is women's poverty. As feminists have long pointed out, women under global capitalism and patriarchy differentially suffer from economic hardship. Much of the most violent porn, as well as much child pornography, is made by western men in the so-called Third World where women and children are more economically vulnerable, with starvation often being the only alternative to working in the sex industry. The sex industry is particularly focused in South East Asia, partly for the troops at military bases, and partly for tourists. The sex industry relies on this unequal distribution of world resources between men and women, and between North and South, in order to recruit or coerce women and children into working for it.

The sex industry in Britain shows a similar pattern at work. A high percentage of both male and female runaways, or young people who are homeless, become involved in the sex industry. Many are leaving care and have nowhere to go and many have left home to escape sexual or other abuse. Pimps are known by social services to hang around care homes and homeless hostels trying to 'recruit'. A project in Manchester recently showed that 70 per cent of young runaways have been sexually exploited for cash. Pimps also know how to make women more vulnerable through drugs and how to make them dependent on prostitution in order to support their habit.

The fact that pornographers have to go to such lengths to make porn, and certain kinds of porn in particular, is significant. If there were any other way they could make that kind of porn, they would. But they can't. And the same goes for pimping and other practices of the sex industry: hanging around care homes, finding vulnerable young women on the street, hooking someone to drugs, are time-consuming procedures. There aren't queues of keen young women begging to be taken into prostitution.

Of course, all this deals only with one side of the porn industry: in fact a great deal of pornography is made 'at home'. The typical pimp is a batterer. Many women who may never have seen themselves as having been involved in the porn industry, have in fact had pornography made of them in the home which has been sold commercially and has been pimped by men they are in relationships with.

For lesbian feminists, therefore, the pornography industry is not only important in that it markets eroticised domination and subordination, but also because it completely relies on institutionalised heterosexuality and male dominance in order to exist. Inequality is eroticised and promoted in the industry's products, and is dependent on it for its production. The industry is a potent example of capitalism, imperialism, racism and patriarchy working together to exploit women and children, and to create a product which is there to justify and maintain the existence of these systems of oppression.

Why then, do we find lesbians who define themselves as feminists, suggesting that the development of prostitutes and pornography for lesbians is the way forward? Lesbian or heterosexual, women go into the sex industry for the same reasons and their participation is brought about by the same life experiences and the same forms of oppression. Can it seriously be argued by FAC or any other woman calling herself a feminist, that somehow the fact that the sale of some women's bodies to more privileged women becomes 'feminist' or about equality, simply because there are no men in the equation? The use of women in pornography and prostitution is brought about by the inequalities of a patriarchal system, whoever the target market may be.

THE WAY FORWARD

In the current climate of hostility to all things feminist, we should not be surprised that the issue of pornography has become central to this backlash. Pornography raises the most contentious areas of debate for the women's movement – the centrality of sexual violence, compulsory heterosexuality, even the existence of patriarchy – and consequently is one of the first areas of feminist analysis to come under attack.

The attack on feminism from within our own movement in a sense mirrors the so-called New Realism in the Labour movement. The right, under Thatcher during the 1980s, became so influential that the left accepted its agenda and took on board a major part of its perspective. We were told that unless we accepted that 'times had changed' and that the class system was no longer its old self, we would never again have a Labour government. The left of the Labour movement was blamed for being alienating; the right decided to 'move with the times' and accept the market, privatisation, ownership of council houses as well as abandoning policies on full employment, nuclear weapons, trade unions and taxation. Meanwhile, the Labour Party continued not to get elected into office, while the Left achieved considerable popular success at local government level (eg the GLC) with policies more radical than any the Labour Party had ever had in its manifesto.

Feminists have been told that we need to 'rethink' our most basic principles. Much of this rethinking has come from women on the left – socialist feminists – who took on their own version of New Realism after the defeat of the Miners' strike in 1985. This demoralisation led to a 'maybe we've been wrong all along' feeling, and hence socialist feminists such as Sheila Rowbotham have written that feminists tried and failed to equalise power relations in sex during the 1980s, seeing this 'failure' as evidence that the project was 'wrong all along'. (*City Limits* magazine 1984) Ten years of feminism was supposed to defeat thousands of years of patriarchy. Since it didn't, Rowbotham concludes we must realise that: 'Sex is about power anyway'. The media has been keen to exploit this thinking in its promotion of 'post-feminism', and through particular women who it has made into 'darlings of the media', such as Kate Roiphie and Camille Paglia.

This onslaught on radical feminist politics both in and outside the movement is a depressing, but an easily anticipated part of the backlash. It is important to recognise this, and to acknowledge that in the current context, patriarchy will find ever new ways of dressing up its attack on us. As lesbian feminists we shouldn't be unduly daunted by this: radical feminism has never had it easy and never will, until patriarchy is ended.

The relentless, exhausting nature of the recent attacks on our brand of feminism has left many women demoralised. It is time for us to stop getting bogged down in the agenda set by the pro-porn lobby – even within the lesbian community – and to remember that for as long as we do so, the pornographers, and patriarchy in general are able to get on with business as usual.

During the last two years anti-pornography feminists have got over the defeatism of the late eighties and have once again begun to fight the sex industry and, more specifically, the pornography industry.

Whilst recognising that some heterosexual women and some lesbians perceive themselves as having a stake in this industry, we need to remember that the vast majority of women continue to hate porn, to feel abused and degraded by it and that this is our greatest weapon against it.

References

Assiter, A and Avedon, Carol (eds), *Bad Girls and Dirty Pictures – The challenge to reclaim feminism*, Pluto Press, London, 1993.

Segal, L, 'New Thoughts on Old Contradictions', in S Cartledge and Joanna Ryan (eds), *Sex and Love*, The Women's Press, London, 1983.

Segal, L, *Slow Motions. Changing Masculinities, Changing Men*, Virago, London, 1990.

Segal, L, *Straight Sex. The Politics of Pleasure*, Virago, London, 1994.

Sheba Collective (eds), *Serious Pleasure – Lesbian Erotic Stories and Poetry*, Sheba Feminist Publishers, London, 1989.

Miriam, K, 'From Rage to all the Rage: Lesbian Feminism, Sado-masochism and the Politics of Memory', in I Reti (ed) *Unleashing Feminism* Herbooks, Santa Cruz CA, 1993.

Rowbotham, S, 'Passion off the Pedestal', *City Limits* Magazine No 26 March 2–8 1984.

BISEXUALITY AS BACKLASH

SUE WILKINSON

MARKETING BISEXUALITY, DEPOLITICISING SEX

In the rule-breaking, gender-bending present day, bisexuality is being marketed to lesbians and straight women alike as the latest fashion. Mainstream newspapers and women's magazines sport articles entitled 'Why girls just want to have fun with each other' (*The Observer*), 'Want to get ahead? Get a girlfriend' (*The Guardian*), or 'Sappho So Good' (*Harpers & Queen*). 'Lesbian chic' (*New York, Diva, Everywoman*), 'bi-girl frisson' (*Elle*) and 'sexual tourism' (*Harpers & Queen*) are trendy. These articles suggest it's trendy to have sex with a man if you're a *lesbian*, because for a lesbian to have heterosex is 'transgressive'. Similarly the articles suggest it's chic to have sex with a woman if you're *straight*: the risqué glamour of a girlfriend is marketed as the latest fashion accessory for the heterosexual woman.

The image of the new 'sapphic sophisticate' (heterosexual or lesbian) depends on the creation of a dualism between the old-style 'political lesbian' and the new-style 'lipstick lesbian'. Lesbian feminists are caricatured as 'manhating harridans with bad haircuts and no dress sense' (Hamer and Budge 1994 p 11), political 'ugly sisters' left over from the 1970s and 1980s:

> All that late-Seventies radical feminist stuff left me lukewarm. It's not that I didn't understand or sympathise with the intellectual raison d'être; it's just that I really don't think generously pro-

portioned girls like me should wear flat tops and horizontal stripes. If men also happen to find 'chic' lesbians attractive, so what? Why do we keep using men as a reference point when defining ourselves? Why don't we see the mythology of 'lesbian chic' for what it is — an opportunity to shed the old stereotype for a new, more sexually enticing stereotype? Why should all the gay boys have all the glamour and, therefore, all the fun? (McCauley, quoted in *Diva* 1994 p 10)

Camille Paglia, 'the most famous anti-lesbian feminist lesbian feminist' (Bright 1992 p 71) has flatly declared lesbian feminists to be sexually and intellectually inert:

you [don't] understand the degree to which this absolutely sex-phobic, crazed Moonie feminism has taken over the women studies programs. I'm so happy I do not have any of these amateurish, incompetent, resentful angry women trifling with my brain. (Paglia, in Bright 1992 p 73)

And what is Paglia's prescription for the 'sex-phobic' lesbian feminist? Why, to embrace bisexual desires, of course:

I want women to be with women who are straight, who do not close themselves down against male lust. Women, I think, are naturally bisexual. You know, I'm not telling lesbians to stop sleeping only with women, but to leave open a part of the brain toward men and accept male lust and find men extremely attractive and get horny in relation to men and ogle their bodies and do something with them. Then sex with women will be hotter. (Paglia, in Bright 1992 p 82)

Conversely, the sexually adventurous heterosexual woman now gets her kicks from 'weekend lesbianism' or 'sexual tourism': 'dipping into dykedom at parties, returning to straightland by Monday morning'. (*The Pink Paper* 1994) The attraction is no responsibilities, difficulties or obligations: 'She just has carefree sex and waits until the next weekend to look and feel chic again.' (Branner 1994 p 10)

The 1990s woman therefore 'does bisexuality' (even if she calls herself a lesbian feminist) in order to spice up her sex life or to be in the vanguard of fashion. The main effect of the marketing of bisexuality as fashionable is a comprehensive depoliticisation of sex and the concomitant erasure of more than two decades of radical feminist theory. Gone are the analyses of heterosexuality as an oppressive and compulsory institution, and of lesbianism as a radical challenge to hetero-patriarchy. (Harne this volume) There is no representation of heterosex as eroticised dominance and submission, or of lesbian sado-masochism as modelled on heterosexual practice. (Reeves and Wingfield this volume)

Far from being 'new', the contemporary fashion for bisexuality seems to herald a return to sexual hedonism, doing 'whatever turns you on', simply because you like it, or because 'everyone else is doing it'. Sexual desire is clearly privileged over politics: 'Desire will out . . . We choose to acknowledge our desires and *then* find a way to live with them as feminists.' (Weise 1992 p xi, italics in original) Fashionable bisexuality also seems to be based on liberal-humanistic notions of 'self-fulfilment', 'choice', and 'freedom', albeit cloaked in a 1990s gloss of consumerism and (sometimes) therapy-speak:

> each of us has to be true to her own self . . . I CHOOSE every time I fuck. I think about it, like most people do. (Hutchins, quoted in Guidroz 1993 pp 8–9, emphasis in original)

> I make a decision each time I have sex. I choose to honor the purr in my cunt that says 'Gimme'. I choose the thrill of attraction and the promise of pleasure, the clit, the cock, the fire in the eyes. (Queen 1991 p 20)

> [calling oneself bisexual in the 1990s is] the closest approximation of freedom I can find . . . my inner child saying NO to a world where gender determines my desire and behaviour . . . I want to be able to do what I want to, to feel what I feel. (Kaplan, quoted in Elliott 1992 p 236)

The 'new' bisexuality also – paradoxically – reinforces the old idea that there are 'essentially' two sexual identities: lesbian and straight. If a lesbian having heterosex is 'transgressive', there must be some basic, underlying sexual identity which *can* be transgressed. Lesbians who have sex with men once in a while can be reassured that such practice does not mean they have to renounce a 'fundamentally lesbian' sexual identity. Likewise, the notion of 'essential' sexual orientations provides a safety-net for heterosexual women who occasionally have sex with women: they remain certain that they are 'heterosexual really', returning securely to the arms of their men after a little lesbian 'fun'.

BISEXUALITY FOR LESBIANS

Given the pressure on *all* women to have sex with men, it is perhaps not surprising that strenuous attempts are made to 'sell' heterosexual activity to lesbians, with or without an explicit bisexual tag. The message that sex with men is 'okay', 'normal', or even 'a good thing' for lesbians (or lesbian-identified bisexuals) is being marketed as: just a 'sport fuck', as 'hot sex'; as 'healing'; and as 'forbidden, therefore transgressive'.

The first of these strategies is to present sex with men as 'no big deal', just a 'sport fuck' (Elliott 1991). Apparently a 'sport fuck' is likely to occur in situations 'such as travel', when 'a good time with a kindred spirit' just happens along. '[W]hen companionship is appreciated, it doesn't make sense to stand on ceremony and refuse the lagniappe of a night shared with an interesting person.' (Elliott 1991 p 328) A variant on this is along the lines 'I wanted sex and it just happened to be a man who was available':

I'm as horny as hell and the club has just closed. The sidewalk is littered with fags, a friend of a fag walks over to me and offers his pound of flesh. I accept. Tit for tat. Dick for clit, what the fuck, Saturday night in the West End. (Taylor 1994 p 52)

It often seems to help to suggest that 'it's quite common' or that 'all lesbians do it sometimes'. So, in answer to the question, 'How can you be a lesbian and sleep with boys?', one woman said:

Easy. I am a lesbian and I sleep with guys every once in a while. Which I know many dykes do but they're just scared to admit thinking that women will see them in a different light. Most dykes get the seven-year itch even when they don't admit it to themselves. (unnamed woman, quoted in *Quim* 1994 p 55)

Surveys of sexual behaviour which emphasise the numbers of 'lesbians' who have/have had sex with men (for example Chapman and Brannock 1987; Saghir and Robins 1973) are often cited to support the 'sport fuck', most famously the 1987 Kinsey Institute survey conducted at the Michigan Women's Music Festival (in which 75 per cent of a sample of 262 women currently calling themselves lesbian said they had had sex with men since age 18, 46 per cent in the last seven years): see, for example, Bright (1992 pp 136–7); Elliott (1992 pp 235–6); and Hutchins (1993 p 8). Similarly, research which claims that self-identified 'lesbians', 'heterosexuals', and 'bisexuals' do not show clearly distinguishable and distinctive patterns of sexual behaviour (for example Blumstein and Schwartz 1976) is invoked to support the argument that bisexuality is poorly understood by lesbians, and that a greater awareness of the similarities in the experience of lesbians and bisexuals could lead to increased affiliation between them: see, for example, Rust 1992.

An opposite strategy to 'the sport fuck' is to present the deliberate choice of sex with men as 'fun' for 'lesbians', or as 'hot sex' per se:

I knew I had lesbian blood. So why did I continue to fuck men? For fun, for one thing – for the near effortless heat of it . . . and, amazingly, the more comfortable I became with being a dyke, the more fun I had having sex with men! (*Queen* 1991 pp 18–19)

Objectification, if not veneration, of the penis is a recurrent theme – what's 'new' about this is that it's now being done by 'lesbians', including so-called 'lesbian icons'. The (in)famous August 1993 issue of *Vanity Fair* (with cover photo of scantily-dressed supermodel Cindy Crawford 'shaving' masculine-attired singer k.d. lang) includes a picture of k.d. lang licking a dish, captioned 'I have a little bit of penis envy? They're ridiculous but they're cool', followed by an admission that 'I admire the male sexual drive because it's so primal and so animalistic' (quoted in Raymond 1994 pp 631–2). Camille Paglia's most flamboyant notions, which have been characterised as 'erecting a new lesbianism *based around men*' take such views to even greater extremes:

> I'm trying to bring a whole new kind of sexual sophistication to feminism, to allow even women who are openly lesbian, as I am with my lover, to say that we regard the penis as hot. It's natural for any woman, lesbian or not, to regard the penis as hot; your body naturally responds to that. (Paglia, quoted in Chauchard-Stuart 1994 p 60)

A variant on the 'hot sex' theme presents sex with men as 'therapy' or 'healing' for 'lesbians' wanting to improve their sex lives. At the forefront of such advocacy is self-proclaimed 'sexpert' JoAnn Loulan. (Stein 1993 p 15; see also Jeffreys, this volume) 'Therapeutic' advocates write, for example, of the benefit of transposing sexual techniques learnt in relationships with women lovers into a relationship with a (bisexual) man:

> I taught him about lesbian sex, about arousal and pleasure. I told him that traditional sex was too goal-oriented ... Bringing my lesbian sexual self into a relationship with a man was very healing. We took the focus off intercourse, put it onto pleasure and built a trusting safe place for me to heal. (Gonsalves 1992 p 122)

Psychologists involved in the North American lesbian sex therapy 'industry' (see Kitzinger and Perkins 1993, and this volume) have long advocated sex with men and/or sado-masochistic techniques as ways of 'spicing up' a flagging sex life (for example Nichols 1987a; Tessina 1989). Therapists who find such practices problematic are castigated as 'intolerant' (Roth 1989 p 295), 'rigid and punitive' (Toder 1978 p 113), 'erotophobic' (Nichols 1987b p 122), or 'heterophobic' (Roth 1989 p 291), and even recommended to undergo a training process known as Sexual Attitudes Reassessment, which is 'designed to help participants get in touch with and become more comfortable with their sexuality' (Hamadock 1988 p 211).

The lesbian feminist 'doctrine', 'party line', 'political correctness', 'ideological purity', or 'judgemental moralism'[1] is widely castigated as a major obstacle to 'lesbians' having sex with men. There has been a recent spate of books promoting bisexuality with anti-lesbian arguments (such as Bright 1992; Bristow and Wilson 1993; George 1993; Hutchins and Kaahumanu 1991; and Weise 1992), the most offensive of which claims that 'real lesbians (who have no contact with men or IV drugs)' are 'little more than a political myth' (Bright 1992 p 136). While many of the contributors to such anthologies simply celebrate the joys of bisexual sex, some do argue for a bisexual politics subsuming, or explicitly oppositional to, lesbian feminist politics:

> Bisexuality could even be seen to be lesbianism of post-feminism. Feminist bisexuality is a statement that says, 'Loving women now is a given; we know we love women, we know we want to be with women; and now we're strong enough to love men. On our terms.' (Choe 1992 p 22)

A common theme here is that 'lesbians' having sex with men is primarily about defiance and rule-breaking, 'freedom' and 'flaunting it': sex with men is especially exciting or 'transgressive' precisely because it is seen as 'forbidden' by lesbian feminists.

A number of (ex) 'lesbians', including singer Holly Near (1990) and writer Jan Clausen (1990), have written about the experience of sex with men. Clausen's relationship with a man 'affords an exhilarating sensation of risk-taking' (1990 p 15): in part because her lover is black, and 'the racial difference is at least as charged with tension, fascination, promise and difficulty as is the sexual one' (p 16). She does not identify as bisexual (see also Bart 1993) because 'bisexuality is not a sexual identity at all, but a sort of anti-identity, a refusal (not, of course, conscious) to be limited to one object of desire, one way of loving,' (Clausen 1990 p 19), and she continues (as does Holly Near) to march in Lesbian and Gay Pride parades. While the participation of bisexuals in Pride Marches is a political issue of some complexity, one of its specific effects is endorsing 'lesbians' having

---

[1]The references for these epithets are as follows: 'doctrine' – Elliott (1991 p 326); 'party line' – Silver (1993 p 15); 'political correctness' – Elliott (1992 p 234), Loulan (1984 p 24), Terris (1991 p 57) and Wilson (1993 p 133 and 114); 'ideological purity' – Weise (1992 p xiv); and 'judgemental moralism' – George (1993 p 57).

sex with men as a typical – and acceptable – practice, fuelling anti-lesbian protest targeted at (radical feminist) lesbians who do not share this view. Julia Penelope (1993) documents a 'Lesbian bashing' campaign of this type surrounding the 1989 Pride March in Northampton, Massachusetts. A member of the March Committee, challenged about the lack of lesbian speakers, claimed 'All Lesbians are really bisexual. They all sleep with men'; a local newsletter dubbed the lesbians organising the March 'lesbian fascists from hell', accusing them of 'oppressing' bisexuals; and bathroom graffiti appeared in a local shop saying 'Lesbians are sexual Nazis, and Bisexuals are their Jews'. (Penelope 1993 pp 8 and 16)

For many young lesbians in the 1990s, a 'bad girl attitude' is a crucial fashion accessory or lifestyle, nurtured and sustained by media hype. The May 1994 issue of *Quim*, the sex magazine 'for dykes of all sexual persuasions', includes an article entitled 'Sex Toy Boys', on 'lesbians' sleeping with boys and men. It is clear that it is the 'forbidden' aspect of sex with men that provides the turn-on: 'fucking' (or more commonly 'getting fucked') is repeatedly described – with some relish – as 'perverted', 'nasty', 'dirty'. Very similar material appears in the Spring 1993 issue of the Canadian 'feminist quarterly' *Fireweed* (whose editorial lauds 'smut'), particularly in a piece called 'Dykes and Dicks':

> We cruise straight boys and faggots, young thugs and older gentlemen, drag queens and skate rats, leather boys and suits. We cruise our co-workers, our brothers, our uncles and our friends. We have violent fantasies and fantasies that are too sweet for words. We have rape fantasies and incest fantasies. Sometimes the boys are on top, sometimes the boys are on the bottom, and sometimes we are the boys ourselves. We're dykes and boys are forbidden, so naturally we want 'em. (Thomas 1993 p 54)

Queer theory (see Parnaby this volume; Jeffreys 1994; Kitzinger and Wilkinson 1994; Wilkinson and Kitzinger 1995) provides an explicit context – and justification – for 'lesbians' having sex with men as 'transgressive' (Wilson 1992). This is particularly so when they partner (or imitate) gay men:

I saw a performance by Christine Taylor, a bisexual woman, in which she talked about her lust for gay men, and her distaste for straight ones. I am a lesbian, but I could relate. How can you lust after a straight man? But a man whose sexuality endangers him and you? Aaah. . . . queerness, renegadeness, danger. Fantasizing lesbian sex, sex in public, sex with strangers, they don't work any more. Aaah, but sex with a man, that would be transgressive. (Lizard, in *Kiss and Tell* 1994 pp 57–8)

Sex between gay men and lesbians is also coming out of the closet . . . Now people talk openly of their opposite-sex-same-sexuality lovers and at the party after the s-m Pride March a gay man and a lesbian had sex on the dance floor, but it wasn't heterosexuality. You can tell. (McKerrow, cited in Eadie 1992 p 150)

By creating a fantasy world of ambiguity, indeterminacy and charade, Queer Theory aims to deconstruct – and transcend – the categories of homosexuality and heterosexuality. However, paradoxically, these very categories are *reinforced* by 'transgressive' sexual acts and identities. It is not possible deliberately to 'transgress', to break a rule or overstep a boundary, without a clear knowledge of those rules and boundaries, the existence of which is thereby reinforced.

BISEXUALITY FOR STRAIGHT WOMEN

Lesbians have always been under pressure to have sex with men, but the widespread contemporary advice to the heterosexual woman to 'get a girlfriend' is relatively new (for some earlier – and more circumscribed – examples, see Faderman 1992). How is it that the spectre of lesbianism as sin or sickness has been overcome such the women having sex with women is now 'chic'? Lesbianism sells to *straight* women (just as it always has to straight men). Of course, the 'brand' of lesbianism has to be appropriately 'packaged', but this is a 1990s marketing success story:

How do you sell a lesbian? Easy. Slap some lipstick on the controversy, hit the mainstream, and watch the ratings rise. From diesel dyke to Sapphic sophisticate in a few years, the lesbian image has never looked so sexy – or so lucrative. (Briscoe 1994 p 57)

The 'lipstick lesbian' success story hinges around a series of 'messages' to straight women about sex with women: it's 'sweet sensations'; it's 'safer sex'; 'you can be a weekend lesbian'; and 'you won't turn into a dyke'. In all of these, *reassurance* is the keyword. In contrast to the promised titillation of 'transgression' for the lesbian who sleeps with men, the heterosexual woman who has a 'lesbian' affair is reassured that she remains within the bounds of normality, that her straight identity is not under threat, that she is just having a little fun.

Heterosexual women are enticed to have sex with women by playing on their disappointments with men:

> We're all for the phallus in general, and we know that it's supposed to be the source of the most exquisite pleasure you'll ever experience, and we keep hoping it will be, but when we get down to your common or garden penis, we find it doesn't always do the trick. (Tennant and Cripps 1994 p 124)

The promise is that it will be different with women – and an explicit contrast may be set up: 'goodbye phallus and sandpaper kisses, hello soft skin and sensational sex' (Clarke, quoted in O'Sullivan 1994 pp 88–9). Fashion models (Branner 1994 p 10) and 'beautiful bare-breasted women' (Clarke in O'Sullivan 1994 p 89) abound, and magazines extol the 'sheer, sensuous pleasure of flesh on flesh', along with images of the 'light touch', 'soft skin', and 'perfumed silk' (Tennant and Cripps 1994 pp 123–4). The newly initiated describe sapphic sex as: 'sweet, playful fun'; 'like going on holiday'; 'very exciting, enjoyable and there's a real element of fun'; and as 'more fun, safer and you don't play games. You are not going to get hurt by other women because they are basically into the same thing as you, having a laugh'. (all heterosexual women, quoted in Tennant and Cripps 1994 pp 125–7)

Sex with women is also marketed as 'safe sex in the naughty Nineties' (Tennant and Cripps 1994 p 123). It's much 'safer' than sex with men for the woman who is concerned about HIV/AIDS. In a 1989 *Harpers & Queen* article, 'Bra-Crossed Lovers' (one of the earliest to identify bisexuality as fashionable), Nicola Shulman explains ('one of the most intriguing phenomena of the late eighties' (women 'turning in droves to lesbianism') in this way:

> In fact, it's being taken up by girls who ultimately want a man. To attract said man they need a clean bill of health. Why lesbianism? It's safe – from AIDS! (Shulman, quoted in O'Sullivan 1994 p 88)

Hamer and Budge (1994) extend O'Sullivan's (1994) argument that HIV/AIDS has forced mainstream culture to engage with 'sexual diversity', suggesting that 'the spectre of AIDS' has also encouraged the promotion of images clearly differentiating lesbians from gay men and emphasising *lesbian* sexual safety. 'Devoid of the grimly profound themes of sickness and death' they say, 'lesbian sex has been able to emerge as "exciting, exploratory and glamorous".' (Hamer and Budge 1994 p 10)

Perhaps the most importantly reassuring message purveyed to the heterosexual woman about to engage in 'lesbian' sex is that it will be a purely temporary affair. Dubbed 'weekend lesbians' (Branner 1994) or 'sexual tourists' (*The Pink Paper* 1994; *Harpers & Queen* 1994), straight women 'straying across the sexual divide' (Tennant and Cripps 1994 p 123) are left in no doubt that they can return to their men at any time. Even when Madonna is seen dabbling in lesbian sex in her pornographic essay *Sex*, it is profoundly reassuring to know that 'one merely needs to turn the page to find our intrepid heroine safely back in the arms of men' (Susan, in *Kiss and Tell* 1994 p 57). The 'weekend lesbian' has a boyfriend 'who, incidentally, is built on heroic proportions and will never run low on testosterone'; or she may be 'married and expecting her first child'. She *always* 'kisses and tells': 'Her then boyfriend, now husband, couldn't possibly have minded'; 'My boyfriend doesn't mind if I go with women'; and she'll 'probably boast about it to [her] friends in the morning' (all heterosexual women, quoted in Tennant and Cripps 1994 pp 124–7). Indeed, for Branner (1994 p 10) a defining characteristic of the 'weekend lesbian' is that she 'doesn't forget to brag to at least two co-workers or a boyfriend or husband about her weekend's exploits'. Heterosexual women who have sex with other women remain certain they are straight, not lesbian, and that they won't 'turn into dykes' by indulging in 'lesbian' sex. After all, they are very different from 'real' lesbians. They are just 'girls who want to have fun', 'beautiful things', with 'no hint of the butch about them', 'subtle seductresses' (Tennant and Cripps 123); they are:

Attractive, middle–class, clever girls . . . so profoundly acceptable to society that they can afford to fool around a little. The only label they have to adopt is that of 'sexual being'. Their femininity is far from threatened by experiments in lesbianism; in fact it's probably enhanced by it. (Tennant and Cripps 1994 p 124)

'Real' lesbians (lurking in the wings as a dreadful warning) are 'sleeping bags with legs'; 'androgynous, dungareed, cropped–headed dykes with shoulders like the back of a sofa'; 'feminist guerrillas who trim their hair with the coarse plate of the cheese grater' or 'persons with Eton crops and monocles who drink stout from straight glasses and call each other Jim' (Wolff, Clarke and Shulman, all quoted in O'Sullivan 1994 pp 88–90). On the other hand, should our sexual adventurer covet today's cachet of the 'lesbian' epithet, enter a new character:

Lipstick Lesbian aka Lesbian Chic, the lesbian re–invented and sanitised. Gone are the dungarees and man–hating slogans. The new lesbian doesn't bite or scratch, she even wants to have babies, is just like me and you . . . Have they finally taken the feminist out of lesbian, the outlaw out of being out? (Smyth 1994 p 18)

Yes, with 'today's brand . . . more interested in looking and feeling sexy than in radical sexual politics' (Cash, quoted in *Diva* 1994 p 11), the heterosexual woman can call herself a 'lesbian' without having to be a dyke and/or a feminist.

THE POLITICS BEYOND THE HYPE

Whether presenting sex with men as 'transgressive' for lesbians, or sex with women as 'chic' for heterosexual women, the marketing of bisexuality as fashion functions primarily to depoliticise sex. Women's oppression in heterosex and lesbian feminist politics of resistance are both erased by an individualistic focus on pleasure, style and fashion. Lesbianism becomes no more than the latest trend – a girlfriend is a heterosexual woman's fashion accessory, 'lesbians' unproblematically have sex with men and the politics of lesbian feminism are obliterated.

The 'new' writing on bisexuality presages a return to sexual hedonism, in its clear privileging of desire over politics. Many contributors to this trend are utterly dismissive of lesbian feminism, which is seen as an idealistic 1970s throwback at best, and as a vindictive, 'politically correct' moralism at worst. In this way, contemporary writing on bisexuality continues to be actively antithetical to radical/revolutionary lesbian feminism.

Acknowledgement

With thanks to Celia Kitzinger for helpful comments on earlier versions.

References

Bart, P, 'Protean woman: The liquidity of female sexuality and the tenaciousness of lesbian identity', in S Wilkinson and C Kitzinger (eds), *Heterosexuality: A 'Feminism & Psychology' Reader*, Sage Publications, London, 1993.

Blumstein, P W and Schwartz, P, 'Bisexuality in women', *Archives of Sexual Behaviour*, 1976, 5 (2) pp 171–81.

Branner, A C, 'Weekend lesbians', *off our backs*, July 1994, pp 10–11.

Bright, S, *Sexual Reality: A Virtual Sex World Reader*, Cleis Press, San Francisco CA, 1992.

Briscoe, J, 'Lesbian hard sell', *Elle*, May 1994, pp 57–60.

Bristow, J and Wilson, A R, *Activating Theory: Lesbian, Gay, Bisexual Politics*, Lawrence and Wishart, London, 1993.

Chapman, B E and Brannock, J C, 'Proposed model of lesbian identity development: An empirical examination', *Journal of Homosexuality*, 1987, 14 pp 69–80.

Chauchard-Stuart, S, 'The dyke from hell?', *Phase*, No 3 May 1994, pp 59–61.

Choe, M M, 'Our selves, growing whole', in E R Weise (ed), *Closer to Home: Bisexuality and Feminism*, Seal Press, Seattle WA, 1992.

Clausen, J, 'My interesting condition', in *Out/Look: National Lesbian and Gay Quarterly*, 1990, 7 pp 10–21.

Diva, 'Lesbian chic', 1994 No 1, pp 10–11.

Eadie, J, 'Activating bisexuality: Towards a bi/sexual politics', In J Bristow and A R Wilson (eds), *Activating Theory: Lesbian, Gay, Bisexual Politics*, Lawrence and Wishart, London, 1993.

Elliott, B, 'Bisexuality: The best thing that ever happened to lesbian-feminism?', in L Hutchins and L Kaahumanu (eds), *Bi Any Other Name: Bisexual People Speak Out*, Alyson Publications, Boston MA, 1991.

Elliott, B, 'Holly Near and yet so far', in E R Weise (ed), *Closer to Home: Bisexuality and Feminism*, Seal Press, Seattle WA, 1992.

Faderman, L, *Odd Girls and Twilight Lovers: A History of Lesbian Life in Twentieth Century America*, Penguin, New York, 1992.

Fireweed Sex and Sexuality, 1993, Vol 2, Issue 38

George, S, *Women and Bisexuality*, Scarlet Press, London, 1993.

Gonsalves, S, 'Where healing becomes possible', in E R Weise (ed), *Closer to Home: Bisexuality and Feminism*, Seal Press, Seattle WA, 1992.

Guidroz, K, 'Out and proud, bi and sexual: An interview with Loraine Hutchins', *off our backs*, (Sex Issue Part 1), Aug-Sept pp 8–10.

Hamadock, S, 'Lesbian sexuality in the framework of psychotherapy: A practical model for the lesbian therapist', in E Cole and E Rothblum (eds), *Women and Sex Therapy: Closing the Circle of Sexual Knowledge*, Harrington Park Press, New York, 1988.

Hamer, D and Budge, B (eds), *The Good, The Bad and The Gorgeous: Popular Culture's Romance With Lesbianism*, Pandora, London, 1994.

Hutchins, L and Kaahumanu, L, *Bi Any Other Name: Bisexual People Speak Out*, Alyson Publications, Boston MA, 1991.

Jeffreys, S, 'The queer disappearance of lesbians', *Women's Studies International Forum*, 1994, 17(5) pp 459–72.

Kiss and Tell, *Her Tongue on My Theory: Images, Essays and Fantasies*, Press Gang Publishers, Vancouver, 1994.

Kitzinger, C and Perkins, R, *Changing Our Minds: Lesbian Feminism and Psychology*, Onlywomen Press, London: New York University Press, 1993.

Kitzinger, C and Wilkinson, S, 'Virgins and queers: Rehabilitating heterosexuality?', in B Schneider (ed), *Sexual Identities/Sexual Communities*, a special issue of *Gender and Society*, 1994, 8(3) pp 444–63.

Loulan, J, *Lesbian Sex*, Spinsters Ink, San Francisco, CA, 1984.

Near, H, *Fire in the Rain, Singer in the Storm*, William Morrow, New York, 1990.

Nichols, M, 'Doing sex therapy with lesbians: Bending a heterosexual paradigm to fit a gay lifestyle', in Boston Lesbian Psychologies Collective (ed), *Lesbian Psychologies: Explorations and Challenges*, University of Illinois Press, 1987a.

Nichols, M, 'Lesbian sexuality: Issues and developing theory', in Boston Lesbian Psychologies Collective (ed), ibid, 1987b.

O'Sullivan, S, 'Girls who kiss girls and who cares?', in D Hamer and B Budge (eds), *The Good, The Bad, and The Gorgeous: Popular Culture's Romance With Lesbianism*, Pandora, London, 1994.

Penelope, J, 'Lesbianville, USA?', *off our backs*, (Sex Issue Part Two), Oct 1993, p 8 and 16–17.

The Pink Paper, 'Sexual tourism', 27 May 1994.

Queen, C A 'The Queer in me', in L Hutchins and L Kaahumanu (eds), *Bi Any Other Name: Bisexual People Speak Out* Alyson Publications, Boston MA, 1991.

Raymond, J, 'The politics of transgender', *Feminism & Psychology: an International Journal*, 1994 4(4) pp 628–33.

Roth, S 'Psychotherapy with lesbian couples: Individual issues, female socialization, and the social context', in M McGoldrick, C Anderson and F Walsh (eds), *Women in Families: A Framework for Family Therapy*, Norton, New York, 1989.

Rust, P C, 'The politics of sexual identity: Sexual attraction and behaviour among lesbian and bisexual women', *Social Problems*, 1992 39(4) pp 366–83.

Saghir, M T and Robins, E, *Male and Female Homosexuality*, Williams and Wilkins, Baltimore, MD, 1973.

Silver, N, 'Coming out as a heterosexual', in E R Weise (ed), *Closer to Home: Bisexuality and Feminism*, Seal Press, Seattle WA, 1992.

Smyth, C *Lesbians talk Queer Notions*, Scarlet Press, London, 1992.

Smyth, C, 'Playing it straight', *Everywoman*, April 1994, pp 18–19.

Stein, A (ed), *Sisters, Sexperts, Queers: Beyond the Lesbian Nation*, Plume, New York, 1993.

Taylor, C, 'Boy meat', *Quim*, 1994, no 5 p 52.

Tennat, L and Cripps, C, 'Sappho so good', *Harpers & Queen*, June 1994, pp 123–27.

Terris, E, 'My life as a lesbian-identified bisexual fag hag', in L Hutchins and L Kaahumanu (eds), *Bi Any Other Name: Bisexual People Speak Out*, Alyson Publications, Boston MA, 1991.

Tessina, T, *Gay Relationships*, Jeremy P Tarcher, Los Angeles, CA, 1989.

Thomas, T, 'Dykes and dicks', *Fireweed*, 1993 issue 38 pp 54–60.

Toder, N, 'Lesbian sex problems', in G Vida (ed), *Our Right to Love: A Lesbian Resource Book*, Prentice Hall, Englewood Cliffs, NJ, 1978.

Weise, E R (ed), *Closer to Home: Bisexuality and Feminism*, Seal Press, Seattle, WA, 1992.

Wilkinson, S and Kitzinger, C (eds), *Heterosexuality: A 'Feminism & Psychology' Reader*, Sage Publications, London, 1993.

Wilkinson, S and Kitzinger, C 'The queer backlash', in D Bell and R Klein (eds), *Radically Speaking: Feminism Reclaimed*, Spinifex Press, Melbourne, Australia, 1995.

Wilson, E, 'Crossed wires in the gender debate', *The Guardian*, 2 May 1992.

Wilson, E, 'Is transgression transgressive?', in J Bristow and A R Wilson (eds), *Activating Theory: Lesbian, Gay, Bisexual Politics*, Lawrence and Wishart, London, 1993.

THE ESSENTIAL LESBIAN

SHEILA JEFFREYS

In the last decade there has been a startling return to biological arguments to explain homosexuality. This regression to biologism has come from gay male researchers in particular. It is but one example of the retreat to Victorian values in gay theory and practice which is taking place in the present. In the queer politics of the 1990s there is much evidence of a return to the values of the 1890s. The theories of Victorian sexologists are being recycled as the truth about lesbians and gay men as we approach a new century. Along with biologism we see a fresh insistence on the minority status of homosexuality for women and men. The deviancy of this minority status is being celebrated again. There is a return to the idea that homosexual relations are inevitably founded on hierarchy and modelled on hetero-relations. The masculine lesbian, the congenital, original, genuine invert of the sexologists, roams lesbian culture in the 1990s as she did in the case studies of one hundred years ago.

Opposition to the stereotypes and hostile ideology of sexology, particularly the idea that sexual orientation was biologically based, was fundamental to the activism of gay liberationists and lesbian feminists in the 1970s. The 1960s and 1970s were the great decades of social constructionism. Social theorists vigorously opposed biological arguments about racial inferiority, gender differences, and mental illness. It was recognised that the biological explanations provided the scientific basis for conservative social engineering. Biological arguments, arguments from nature, could be used to assert the rightness and inevitability of women's subordination, of racial inequality, of heterosexual hegemony and of drugs and institutions for those suffering from mental ill health. In the 1980s the confidence in social constructionism was rocked by the adherence of some lesbians and gay men to a fresh wave of biological determinism to explain sexual orientation. Some lesbian theorists have even begun to assert that butch-femme role-playing and masculinity and femininity in their stereotypical forms are natural, even unavoidable, for lesbians.

The renewed faith in biology comes mainly from male gay theorists but it is affecting lesbians too. The impact on a new generation of lesbians was impressed upon me when I was recently interviewed in the UK for a student newspaper by a young lesbian. I explained my progression to lesbianism through a kind of sexual neutrality in my teens, and eight years of heterosexuality in my twenties to political lesbianism at 28. She assured me that I must have been a 'latent' all along. I was not comforted by this assurance since my choice of lesbianism is a source of considerable pride and sense of achievement and not something I wish to relegate to biology.

It is not surprising, though, that it is mainly from gay men that the new enthusiasm for biology comes. Gay activists never subscribed to the slogan 'Any man can be gay' when lesbian feminists were wearing badges saying 'Any woman can be a lesbian'. At the turn of the last century male gay rights campaigners, such as Edward Carpenter, adopted the biological arguments of sexology with great relief and hope that the idea that they could not help themselves could form the basis of a plea for public sympathy. Traditional gay male politics continued to rely on this idea. Lesbians are often surprised to discover how deep the reliance on biology goes among some gay men, even sometimes those of otherwise progressive politics. When teaching a lesbian and gay studies evening class in the early 1980s I found that the gay male students were swift to express some belief in biology. The majority of lesbian students expressed complete rejection of the idea. The lesbians had very often been heterosexual, wives and mothers, and had often not thought of loving women until well past their teens. A biological explanation would not have made sense in terms of their experience or their politics.

A considerable difference over biology between male gay and lesbian-feminist activists was evident in the campaign in the UK against Section 28 of the Local Government Act 1988. Prominent gay speak-

.ers went on television to argue that the amendment against the 'promotion of homosexuality' was a nonsense because homosexuality was innate and couldn't be promoted. Lesbian activists were amazed. This was the opposite of lesbian-feminist politics and judging from debate on the amendment in the House of Commons it seemed that it was lesbian-feminist efforts precisely to promote lesbianism that were causing alarm in conservative legislators. There seemed to be a fundamental political difference here, and even though some gay activists were critical of this biological position they were not in the ascendant. (Alderson and Wistrich 1986 pp 3–8).

In 1987 there was a lesbian and gay studies conference in Amsterdam for which the theme was 'Essentialism versus Social Constructionism'. This seemed to be a controversy which was pressing for those who had planned the conference. The introduction to the collected papers states 'For a decade there has been a growing controversy among gay and lesbian scholars centring around two rival scientific theories and their implications for homosexuality, *essentialism* and *constructionism*.' (Altman et al. 1989 p 6).

Lesbian feminists were merely puzzled that a question they thought had been answered twenty years before should excite so much interest in 1987. The fact that such a question could be seen as important enough to stage a whole conference around suggested that a belief in essentialism must be alive and well somewhere outside the lesbian-feminist community. Lesbian-feminist theorists were still busily challenging the institution of heterosexuality, suggesting that all women could make the choice to be lesbian save for the restrictions imposed by compulsory heterosexuality. Considering whether they were essentially lesbian was a non-question.

In the 1990s the rollback of social constructionism carries on apace with the help of male gay medical researchers who are 'finding' gay brains and genes. In 1991 Simon LeVay published his finding of an area within the brains of gay men which distinguished them from heterosexuals. In 1992 Dean Hamer published his research which has been seen, erroneously, as uncovering a gay gene. LeVay studied the brains of gay men who had died from AIDS and of men who claimed they were not gay who had died from the same cause. He apparently found that a tiny area of the hypothalamus was on average twice as large in heterosexual men as in either heterosexual women or homosexual men. He suggested that varying hormone levels before birth 'wired' the hypothalamus for either heterosexuality or homosexuality.

LeVay sees his work as having positive outcomes in ending discrimination against gays. He had always believed that homosexuality was biologically determined and set out to prove it so that anti-gay discrimination might be opposed on the grounds that gays were condemned by nature to their behaviour and must be treated with the mercy that should be shown to any group who cannot help themselves. LeVay has not yet had access to the brains of lesbians but is convinced that he will find that their brains resemble those of heterosexual men in the crucial area.

As turn-of-the-nineteenth-century sexologists based their understanding of homosexuality on the idea of gender confusion, so do their counterparts today. Despite all the best efforts of feminists and gay liberation activists to dismantle the idea that gay men were somehow innately feminine and lesbians somehow innately masculine this idea flourishes today. It seems that all biological understandings of homosexuality are based upon the idea of gender transposition and if you believe that gender is a social construction then it is hard to take any biological explanations seriously. Gay activists who support the notion of biological determinism tend to lose all their political sense around gender.

Peter Tatchell, for instance, a British gay activist, produced some astonishing stereotypes of lesbians and gay men, clearly based upon the idea of gender transposition, when explaining why parents should not abort gay foetuses:

> Compared to heterosexual males, gay men tend to be more sensitive and caring . . . and are disproportionately involved in the creative arts and caring professions. Lesbians are generally more independent and assertive than heterosexual women. These attributes are of immense individual and social value. (*Rouge* issue 14 1993 p 11)

These views replicate very precisely those of Carpenter in his book *The Intermediate Sex*. For the 1890s they were a radical defence of the social value of homosexuality. In the 1990s they look very old fashioned and apologetic.

LeVay believes in gender transposition, too. The area that he found in the hypothalamus to indicate male homosexuality is smaller than that in apparently heterosexual men and similar in size to that of women. The women's brains he examined were undifferentiated as to sexual orientation, which is a major flaw in his research technique. He believes that biology is responsible for differences between males and females in behaviour. He thinks that women are more verbally competent than men and men more spatially competent than women by reason of brain differences.

He manages to associate these brain differences with the fact that gay men are 'less strongly right-handed than straight men'. (Campaign 1992) LeVay is clearly prepared to believe that any number of stereotypical differences between men and women are the result of biology with no evidence whatsoever apart from his hunches. Most worryingly he believes that 'male and female sex drives are biologically determined'. One fundamental insight of feminist theory is that male sexual behaviour is learned and not natural. There would be no hope otherwise of women's freedom from sexual violence. LeVay's wisdom suggests otherwise:

In general, throughout the entire mammalian kingdom, men are more promiscuous than women. Males have the potential to father an unlimited number of offspring. It's cheap for them to inseminate a female, so it's in their interest to be as promiscuous as they can. For a female, it's quite different ... There's no question in my mind that this characteristic is biologically determined. There's something in the brains of males and females that causes them to be this way. Now if you look at gay man and lesbians, this trait is not sex-reversed. In fact, this trait in gay men is no longer restricted by women's unwillingness – so the sky is the limit. Most straight men don't get as much sex as they want because women won't let them. (Ibid.)

LeVay shows us that biological arguments about 'gay genes' can lead directly into biological arguments that justify women's oppression.

It is worrying that the LeVay theory has been treated enthusiastically by some of the gay press and at least with sympathetic curiosity by the rest. The return to essentialism is in full swing it seems. Feminists have been particularly hostile to biological determinist explanations because the very idea of feminism, the possibility of its birth, depends on fighting the idea of biologically constructed psychological differences between the sexes. After a good grounding in such a battle it is not possible for lesbian feminists to be sanguine about biological explanations of homosexuality. Gay men can be because their freedom as men does not depend to the same extent on fighting biologism.

Women's 'difference' or femininity has been explained in lesbian-feminist theory as a male invention, and the subjection of women to femininity as a projection on to women of men's fantasies, or as one separatist put it:

> Men project onto females all of their own deficiencies (cowardice, illogicality, inanity, dishonesty, treachery, pettiness, etc.) and they push onto females an array of male-invented feminine mannerisms and styles that encourage weakness, dependence, submissiveness and general fuckability. (Bev, Strega & Ruston 1990)

Femininity has been experienced by lesbian feminists simply as brutal restriction of freedom, as torture of the body. Lesbians have been freer to abandon its dictates and express total rejection. The same writer makes femininity sound quite brutal:

> We're supposed to believe it's natural to want to mince along on stilted shoes, face masked with stinking, lurid chemicals, nails bloody talons, dieted-jazzercized-depilated-plastic-surgeried bodies encased in exposing dresses, voices unnaturally high, gestures 'cute' and aggressively flirtatious, and minds focused on pleasing men at all costs. (Ibid.)

Heterosexual feminists have demolished the myth of femininity effectively, too, most notably Naomi Wolf in *The Beauty Myth* (1990). She, like other feminist theorists before her, shows how the fashion and beauty industries encourage women to do grave damage to their bodies and even starve themselves to death through eating disorders. What is surprising then is that femininity is being reintroduced presently into lesbian culture as a new and revolutionary erotic possibility.

In the 1970s lesbian feminists, myself included, wore badges saying 'Any woman can be a lesbian' and we believed it. We believed it not just on good political grounds such as our resistance to biological theories of gender or sexual behaviour, but because for many of us it was our experience. Thousands of women who had not knowingly considered lesbianism as a possibility, left men and committed all their emotional and sexual energies to women, and are still so committed today. (see Jeffreys in Holdsworth 1988) The idea of political lesbianism, as this phenomenon was generally called, was controversial at the time. Political lesbians were accused by some of not being 'real' lesbians since they were seen as turning to women for political reasons rather than out of a lifelong determination. But no lesbian feminists would have thought of arguing that lesbians and heterosexual women were simply two distinct biological categories.

Joan Nestle, the leading propagandist of the new lesbian role-playing, does state categorically 'I think the phrase, *every woman is a potential Lesbian*, is no longer useful'. (Nestle 1990 p 124) She says it was simply a 'rhetorical device' and that now is the time for lesbians and heterosexual women to simply recognise their different 'choices'. Lesbians must now 'stop bullying women into sexual stances, to end the assumption that only Lesbians make choices.' The 'bullying' she has in mind probably comprises the exciting theoretical work by lesbian feminists such as Adrienne Rich and Monique Wittig who analyse heterosexuality as a political institution. A new determinism which reifies the sexual categories of the male supremacist sexual system has crept in here under the rhetoric of choice. It is from the pornographers of the new role-playing, the therapists of role-playing, that the new essentialism flows. This is not particularly surprising, because at the root of a belief in role-playing there is inevitably an essentialist foundation.

Femininity and masculinity returned to the lesbian community in the context of the rehabilitation of role-playing in the early 1980s. Though there are lesbians who were unaffected by such developments, the lessening of gender fetishism in the 1960s and the impact of feminism provided a liberation for many of those lesbians who had previously used roles. Julia Penelope is a lesbian theorist who had chosen to abandon butch role-playing. She was horrified to see a revalidation and in 1984 she attacked the new role-playing from a strong and clear radical feminist perspective:

The impulse to revive the labels 'butch' and 'femme' and inject some political respectability into their meaning (however belatedly) by talking about 'gut feelings', 'intuitions', and 'power' is the lesbian manifestation of the contemporary right wing backlash, further encouraged by 50s nostalgia ('Happy Days'), and the illusion of security we get by going back to what we imagine to have been 'better days', (usually because we didn't live through them), and talking about 'reclaiming our heritage'. (Penelope 1984 p 42)

As Penelope points out, the new role-playing was legitimated with appeals to lesbian history, usually the 1950s.

Another lesbian who abandoned the butch role explains that she defined herself in the mid-1950s as a butch and aspired to be a 'Big Bad Butch' who saw femmes as 'too sissy or too inadequate to be butch'. She is amazed that any lesbians today could 'plead ignorance of the woman-hating elements which permeated the traditional butch-femme identities':

It's easy to feel nostalgia for the good old, bad old days . . . There's a thrill to conquest. There's a thrill to overpowering someone, either literally or figuratively. But for me those old roles were terribly crippling and it took a long time to free myself from their grip. (Koertge 1986 p 103)

She explains that the rigidity of roles was alleviated by the 'hippie sixties' which allowed men to wear beads and long hair. But what she describes as the 'big breakthrough' came with the women's liberation movement through which she learned to 'combine strength with sensitivity, and to widen our conceptions of sexuality and sensuality'. She concludes:

At this point it seems mad to jeopardise this ethos for the cheap thrills of black leather jackets and dolly dresses . . . We no longer have any excuse for letting the popular punk culture define for us what is sexy, what is romantic, what is worth living for. (Ibid.)

But the pursuit of 'cheap thrills' through role-playing within the lesbian community has burgeoned through the 1980s and into today and is indeed jeopardising the survival of the lesbian-feminist critique of masculinity and femininity. The imitation of the political class system of heterosexuality demonstrates a staggering exactitude in recent role-playing literature. The role-players see no humour in their project, even in its more unlikely manifestations, perhaps because humour would puncture the erotic buzz that is supposed to be one of the main benefits thereof. *The Persistent Desire*, a role-playing anthology edited by Joan Nestle, reveals the extraordinary lengths to which the promoters of role-playing are prepared to go in their imitation of some of the most politically oppressive aspects of heterosexuality. The role-playing propagandists reject any suggestion that their practice could be politically constructed and derived from the oppression of women.

One article by Paula Austin a 'black self-identified femme' gives a representative picture of the way this role-playing imitates old-fashioned heterosexuality. Austin realises she is a femme while in a relationship with a lesbian named Rhon. Austin opines that 'I was convinced she had hidden somewhere in the recesses of her clothing a penis.' Rhon is attractive because she is 'hard, the hardest dyke I had ever been with.' About another lover Buddy, she writes 'I love the hardness, the hint of power and violence, the strength, the inkling of being owned.' Austin confesses to angst over her 'femme-ininity' and whether it is politically correct but clearly decides to disregard her concerns. This is her description of her 'femme-ininity':

Being femme for me means wearing a short, tight skirt, garters, and three-inch heels when I'm going out. It means standing in front of the mirror putting on mascara and reddish brown lipstick. It means shopping for a low cut blouse to reveal a hint of cleavage some nights. It means smiling, or sometimes pouting, when my woman puts her arm around my waist and, with her other hand, turns my face up to kiss hers. It means whispering, 'I'm yours, own me,' when she makes love to me. It means feeling sexy. (Austin 1992 pp 362–5)

This, like other descriptions of the new role-playing, has a Mills and Boon quality. But what is ironic is that within heterosexuality women are refusing such gendered inequality. A generation of heterosexual young women would find such material for a heterosexual audience frankly embarrassing and even Mills and Boon are having to market slightly more egalitarian models today. The 'hint of power and violence' that excites Austin is likely to mean real abuse in heterosexuality and often means such in lesbian relationships too.

The model role-playing relationships described in the anthology have a flavour of down home, folksy, working class, heart of America, 1950s heterosexuality. Femmes welcome their butches home after a hard day, usually performing manual labour but sometimes a professional occupation, and proceed to offer them comfort against a harsh world. As Nestle expresses this, 'When she comes home to me, I must caress the parts of her that have been worn thin, trying to do her work in a man's world.' (Nestle 1992b p 348)

One wonders what the femmes are supposed to do all day, bake cakes? Then the femme is supposed to make her butch feel safe enough to let herself be vulnerable, revealed in being made love to, but her masculinity must be protected: 'I know how to make love to/Your woman's body/Without taking your masculinity away.' (Califia 1992b p 418) The role of the femme, like that of the traditional housewife, is to nurture the power of her butch so that she can retain her place in the male ruling class and her power over her. Though this might seem very perplexing from a feminist perspective, the idealisation of precisely the power dynamics that keep women subordinate and abused within heterosexual relationships is seen as positive by the new role-players. But then they seem to have asserted a declaration of independence from the feminist movement. Some repudiate their previous feminism, others say they have never been feminists.

Lyndall MacCowan, a femme, explains in *The Persistent Desire* that she never identified with feminism or with being a woman. She says that when she came out in the 1970s:

It would've been heretical then, as it still is now, to be a lesbian and assert that feminism has little meaning for me – imagine trying to be an atheist in fourteenth-century Europe. Yet such a statement is true, and it's important to say it, because feminism has come to overshadow lesbianism's meaning. It's not that I don't believe women are oppressed, but I've never been able to identify myself with that all-encompassing group 'woman'. I've never been anywhere near being as oppressed as a woman as I am as a lesbian.

MacCowan states that being a lesbian means 'knowing that I am not a woman'. (MacCowan 1992 pp 309–11) Yet being a lesbian femme actually subjects her directly to the oppression of women. Paula Austin writes about the difficulty of having to suffer men's sexual harassment because she looks like a heterosexual woman and one might have thought that MacCowan who favours similar apparel would have the same problem.

Angry statements about the authoritarian and bullying behaviour of lesbian feminists towards those in their ranks like MacCowan or JoAnn Loulan who really wanted to be femmes are common in this role-playing literature. This approach relieves these writers of responsibility for having consciously espoused feminist ideas in the 1970s. Rather than really being silent victims when they were in the lesbian-feminist movement, it is likely that they have simply changed their minds to fit the fashion of the conservative backlash.

It is in the explanations offered for role-playing that the essentialism behind butch-femme ideology is clearest. Baldly biological explanations are not usually suggested though even these are returning in some areas. Loulan suggests that homosexuality is hereditary, an idea abandoned even by most sexologists once psychoanalysis caught on before the Second World War:

Some of us are just born that way. It probably is genetic; homosexuality does run strongly in some families. I know a woman who has six brothers and sisters and all but one are gay.

She says 'we can depend' on stories of homosexuality running in families 'to prove that yes, one of the components is our DNA'. (Loulan 1990 pp 193–4) It does seem surprising that the fact that the vast majority of lesbians and gay men have heterosexual parents does not shake the appeal of the hereditary argument. Interestingly she wants to use a combination of explanations using genetics for some and 'choice' for others. The genetic variety are apparently self identified, if you say you are a genetic than you are. This combination is reminiscent of the old sexological idea that homosexuals were divided into inverts and perverts. Inverts were the congenitals who couldn't help it and deserved sympathy and the perverts had deliberately chosen to be bad. It is interesting that the thinking of someone like Loulan who did have a brush with feminism in the 1970s could revert so easily to traditional sexology.

It suggests a deeply rooted conservatism which her experience of feminism was not sufficient to alter. Loulan has anxieties about suggesting that all homosexuality is genetic because she is aware this could be used to suggest a 'genetic defect' and she does not think lesbianism is 'pathological'. In explaining role-playing Loulan opts for a psychological explanation in terms of archetypes. She says that lesbians have certain archetypes buried deep within their collective unconscious which cannot be argued with. Each one is 'an image that determines behaviour and emotional responses unconsciously.' (Bolen, in Loulan 1990 p 17)

Role-playing is then not the result of a biological but a psychological determinism. The commonest lesbian archetypes are 'the concepts of butch and femme and then recently androgyny as well'. (Ibid. p 20) Archetypal role-playing is apparently so determining that all lesbians are somehow connected to role-playing even if they won't admit it. She describes 'this lesbian eroticism of butch and femme' as something 'which each of us has a connection to, which each of us has been made to deny, put down, and be ashamed of '. (Ibid. p 29) This leaves those who still want to deny it in some sort of false consciousness.

Her audiences tend to be in this benighted state. She says that when she asks audiences whether they have ever rated themselves on a butch-femme scale, 95 per cent say they have, but when asked if role-playing is important to them then 95 per cent say it is 'unimportant in their lives' (Ibid. p 43) The only explanation, for Loulan, is that 95 per cent of lesbians are in denial and it is Loulan's sad duty to try to open them up to the delights of role-playing. Sexologists have traditionally taken on such awesome responsibilities and not quailed at the idea of having to change women's sexual behaviour en masse to fit in to their prescriptions. (Jeffreys 1985)

Joan Nestle, in a 1985 panel on role-playing, offered a version of the archetype theory. She says that when she met a butch she experienced 'some kind of basic, prehistoric foreknowledge of each other' (in Loulan 1990 p 98). Another panel participant, Jewelle Gomez, asserts that role-playing is natural and inevitable. She sees butch and femme as representing the 'two poles that nature presents each of us with.' (Ibid. p 49) As evidence she presents folk wisdom and the yin and yang of Eastern religion. She considers that this ancient wisdom was lost in western European puritanical religion which caused people to forget that 'there are two sides within individuals'. Presumably feminism, which questioned the folk wisdom of all patriarchal ideologies about the essential nature of gender, shared in this tragic forgetting. This essential dualism she describes as 'a natural principle, a natural, psychological, biological, emotional, physiological principle.' (Ibid. p 50) This doesn't leave much space for conscientious objectors.

There are lesbian academics as well as sex therapists involved in promoting the new essentialism of role-playing, Saskia Wieringa is an anthropologist who claims once to have made the mistake, because of a feminist consciousness, of seeing butch-femme culture in the West as 'rather outdated'. Then she experienced the lesbian-bar culture of Jakarta and Lima and realised 'how narrow my own so-called *political lesbianism* was.' (Wieringa 1989 p 215) The discovery of something similar to western role-playing in other cultures convinced her of the poverty of social constructionist approaches to lesbianism. She decided that psychobiological factors must be involved. The existence of role-playing in cultures outside the West could be used to support a feminist social constructionist approach. If lesbian role-playing is related to heterosexual role-playing then we would expect it to be particularly strong in periods and in cultures in which gender differentation was enforced most strictly within heterosexuality. This might explain the bar culture of Jakarta and Lima more easily than the invention of some role-playing essence.

Feminist explanations of role-playing which link it to male supremacist sex roles are roundly rejected by its proponents. Loulan attributes the feminist idea that role-playing lesbians are 'mimicking male/female roles' to lesbian self-hatred, our fear that lesbians are just an inferior version of heterosexuality. She says that 'somewhere in our deepest homophobic selves, we agree that lesbians are an ersatz version of the heterosexual model', whereas in fact 'butch and femme have nothing to do with male and female'. (Loulan 1990 p 48) Role-playing is 'something profoundly female' which instead of deriving from male/female derives from some other root, an archetype or principle from which both male/female roles and lesbian ones stem, a dualism in nature. This means that rather than imitating a heterosexual original, lesbians get their roles independently and from the same source in nature as heterosexual men and women do. It is quite surprising, then, that the great original dualism in nature should be so specific about who does the vacuuming and gossiping, but it does seem to be. This is Loulan's description of 'femme energy':

> A certain lightness, a certain sparkle, a certain interest in every single little detail about what my best friend said to that person she met in the grocery store. A connection to gossip columns filled with people I don't know and will never meet. (Ibid. p 102)

Presumably lesbians suffering from depression could not be femmes, since they would lack the required sparkle. Respondents to her survey who identified as femme annoyed Loulan by being 'most likely to initiate cleaning and decorating the house, doing childcare, organizing social activities, and doing the actual socializing.' (Ibid. p 48) She feels this is too like male/female roles. It might even suggest that femmeness has something to do with learnt female subordination rather than the great archetypes in the sky.

Lyndall MacCowan asserts that masculinity and femininity in heterosexuality are just two genders and really there could be many more. Butch and femme are genders too, – 'lesbian-specific genders' – and part of the potentially great variety. She believes that 'gender systems are a cultural universal' and that it is not true that 'a gender system always implies sexism or homophobia'. Gender is only oppressive if limited in a particular society to two and 'rigidly correlated' with biological sex. According to this unusual interpretation of gender as simply an erotic category, she sees 'androgyny' as a lesbian gender too. Clearly role-players have to repudiate a feminist analysis of gender if they are to have self-respect and believe their games are harmless. So they seek to create confusion about what gender is.

A feminist analysis sees gender as being a political category, deriving from the political class system into which human beings are placed in accordance with possession or non possession of a penis. Those possessing the masculine gender form not simply an interesting erotic category, but the ruling class in the system of oppression called male supremacy in which women are suffering and dying. The power difference between these two gender classes is eroticised to be what is understood as sex under male supremacy. Therefore many, to have sex, need to have a gender and relate to someone of the opposite gender. 'Gender' as a way to get sexual kicks is directly derived from gender the regulating mechanism of the class system of male supremacy. MacCowan ends her piece by saying it is 'time we reclaim the right to fuck around with gender'. (MacCowan 1992 pp 318 and 323) But it is difficult to see how the slavish repetition of the feminine role to which a woman has been brought up, trying to live as a Mills and Boon heroine, is 'fucking around' with anything at all.

And the opportunities for heterosexual women to thus 'fuck around' seem even more limited. If they try femininity no one will notice and if they try masculinity they might meet some opposition from men.

Lesbian feminists who oppose role-playing are called 'androgynes' in role-playing literature. Lesbian feminists do not generally use this word to apply to themselves because it does not mean the elimination of masculinity and femininity which is the feminist project. Androgyny represents the combination of masculinity and femininity in one person. Janice Raymond sees the idea of androgyny as fundamental to justifying heterosexuality as a political institution:

... hetero–reality and hetero–relations are built on the myth of androgyny. 'Thou as a woman must bond with a man' to fulfil the supposed cosmic purpose of reunifying that which was mythically separated into male and female. Arguments supporting the primacy and prevalence of hetero–relations are in some way based on a cosmic male–female polarity in which the lost halves seek to be rejoined. (Raymond 1986)

Androgyny is a concept that lesbian feminists reject. It can be no accident therefore that role-players use it to refer to feminists. They are seeking to draw those who specifically reject and seek to dismantle gender back under its poisonous rule. Loulan calls the feminist project of demolishing hierarchies of power and seeking equality the 'androgynous imperative'. She is particularly dismissive of any pursuit of equality in sexual relationships:

> The lesbian who subscribes to the androgynous imperative idealizes a relationship that has no differences in power. There is no way to keep a relationship of any sort power-free. The fact that there are two people exchanging energy means that they are passing power back and forth. (Loulan 1990 pp 73 and 76)

It is the exciting erotic possibilities offered by the power differences being introduced to or formalised in lesbian relationships through role-playing that explains its new popularity. It does not derive from nature, psychological imperative or tradition.

The new role-players appeal to lesbian history to legitimate their practice, as if they are simply continuing an honourable tradition.

I have argued elsewhere that those seeking to rehabilitate role-playing in the 1980s were doing so for rather different reasons, specifically erotic ones (Jeffreys 1989). The new role-playing is a variety of the newly fashionable sado-masochism.

It does not resemble its historical counterpart because gender roles have been exploded by feminist theory and are no longer compulsory, certainly not for those now promoting them who are well versed in such theory. The political repression of the 1950s had made role-playing a form of protection when one of a lesbian couple could 'pass' in the street, and had made it difficult for some lesbians to think beyond gender difference because of the blanket propaganda of separate spheres and women's difference that pervaded that decade. The 1980s and 1990s are a very different time. A far-reaching feminist critique of heterosexuality from Jill Johnston to Adrienne Rich and Monique Wittig has spelled out the emptiness of traditional heterosexuality and named it as an institution of political control of women. An imitation of the rules of this institution could not be performed out of ignorance in the 1980s by those who had been steeped in feminist theory.

Role-playing in the 1980s is the soft pornography compared with the hard-core pornography of lesbian s-m. It provides the thrill of eroticised power difference without the extremes of violence and vulgarity. Merrill Mushroom describes the advantages of role-playing using the catchwords of s-m such as vulnerability, trust and power:

> The basic dynamics of butch-femme relating involve power, trust, vulnerability, tenderness and caring. When I as a butch demand of my lover 'Give it to me, baby, now', being as deep inside her as I can penetrate; and she completely releases herself and *flows* out to me . . . Sometimes I want her to take me right away, and then I seduce her the way a femme seduces a butch — seduce her into taking me instead of wanting me to take her. Sometimes her own butch streak will dominate, and she will Have Her Way with me, and I will let her. (Mushroom 1983 p 43)

Mushroom still sees herself as a butch despite a little controlled role swapping. The disadvantages of role-playing are forgotten in this new version which is supposed to be just playing rather than for real. There are other reasons for the revitalisation of role-playing. Lesbians are wanting to describe problems in their relationships, particularly around sexuality, and in the absence of a feminist language, now that feminism is so despised and discarded, the language of role-playing appears useful.

Sex therapist JoAnn Loulan in her book *The Lesbian Erotic Dance* expresses her view that role-playing is about the construction of erotic categories. Butch-femme for her is about how to choose a sexual partner and what to do with them. For her lesbianism is a sexual practice and it is the sexual practice itself, doing it, which makes lesbianism revolutionary. Feminist criticism of role-playing is referred to by its propagandists as 'desexualising' lesbianism. Loulan feels she 'can't help commenting on the desexualizing of our culture' (Loulan 1990 p 203). Contributors to the *The Persistent Desire* make the same argument. Madeline Davis remarks:

> Frankly, I don't understand not being role identified. Sure, I believe

them when they say that they are not, but it all seems so 'the same' to me and sort of boring. They're too busy holding hands and swaying and singing about 'filling up and spilling over'. (Davis 1992 p 270)

Arlene Istar complains about feminism, 'We have limited our options by desexualizing our community'. (Istar 1992 p 382) Lyndall MacCowan explains that 'butch and femme are gender constructions that arise from a sexual definition of lesbianism' (MacCowan 1992 p 306) and that 'Butch-femme has been made invisible because lesbian sexuality has been made invisible' and goes on to an explicit repudiation of lesbian feminism's temerity in giving lesbianism a political meaning.

Role-playing sexuality as demonstrated in collections such as *The Persistent Desire* imitates classic heterosexual fellatio and intercourse fairly religiously in order to realise the potential of these practices for sado-masochistic satisfactions. One butch helpfully explains the excitement of penetration for her: 'fucking between equals is passionless. When we fuck we possess. When we get fucked we become the possession.' (Brown 1992 p 411) Joan Nestle describes being fucked with a dildo: '. . . she reaches down and slips the cock into me . . . she starts to move her hips in short strong thrusts.' (Nestle 1992 p 350) Pat Califia has a poem in the collection about wishing she had a cock, with lines like 'Imagining the swell and rigid length/shoved into you,' 'Fucking you until I come,/Staying in you until I get hard again'. The words used for fucking in the poem are 'shove and thrust and hump', 'drill', 'hurt and fill and punch into you'. (Califia 1992 pp 423–4)

More surprising than the imitation of brutal sexual intercourse is the practice of cocksucking. This means performing the act of fellatio on a dildo. Jan Brown explains that the reason for this practice is that it is the ultimate in dominance and submission. 'It is about the urge to dominate, take, and degrade. It is about the fierce need to submit. To serve somebody.' (Brown 1992 p 413) Nestle also describes cocksucking. Lest it lack erotic potential for the woman strapped into it Nestle invents a variation. 'I take one of her hands and wrap it around the base so she can feel my lips as I move on her . . . licking the lavender cock.' (Nestle 1992 p 349)

The role-playing practices described, in their determination to imitate traditional heterosexual sex, include non-consensual violence. The Pat Califia poem above about drilling and hurting also mentions the butch's alcoholism and violence. Scarlet Woman writes about what would in a heterosexual context be liable in some jurisdictions to the charge of marital rape. The woman wakes 'under fast hands alarmed into instant arousal' and 'you move in faster than I can trust you' while 'my brain is asleep'. (Scarlet Woman 1992 p 352) But this is represented as acceptable because the victim does get aroused in the course of the event. It is perhaps not surprising that when the dynamics of heterosexuality are imitated down to the very dynamics of activity and passivity then rape is likely to become a real possibility between women.

It is an open secret among proponents of lesbian sado-masochism that the sexuality of cruelty is linked with childhood sexual abuse. Practitioners defend s-m by stating that it is the only way they can experience sexual pleasure because their abuse has tied abuse and pleasure so closely together for them that any possibility of an eroticism of equality is locked out. From the writings of role-players it seems fairly clear that there are similar links between the compulsiveness of the mild s-m practice it involves and women's oppression. Jan Brown in *The Persistent Desire* tells us that she worked as a street prostitute at seventeen. As an adult butch she tells us that she and her role-playing friends lied to feminists to try and make their sexual practices appear respectable. 'We explained to them that even though many of us might jerk off to gang rape, torture, daddy in our beds, and other undeniably incorrect imagery, it was really nothing to lose sleep over.' They emphasised the difference between fantasy and reality and that they were in control of their fantasies. But she says, 'we lied'. In fact it is the lack of control that is attractive. The power of the fantasies lies:

> . . . in the lust to be overpowered, forced, hurt, used, objectified. We jerk off to the rapist, to the Hell's Angel, to daddy, to the Nazi, to the cop, and to all the other images that have nothing to do with the kind of lesbian sex that entails murmurs of endearment, stroking of breasts, and long, slow tongue work. And, yes, we also dream

of the taking. We dream of someone's blood on our hands, of laughing at cries for mercy.

We wear the uniform and the gun; we haul our cocks out of our pants to drive into a struggling body. Sometimes we want to give up to the strangler's hands. Sometimes, we need to have a dick as hard as truth between our legs, to have the freedom to ignore 'no' or to have our own 'no' ignored.

Brown explains that the fantasies arise directly from the oppression of women because 'many of us have graduated from the university of self-destruct'. They are 'street survivors, incest survivors', have lived with 'abusive boyfriends' or 'substance abuse' and 'carry many kinds of scars'. But the sex that is eroticised cruelty is their salvation and 'keeps us alive – out of prisons and locked wards, abusive relationships, and bad-odds fights in bars'. (Brown 1992 pp 411–12) Brown explains quite straightforwardly how role-playing eroticises the real material experience of brutality.

A poem in the *Femme-Butch Reader* makes the same point. Sonja Franeta's poetical narrator explains that she would listen to the sounds of her father beating and abusing her mother and 'discovered how to rub/the hurt away directly on myself'. (Franeta 1992 p 375) She was beaten herself. Once again eroticised cruelty is seen as the answer in which 'our pain will turn to pleasure' and is expressed this time in belt buckle, boots, leather jacket, knife and being 'tough'. The idea that role-playing sexuality like other forms of s-m is some kind of religious ritual of masochism that will save or compensate for real pain is a common refrain.

It is not just libertarian role-players who fall into the essentialist fallacy. Three radical separatist lesbians living in Oakland, California who have unimpeachably feminist perspectives on sado-masochism and femininity, are using the idea of butchness and femmeness in ways which share some of the deeply problematic implications of the libertarian perspective we have seen above.

Bev Jo, Linda Strega and Ruston attack what they see as the oppression of butches by femmes. They do not see butch and femme as erotic categories at all. Their definitions are political. They see butches as 'those who, as girls, rejected feminization, and refused to play the role designed by men for women' and femmes as 'those who accepted the feminine role, to various degrees, as girls'. (Jo, Strega, Ruston 1990 pp 140–1) They reject the idea of role-playing entirely and believe that lesbians should be eschewing any 'masculine' or 'feminine' behaviour. But they believe that butch and femme are categories that all lesbians fall into without exception, that they are the 'basic core identities' that 'all Lesbians have'. (Ibid. p 139) They ask, 'Is it possible to be neither Butch nor Femme' and reply, 'no'. (Ibid. p 157) They seem to have decided to use the role-playing vocabulary in order to address a significant political question.

This is the difference in experience between lesbians who have always looked like lesbians and suffered punishment for lesbian visibility, and those lesbians who 'passed' by adopting feminine clothing or who came out as lesbians after some time of living as heterosexual and gaining the privileges that long-time lesbians were unable to acquire. They define the lesbians who carried the standard of lesbian visibility as brave heroes of lesbian liberation and as butches. Joan Nestle, who comes from a very different politics, makes the same point. Indeed the admiration for the visible butches expressed by the new femmes seems to emanate from some understandable guilt about their assumption of the privileges of passing. Femmes, as many of them point out, are only visible when on the arm of a butch. Jo, Strega and Ruston have a very different approach. They call upon all lesbians to simply relinquish the privileges of passing and give up femininity so that 'butches' would no longer suffer for their visibility. That is a more dynamic lesbian-positive solution. But their use of role-playing vocabulary in situations in which it hardly seems appropriate does undermine the important political points they are making.

To say that children as young as two, by making a decision to accept or reject femininity, are locking themselves in to a system whereby they will all their lives be oppressing butches or be oppressed as butches does smack of essentialism. It rigidifies butch-femme categories and does not allow for change. They seek to reverse what they see as the oppression of butches by femmes but in doing so create a new hierarchy. Butches, who they see as fairly rare, possibly only five in one hundred lesbians, are 'much closer to our inborn, natural state' of being female. Femmes will never be able to become that 'natural' and so are relegated to being in an inferior category all their lives. The creation of such unnecessary divisions cannot help the building of lesbian-feminist community. Two lesbians who look and behave identically, both in plaid shirts, jeans and boots, may in fact, according to this analysis, remain in different status categories all their lives.

According to this analysis butches and femmes can be recognised by the cognoscenti on sight even if they do not themselves know what they are; 'You can usually tell when you first meet someone whether she's Butch or fem.' (Ibid. p 147) Some clues to recognition are provided under the heading 'One Honest Fem's Self-Recognition List'. Said femme explains that when she meets other lesbians she feels 'less difference with fems' and with a butch she feels a 'potential barrier'. She feels herself 'moving like a Fem, and automatically using some feminine gestures'. (Ibid. pp 150–51). What is more she finds that 'feminine activities like sewing, needlecrafts, cooking, and other things designated as "women's work" ' feel like things that belong to her and to her 'sphere of activity'. It seems that the great archetype in the sky is at work again. Yet the work of these three lesbians contains much clear and cogent feminist analysis, such as Linda Strega's of the movement towards femininity in the lesbian community in the 1980s. Linda Strega calls lesbian femininity the 'Big Sell-Out'. She explains that other lesbians have 'verbally assaulted' her at social gatherings about why she wanted to 'wear a uniform' (Ibid. p 163). This social assault on what lesbian feminists had always tended to wear, shirts and jeans, is the parallel of the literary assault carried out by the role-players such as JoAnn Loulan and sex therapists like Margaret Nicholls. As Strega points out, those who might with more justice be seen as wearing uniforms are surely the lesbians who choose to imitate traditional male-designed femininity. Somehow the newly feminine lesbians see themselves as truly courageous to challenge that tiny fraction of the western world that does not enforce compulsory femininity on women, lesbian feminists. Strega suggests that rather than being an act of heroism, the return to femininity is about passing to gain privilege.

In the late 1980s it became more and more difficult to state that such and such a woman 'looked like a lesbian'. Angry lesbian protestors would say that there was no such thing as 'what a lesbian looked like'.

Well, like Strega, I think that is not so. There has been a historical tradition of lesbians rejecting femininity in different ways and to different extents but the rejection of femininity has been, I would suggest, a common theme. Lesbians have tended to assert human dignity against the social indignities of male-designed femininity. The lesbians at feminist discos in the 1970s and early 1980s did not look vastly different from the lesbians at traditional lesbian discos; shirts, T-shirts and jeans predominated, and short hair. The political strategy of looking like lesbians is more than just a personal desire to be warm and comfortable and possessed of freedom of action, very useful in a world where men attack women. It is an important strategy for the creation of lesbian freedom. In the workplace, in their families of origin, on the street, lesbians who 'look like lesbians', and their attackers do know what that means, are at risk. The more that lesbians and heterosexual women reject femininity the easier it becomes for other women to escape degrading feminine norms and the more difficult it becomes to discriminate against lesbians.

The new role-playing is the fundamentalism of lesbianism. As fundamentalism in all patiarchal religions is founded upon and designed to maintain the oppression of women through the enforcement of male dominance and female submission, so too is lesbian role-playing. It requires the same enthusiastic self abasement from women and achieves it. It is explained by the same mythology of biology or yin and yang. Lesbian role-playing needs to be explained as part of the very grave worldwide backlash against the liberation of women in which some women are indeed embracing their oppression with slavish obedience and compulsive repetition, but plenty more are rebelling. The erotic dance of role-playing, the rhythm that Loulan rhapsodises about, is the rhythm of slavery, male dominance and female submission, an old rhythm indeed, but not natural.

This article is substantially based on a chapter with the same title, originally published in Jeffreys, Sheila, *The Lesbian Heresy*, Spinifex, Melbourne, Australia 1993; and The Women's Press, London, 1994.

References

Alderson, L and Wistrich H, 'Clause 29: Radical, Feminist Perspectives', in *Trouble and Strife* No 13, 1988.

Altman, D *et al* (eds), *Which Homosexuality?*, Gay Men's Press, London, 1989.

Austin, P, 'Femme-ism', in J Nestle (ed), *The Persistent Desire*, Alyson, Boston, MA 1992.

Bolen, quoted in Loulan (1990)

Brown, J, 'Sex, Lies and Penetration: A Butch Finally Fesses Up', in J Nestle (ed), *The Persistent Desire*, Alyson, Boston MA, 1992.

Califia, Pat, 'The Femme Poem', in J Nestle Ibid.

Campaign, *Are We Born To Be Gay?*, No. 19, October 1992, Australia.

Carpenter, E, *The Intermediate Sex*, George Allen and Unwin, London, 1908.

Davis, M, 'Epilogue, Nine Years Later', in J Nestle, (ed), *The Persistent Desire*, Alyson, Boston MA, 1992.

Franeta, S, 'Bridge Poem', in J Nestle, Ibid.

Holdsworth, A, *Out of the Doll's House*, BBC Publications, London, 1988.

Istar, 'Femme-Dyke', in J Nestle (ed), *The Persistent Desire*, Alyson, Boston MA, 1992.

Jeffreys, S, 'The Invention of the Frigid Woman', in S Jeffreys, *The Spinster and Her Enemies*, Pandora, London, 1985.

Jo, Strega and Ruston, *Dykes-Loving-Dykes*, Battleaxe Books, Oakland CA, 1990.

Koertge, N, 'Butch Images 1956–86', in *Lesbian Ethics* Vol 2 No 2, 1986.

Lesbian History Group, *Not a Passing Phase: Reclaiming Lesbians in History (1840–1985)*, The Women's Press, London, 1989.

Loulan, J, *The Lesbian Erotic Dance*, Spinsters, San Francisco, 1990.

MacCowan, L, 'Re-collecting History, Renaming Lives: Femme Stigma and the Feminist Seventies and Eighties', in J Nestle (ed), *The Persistent Desire*, Alyson, Boston MA, 1992.

Mushroom, Merrill, 'Confessions of a Butch Dyke', in *Common Lives, Lesbian Lives*, No 9, 1983.

Nestle, J, *A Restricted Country: Essays and Short Stories*, Sheba, London, 1988.

Nestle, J, *The Persistent Desire: a Femme-Butch Reader*, Alyson, Boston MA, 1992a.

Nestle, J, 'My Woman Poppa', in *The Persistent Desire*, Ibid., 1992b.

Penelope, J, 'Whose Past Are We Reclaiming?', in *Common Lives: Lesbian Lives*, No 13, 1984.

Raymond, J, *A Passion for Friends: Towards a Philosophy of Female Affection*, The Women's Press, London, 1986.

Rouge, Issue 14, 1993.

Scarlet Woman, 'Roll Me Over and Make Me a Rose', in J Nestle (ed), *The Persistent Desire*, Alyson, Boston MA, 1992.

Wieringa, S, 'An Anthropological Critique of Constructionism: Berdaches and Butches', in D Altman *et al* (eds), *Which Homosexuality?*, Gay Men's Press, London, 1989.

Wolf, N, *The Beauty Myth*, Vintage, London, 1990.

section three

REPRESENTATIONS OF LESBIANS IN THE MEDIA AND POPULAR CULTURE

This section argues that recent and current representations of lesbians in print and in other parts of the media popular with lesbians give conservative and anti-feminist messages about lesbian identity and lesbian community. In this way, they contribute significantly to the depoliticisation of the lesbian community and support a right-wing version of this community by subverting and undermining radical feminism.

Elaine Miller examines how the backlash against feminism is influencing written accounts of lesbian history in the 1990s which are mis-representing radical lesbian feminism and, in some cases, distorting historical truth to validate currently fashionable anti-feminist constructions of lesbian identity. She outlines a lesbian-feminist approach to lesbian history, arguing that the value of such an approach lies in its potential for uncovering the power dynamics of history in ways helpful to women's liberation, by opening up, for example, a debate on the historical connection between lesbianism and feminism and putting present day feminists in touch with feminists of the past.

Elaine Hutton examines the way lesbians are represented in contemporary magazines, newspapers, cartoons and popular fiction that are produced specifically for and sometimes by lesbians and gay men. She exposes the 'disappearing' of radical lesbian feminists as well as implicit and explicit attacks on them. She demonstrates that the new lesbianandgay conservatism expressed in such publications has influenced different kinds of writing in a more subtle and insidious way; lesbian detective novels, for instance.

Nicola Humberstone analyses representations of lesbians in television programmes. She looks at alternative and mainstream programming, including portrayals of lesbians in popular dramas and soaps. She concludes that the lack of lesbian feminist representations is due to the way the media has demonised feminism, and discusses strategies for more positive representations.

RIGHTING OUR HISTORY

ELAINE MILLER

The lesbian-feminist movement of the 1970s was the most effective challenge to male power mounted in Britain since the suffragette movement. Out of the initiatives of that decade came the notion of lesbian history as a distinct area for research, study, publication, popular reading and general talk among lesbians and it is today one of those 'building blocks of the lesbian community now taken for granted by young women coming out'. (Jeffreys 1994 p ix) Ironically, it is also one of the areas of present-day lesbian community life where the backlash against radical lesbian feminism is operating most virulently. This backlash is now influencing written accounts of lesbian history by attempting to marginalise, caricature or silence radical lesbian feminism and also to validate lesbian sado-masochism, lesbian pornography, butch-femme role-playing, queer politics and 'lesbians' who sleep with men.

In present day accounts of lesbian history, the issue is not only one of different political stances producing different written versions of lesbian history, although those differences are clearly there. The issue is also one of misrepresentation, omission and, in some instances, acceptance of, or at least collusion with, the male agendas of literary and historical texts.

Critics of radical lesbian feminists have suggested that radical lesbian feminists are living in a time warp; that radical lesbian feminism is out of date and nostalgic; that its proponents persist in clinging to the ideals of their youth when they were in the vanguard; that they are now sour-faced at being left behind by what is perceived as 'progress'. Quite apart from the ageism inherent in this image of radical lesbian feminists, the implication here is that history must be discarded in the rush to be fashionable and ground-breaking. On the contrary, I argue here that it is crucial to remember our history precisely so that we can move forward positively. The 1970s was a decade which saw great developments in lesbian-feminist theory and other kinds of lesbian-feminist activism and it is important not to lose sight of the understanding that we gained at that time.

Nor did radical lesbian feminism materialise out of a vacuum in the 1970s. Long before the twentieth century, women were resisting patriarchy to create a world in which sex was not used to control, to flatter egos, to exert power, to inflict cruelty or degradation on another human being. Queer lesbians, in undermining these goals and looking back to a sexuality based on eroticising dominance and submission, can with more reason be described as living in a time warp.

Lesbian feminists objecting to sado-masochism and pornography, butch-femme role-playing and 'lesbians' sleeping with men have also been accused of being anti-sex. Radical lesbian feminism neither is nor ever has been anti-sex, in either theory or practice. It is not sex but oppression as a result of particular socially condoned sexual practices, including sexual violence and the objectification and degradation of women, that this politics opposes. Confusing the two obscures radical feminist analysis of the connections between sexuality and power and has been a singularly effective patriarchal ploy. Many lesbians have been taken in by this confusion, believing they are being radical, rebellious and breaking new and exciting boundaries by engaging in sado-masochism, pornography and other practices that objectify, exploit and degrade women in exactly the ways that feminists have described and rejected after years of hard fought struggle. As a result, the lesbian community is now fractured. There are certain vocal groups who adopt these practices and who, as a consequence, gain a great deal of media support; there are the liberals retreating comfortably into individual lifestylism; and there are the radical feminists who are caricatured as old-fashioned prudes with no sense of adventure or fun. (This stereotype, too, is familiar. It has been used through the ages to silence women who have objected to degradation and exploitation.) This is a tragic division, adding to the ever-difficult task of making gains for women.

This chapter embraces lesbian history, remembers the lesbian feminists of the 1970s warmly and positively, critiques the politics of queer and s–m, is pro-lesbian sex and radical. The particular accounts of lesbian history I critique are: Lillian Faderman's *Odd Girls and Twilight Lovers – A History of Lesbian Life in Twentieth Century America* and Emma Donoghue's *Passions Between Women – British Lesbian Culture 1668–1801*. I have chosen these because their political perspectives reflect the dominant trends in present-day lesbian culture and because they are being widely read and will, no doubt, be highly influential. Faderman's simplistic and distorted picture of 1970s lesbian feminism, in particular, is becoming a received opinion about the true nature of that movement. It is therefore essential to present a feminist challenge to the ideas contained within these texts. Part of this challenge is to remember the good feminist work that has gone before, so that we do not isolate ourselves in time but gain, instead, a sense of our place in the feminist continuum and learn from our history. For that reason, I have included a re-appraisal of Faderman's earlier book, *Surpassing the Love of Men – Romantic Friendship and Love Between Women from the Renaissance to the Present*.

BEGINNINGS

The concept of lesbian history was one of the many creative outcomes of the 1970s women's liberation movement. As more and more women in the movement made the link between feminism and lesbianism and discovered the possibility of a new identity as radical lesbian feminists, the women's history discussion groups which sprang up as a result of consciousness-raising groups and the subsequent release of feminist energy, failed to satisfy them. The historical experience of heterosexual women was central to the work of such groups, but lesbian experience was not. Radical lesbian feminists set up informal, autonomous discussion and study groups and/or began individual reading and research into lesbian history. These included many oral-history sessions in which lesbians shared 'coming out' and other personal experiences.

In the 1970s, many women were more concerned with writing for each other in such publications of the movement as newsletters, magazines, pamphlets and conference papers than in producing academic records of the movement. Academia was quite rightly regarded by many radical lesbian feminists as patriarchal and hostile to their political analysis. It was also seen as crucially important not to separate theory from activism. It was the establishment of feminist presses in the mid-1970s that made possible more formal publications of the movement's history, including the emergence of lesbian feminism. Lesbian feminists also set up their own study groups and, in the late 1970s, often taught adult education classes. (Auchmuty this volume) As interest in lesbian history mounted and more lesbians became aware of how very effectively their foresisters had been 'hidden from history', the vital importance of leaving a record of their own became only too obvious.

So a tradition began. Reading, writing, recording and theorising lesbian history are now all well-established practices. There are opportunities for some lesbian feminists in colleges and universities to get their work on lesbian history into print. This has helped to spread ideas and to encourage further interest among lesbians, an interest that continues to increase today.

WHY DO IT?

Doing lesbian-feminist history has always included but always gone beyond the uncovering of individual lesbians' lives, past and present. These stories are often experienced by lesbians who read or hear about them as personally inspiring and validating and for that reason alone are invaluable. However, they cannot give, on their own, enough insight into the power dynamics of history: an insight essential if lesbian historians are to make a contribution, through the study of lesbian history, to the continuing development of a radical lesbian-feminist ideology which is a historically relevant force for change and which provides a theoretical basis for lesbian-feminist activism.

Radical lesbian-feminist historians postulate and critique two historical constants: patriarchy and heterosexuality. This approach clearly exposes patriarchal values and the relationship between sexuality and male power. It opens up debate on the historical relationship between lesbianism and feminism. It is also about gathering strength from remembering. It documents and celebrates feminist resistance, analysing the struggles and recording the gains. It gives encouragement to feminists. It reveals mistakes made, so that we can learn. It exposes the forces ranged against us, so that we can be prepared. Informative patterns are discovered. One that so often emerges is the pattern of resistance/reaction/retreat/resistance with new formulations of the struggle and of the strategies for engaging with it. These patterns tell feminists what they need to know. They provide what Mary Taylor, a Victorian radical feminist, called 'daylight to fight by' instead of ignorance to flounder in. (Taylor 1890 Ch. 7)

Margaret Jackson, in her recent book *The Real Facts of Life: Feminism and the Politics of Sexuality 1850–1940*, gives a historical perspective invaluable in illuminating current debates among lesbians. Jackson's thesis is that:

> sexuality is and probably always has been (though in different ways at different times) a critical area of struggle between the sexes: that the process by which sexuality is constructed is to a large extent the outcome of those struggles; that female sexual autonomy is the *sine qua non* of women's liberation; and that the history of feminist struggles for sexual autonomy, which includes the history of male resistance, is of vital political importance to our continuing struggles. (Jackson 1994 p 2)

Radical critiques, such as the one that Jackson provides, gives feminists today both the opportunity to learn from feminists of the past and the strength and confirmation that comes from being part of a long tradition of resistance. In particular, it is vital that young lesbians have access to such an analysis, to avoid what Adrienne Rich has called:

> a leak in history . . . The poorer we become, the less we remember what we had . . . The danger lies in forgetting what we had. The flow between generations becomes a trickle . . . (Rich 1993 pp 72–82)

Tracing the historical presence of these bonds of support between women is one of the principal concerns of lesbian–feminist history.

It is concerned with women who loved and were loved by women in the context of feminist resistance to patriarchy and in particular to sexualized violence; with women who loved each other passionately and sexually, whether or not this love was expressed through genital sexual contact; with women who, as lovers, groups of friends and through networks, resisted male power; with women who found out from experience that politics and political activism are capable of transforming desire.

This does not mean that radical lesbian–feminist historians are concerned to trace a fixed identity throughout time. As members of the London Lesbian History Group have written:

> . . . there can never be a fixed definition of what it means to be a lesbian. The task for the lesbian historian is to try to create the past as women living then would have experienced it and to locate lesbians within it. But we must also try to reinterpret the past in the light of our own lesbian–feminist understanding of what was going on . . . (*Not a Passing Phase* 1989 p 14)

Such an approach to history clearly demonstrates that neither radical feminism nor the oppression that its politics seeks to address are particular to a decade or a generation but are part of a long historical process. Within that process, lesbian feminism can be understood 'as a historical project not yet fully realised'. (Miriam 1993 p 14) So often misrepresented nowadays as old-fashioned, out of date, out of touch, the radical lesbian–feminist movement of the 1970s was, in reality, the newest formulation of this ancient and continuing process of feminist resistance: a conflation of lesbianism and feminism on such a scale as to produce a powerful visible presence with its own theoretical base within a mass movement.

The radical lesbian–feminist political philosophy generated then and continuing to develop now still holds that challenge. The current backlash is the reaction to that challenge: the reassertion of patriarchal systems of control in all the subtle, indirect ways illustrated throughout this anthology.

SURPASSINGLY GOOD FEMINISM

Lillian Faderman's first book *Surpassing the Love of Men* is an example of that challenge being made by writing history from a lesbian-feminist perspective. Using a mass of biographical, literary and documentary evidence, Faderman traces feminist resistance to patriarchal power, misogyny and sexual exploitation throughout her chosen period and concludes that lesbian feminism holds the answer to the oppression of women that she has exposed throughout her book:

> ... until men stop giving women cause to see them as the enemy and until there ceases to be coercion to step into prescribed roles without reference to individual needs and desires, lesbian-feminists will continue to view their choice as the only logical one possible for a woman who desires to be her own adult person. (Faderman 1989 p 415)

The political values which inform Faderman's perspective on lesbian history were inspired by lesbian feminism, which she obviously then saw as the ideal form of lesbianism, writing about its 'compelling logic' (Faderman 1985 p 391) and enthusiastically enumerating its considerable achievements.

Her methods of analysis include: feminist deconstruction of male texts and, in particular, critiques of misogynist representations of lesbians and lesbian sexual practices; analysis of available biographical information about these authors and the personal events that surrounded the creation and production of the texts; and analysis of the wider historical context. The connections that these methods enable her to make with the position of contemporary lesbians is extremely illuminating for lesbian feminists.

Faderman exposes to feminist historical analysis the gross oppression of sado-masochism, male-conceived pornography, essentialist notions of female nature and butch-femme role-play. She celebrates women's resistance to all this and their love for each other which she presents as a force for change because of its political potential. This love might or might not have been expressed by genital sexual acts. About this she is scrupulously tentative, since no pre-twentieth-century woman-authored accounts had then come to light. She convincingly critiques the 'evidence' for genital sexual contact between women as either male fantasy or as happening in the mysogynistic context of male sexual exploitation of women.

Faderman's integrity on this matter has been misunderstood as denying the importance of sexual activity in lesbian lives. Given the sources that do and don't exist, how does anyone go about proving it one way or the other? In any case, such recently discovered evidence as the diaries of Anne Lister in no way undermines Faderman's definition of a lesbian as a woman for women, or her thesis of the constant historical presence of patriarchy and women's resistance to compulsory heterosexuality. It is the combination of feminism and lesbianism that has always been the threat.

Faderman presents passion as sexual, whether expressed genitally or not. She also writes supportively about:

> Those lesbians who see sex between women as a vital part of their bond and who refuse to separate it from other aspects of the relationship as male-authored lesbian literature does. (Faderman 1985 p 329)

A further example of her constant connecting and contextualising is her analysis of the situation in Britain and America about the time of militant feminism and the First World War. The social upheaval caused by that war gave women the opportunity to demonstrate beyond doubt that their capacities were equal to men's, with the resulting confusion and anxiety about sex roles. Faderman argues that:

> When women's increasing freedom began to threaten to change the world – or at least parts of Europe and America – many who had vested interest in the old order were happy to believe that women who wanted independence were usually lesbians. It is no coincidence that many laypersons discovered the congenitalists' theories when the women's movement first began to achieve some success at the end of the nineteenth century. (Faderman 1985 p 332)

Nor is it any coincidence that essentialist notions of female nature found a new popularity in the reactionary 1990s.

In *Surpassing the Love of Men*, Faderman makes telling connections between the extreme misogyny that she has demonstrated as existing in eighteenth-century Europe and the prevalence of sado-masochism in the same era. It was, after all, the era of the Marquis de Sade, the master himself:

> Sade took the brutality that existed between the sexes to its gruesome conclusion; if it was enjoyable to torture a woman mentally and emotionally, would it not also be thrilling to torture her body? Some of the worst excesses of the French Revolution, which occurred in the Marquis de Sade's day, revealed this male hostility towards and contempt for women. Not only was the beautiful head of the guillotined Mme. de Lamballe paraded about on a pole but her pubic hair was also cut off and worn by some gentleman as a moustache. (Faderman 1985 p 95)

She also refers to one Nicolas Restif de la Bretonne as someone who fully understood the ugliness of de Sade's views but was never the less 'addicted to them'. In his novel *L'Anti-Justine* (1798) Bretonne describes a sex scene followed by a murder scene, the latter taking up a whole chapter:

> ... the woman dies after the man bites off her nipples and rips her vagina and anus so that 'where there were formerly two holes, there was now one'. He then slices her apart with a scalpel and lancet beginning with her breast and mons veneris. (Faderman 1985 p 96)

Faderman's concern at the cruelty inflicted on women by such practices sharply contrasts with Donoghue's suggestion that the women's whipping club described in the men's pornographic magazine *Bon Tom* (1792) 'offers some fascinating starting points for a history of SM'. (Donoghue 1993 p 215)

Faderman makes other telling connections in her critique of such eighteenth-century male writers as de Brantôme and Francois Mairobert who, she claims, were responsible for establishing the pattern for a whole range of pornography, that is, male-conceived pornography for male use. She goes on to point out that 'classic' eighteenth-century novels such as Samuel Richardson's *Pamela* (1740) and *Clarissa* (1748), Tobias Smollet's *The Adventures of Roderick Random* (1748) and Choderlos de La Clos' *Les Liaisons Dangereuses* (1780–81) are similar in kind if not in the degree of their mysogynistic cruelty: they are subtle and vicious games whose 'fun' depends of the agony and embarrassment of a woman.

SOMETHING ODD HAPPENED ON THE WAY

Surpassing the Love of Men has been a source of great inspiration to lesbian feminists. Lillian Faderman's second book on lesbian history came as something of a shock to them. It is abundantly clear from this second book, *Odd Girls and Twilight Lovers – A History of Lesbian Life in Twentieth-Century America* (1991) that Faderman no longer accepts many of the fundamental principles of radical lesbian feminism. Gone is her critique of patriarchy, misogyny, sexualised violence and pornography, together with her celebration of feminist resistance, female friendship and lesbian passion in the context of love. Gone is her belief that all these things are a political force for change in the interests of women. She no longer admires the 'compelling logic' of the radical lesbian-feminist vision. Instead, that vision is caricatured. Lesbian friendship and love no longer surpass the love of men.

The new book today casts an ironical shadow over that first title. The crux of her current thesis is that lesbians should emulate men. Faderman advocates that lesbians throw off their 'female socialisation' and behave sexually as men have always done; that they give up the 'luxury' of separatism and, in the age of AIDS, support men; that they adopt the values of the gay family (which is not perceived as patriarchal); that they share the excitement of the gay male sexual adventure. This, it now seems, is the path of lesbian liberation. Faderman claims that things are already better for lesbians. She describes lesbians, young and old, as less critical of society and more happy with their lot 'with little interest in confronting society with personal facts'. The closets are apparently filling up again. Lipstick camouflages.

Praising diversity, she has claimed to represent all versions of lesbianism and lesbian feminism fairly. However, during a talk at the

London Lesbian History Group in 1992, she began to outline the contents of her new book but stopped short at the point in the book where she begins her attempted demolition of radical lesbian feminism. Instead, she offered personal stories. Her behaviour on this occasion would seem to indicate her awareness that she has presented a very hostile account of this 'version' of feminism.

To understand how Faderman's belief in radical lesbian feminism turned into an attack on its very foundations, it is helpful to look in more detail at what she is now convinced is the answer to lesbian happiness and power. Her political focus on the present explains her new interpretation of the past. It is obviously impossible for her to validate the current trends in the lesbian 'community' unless she also presents a version of radical lesbian feminism which has no credibility. This is a clear illustration of how backlash operates today in the re-writing of lesbian history.

Odd Girls and Twilight Lovers is a detailed and very readable book. It claims to trace the changing experiences of lesbians throughout this century in terms of our perceptions of ourselves, the attitudes of the social mainstream to us, and the ways in which both of these have shaped the growth of lesbian culture and politics, especially in the big cities of America. She has based her earlier chapters on written sources including some fascinating songs and reviews from the Harlem clubs of the 1920s. The later chapters are based on the 'living voices' of the lesbians she interviewed, whom she consciously chose to reflect how varied lesbians are in age, race, ethnicity and geographical location.

This is an American history and much of the detail applies to the USA, such as the section on Greenwich Village. There are also some differences in the way lesbian feminism developed around the world, but most of the political issues raised by the book, such as separatism, the nature of feminism, the conflicts stirred by the debates on lesbian sexual practice and the emergence of Queer Nation, are familiar to lesbians and lesbian feminists in Britain and beyond. Faderman surveys and then evaluates each decade for its positive and/or negative contributions to lesbian well-being. For eight chapters she skilfully evokes the sense of a unique atmosphere for each period, beginning with the end of the nineteenth century and the era of romantic friendship, proceeding to the influence of the sexologists, continuing with the 'lesbian chic' of the 1920s, detailing the oppressive decades of the 1930s and 1940s and arriving at the bar culture of the 1950s and 1960s.

Then follow the most controversial sections of the book, although these are not acknowledged as controversial by Faderman. They include a critique of 1970s radical lesbian feminism, 1980s debates on lesbian sexual practice and this decade's concerns with 'diversity', 'moderation' and Queer Nation. In the first eight chapters, Faderman adopts a style that gives the sense of a documentation of lesbian history. It is not until her evaluation of radical lesbian feminist activism in the 1970s that her language becomes politically loaded and her massively changed political stance becomes obvious.

Faderman presents, with apparent enthusiasm, the movement among some lesbians towards such practices as sado-masochistic sex, stranger sex, public and casual sex. She appears to see this as a self-generated phenomenon, whereas radical lesbian feminists critique it as related to a re-assertion of capitalist, patriarchal values including commercialisation of all things lesbian, re-emerging fascism and the rise of the political Right in the mainstream. (These connections are explored more fully elsewhere in this anthology.) She describes in detail the rapidly growing business of Kathy Andrews, proprietor of *Stormy Leather* in San Francisco, a shop catering for lesbians who are into sado-masochistic sex, with no hint of a comment on the commercial impetus behind such a venture. This is an interesting reversal of the concern to contextualise which is so evident in *Surpassing the Love of Men*.

In Chapter Ten, *Sex Wars in the 1980s*, it is those lesbians who copy 'the gay male example' who, according to Faderman, now merit the description 'radical'. This is a strange word to apply to such derivative and unoriginal ways of going on. Faderman goes along with this appropriation of the language of radical feminism and even adds to it, giving one of her later chapters the title 'The Struggle to be Sexually Adventurous' and regarding freewheeling sexuality as lesbian routes to liberation, equality and power.

In social constructionist mode, Faderman analyses why the so-called sexual radicals have had only a limited impact on lesbians as a whole. In effect, she asks: why can't a woman be more like a man? The answer that she chooses to give is that women are severely inhibited in the 'struggle to be sexually adventurous', by which she means to experiment with such practices as sado–masochistic and stranger sex. What inhibits women is, she claims, *female socialisation* [my italics]. Lesbians get a double dose of this in their relationships. This implies, according to Faderman, that lesbians have no analysis, no conscious control over their sexual choices. Faderman's opinion of lesbians now is that:

> In their approach to sexuality they have been much more like heterosexual women than homosexual men, who historically and statistically have many more brief encounters. When both parties in a couple are female, it appears that the effects of female socialis-ation are doubled, lesbianism notwithstanding. While a few lesbians have been able to overcome that socialisation, most have not yet been able to. (Faderman 1992 p 254)

In view of the fact that just being a lesbian necessitates one massive rejection of female socialisation, the above hypothesis, from a lesbian, is remarkable. Faderman writes almost with exasperation of how:

> Another attempt to expand the possibilities of lesbian sexuality – lesbian strip shows – illustrates how female values that reflect the ways women have been socialised can infiltrate even the baldest of male sexual institutions when adopted by lesbians (Faderman 1992 p 257)

Disaster! The lesbians started 'bringing to it traditional female values – nurturing, relating, emotionally touching – that had been totally outside the concerns of such entertainment' – just like those lesbians at the Sutro baths who got bored with the orgy room and sat around in their towels talking. The venture, Faderman writes with regret, soon ceased to be 'economically feasible'. The new rallying cry of 'Let's be like the boys!' had been unable to arouse in lesbians 'an alloyed aggressive interest in sex outside love and commitment'. (Faderman 1992 pp 258–9). This is not at all encouraging for those cruising lesbians who went shining torches on Hampstead Heath in London, looking for stranger sex, only to find that the only lesbians to emerge from the trees were their pals.

Clearly, the polarity with radical lesbian feminism is precisely here. Faderman is supporting the view that equality, justice, liberation and happiness depend on women changing their sexual behaviour and behaving like men have traditionally always done: women aping rather than surpassing the love of men.

A further aspect of her focus on the present which explains her new interpretation of the past is her praise of the decade's *moderation and diversity*: new alliances with gay men, acceptance of bisexuality as part of lesbianism, assimilation into the professional mainstream; lesbians, young and old, happier with their lot and with little interest in confrontation. Faderman celebrates the moderation that has replaced 'ideological rigidity'. Although she sees moderation as emerging in a time of right-wing conservatism, she welcomes it as a retort to 1970s radical lesbian feminism rather than understanding it as a tempting survival strategy for today. Her 'evaluation' of radical lesbian feminism turns out to be a sustained attempt to discredit it as a political philosophy and a practical strategy. She constantly uses 'political correctness' as a term of abuse, apparently forgetting all about the aims of radical lesbian feminists: to construct a critique of heterosexuality and patriarchy and to create an alternative. Instead, she writes about their 'fanaticism . . . extremism . . . unrealistic notions . . .' based on 'excessive youth' and 'excessive idealism' when lesbian feminists with 'basic ineptness' and 'youthful inexperience . . . dreamt grandiosely' of 'Utopia'. (Faderman 1992 Ch. 9–10). Accusations against radical lesbian feminism abound. The irony of this particular piece of misrepresentation is that radical lesbian feminism emerged in the 1970s partly as a result of women's dissatisfaction with heterosexual sex and/or partly as a result of more satisfying sexual experiences with women.

Separatism does not appear in the index, although sex-circuses merits inclusion. In view of the AIDS epidemic, separatism is perceived as a luxury. It is also misrepresented as a philosophy that urges women to run away from the world rather than as the necessary political strategy that it is, to increase the collective strength of women to resist patriarchy. At best, she presents radical lesbian feminism as having been useful in 'lessening lesbian guilt', addressing homophobia in the women's movement, sexism in the gay movement and serving as a helpful backdrop generally:

> They played a kind of bad cop in a social drama, which then permitted more moderate activist lesbians to play the good cop. (Faderman 1992 pp 244–5)

Nothing happened, it seems. Radical lesbian feminism is explained as a product of 1960s liberalism and assessed as a project which was, by its very nature, doomed to failure. Faderman no longer takes into account the power of the forces ranged against lesbian feminists. They are dismissed in the language of fundamentalism as 'true believers' and like all true believers, condemned to fanaticism and disappointment.

The lesbian-feminist movement of the 1970s was, in fact, very complex. It grew out of a very clear sense of women's oppression as a class, recognising, exposing and critiquing the use of male violence, especially sexual violence, against women to perpetuate this oppression. It generated active strategies for change, producing intelligent analyses of patriarchy, capitalism and sexuality. It shifted some ideologies. It created a whole culture. (Harne 1994)

Faderman writes about radical lesbian feminism in the past tense with no recognition of its recurring nature as a vital part, in its earlier forms, of the many waves of active feminism throughout history. Nor does she acknowledge the rising defiance of women now in response to their sense of the current backlash against feminism. Nowhere does she take seriously the continued existence of those issues which were the focus of that feminism and which remain the focus for some feminists today: hard issues about living as women in the real world, far distant from Utopia. She totally fails to recognise the potential of this politics as a developing political philosophy and an adaptable strategy responsive to change.

Why, one must ask, has Faderman changed her political position so fundamentally? The notion which informed *Surpassing the Love of Men* was of a connection between the love and passion women can feel for each other and their consciousness of female oppression within patriarchy, however variously and at whatever level that oppression is perceived and experienced. Nowhere is this notion given any serious consideration in the later book. Has Faderman succumbed to political and commercial pressures to present fashionable versions of lesbian history that will get published and widely read?

A further disturbing aspect of *Odd Girls and Twilight Lovers* is the lack of reference to any other books or written sources that provide a different critique of radical lesbian feminism. There is also the question of Faderman's own sources: on whose experiences and perceptions of 1970s radical lesbian feminism does she base her evaluation? What are the current political stances of the particular women she interviewed? What did she do with their answers?

The book is an account of lesbian history written from a very particular political perspective but there is no acknowledgement of this perspective. The misrepresentation is therefore twofold: the trivialisation of radical lesbian feminist ideology, together with implied objectivity.

ALL IN TOGETHER GIRLS

Emma Donoghue's *Passions Between Women – British Lesbian Culture 1668–1801* is another example of how backlash against radical lesbian feminism can operate through the re-writing of lesbian history. Donoghue's aim is to find in history an ancestry for and therefore a validation of every kind of lesbian. 'Kind' is defined with an exclusive focus on sex, lesbians differing, apparently, only on terms of their preferred sexual practices. It should come as no surprise, therefore, that Donoghue's search through a mass of material has produced long and detailed descriptions of erotic and pornographic sexual encounters between women.

She discusses much of the same eighteenth-century material already analysed by Lilian Faderman in *Surpassing the Love of Men* but brings to it an opposing political approach: Faderman applies a radical feminist critique in that book while Donoghue's is libertarian. Where Faderman concentrates on connecting and contextualising to produce feminist political meaning, Donoghue admits that she has space, on the whole, only for the texts themselves. As a result, two very different versions of eighteenth-century lesbian history emerge.

An examination of these opposing approaches to the same eighteenth-century texts by Faderman, the former supporter of radical lesbian feminism, and Donoghue, the current supporter of lesbian sado-masochism, is useful in demonstrating how the writing of lesbian history can be used either to validate or to discredit particular ways of being lesbian in the present.

Donoghue's major, though not sole, interest in a text is the evidence it appears to contain of awareness or knowledge of female genital sexual activity in the eighteenth century, often regardless of the pervasive anti-lesbian agendas of the great majority of such texts. The cover of the book and the inside plate are from an illustration from the 1766 edition of John Cleland's *Fanny Hill or, Memoirs of a Woman of Pleasure* (1749). It shows one woman apparently caressing the genitals of another. One of the women is Fanny, a teenager from the country, the other is the experienced Phoebe. The venue is a brothel and Phoebe is warming Fanny up for sex in the brothel with men. To cut a long story short, rather than spin it out to the five pages that Donoghue takes to summarise the sexual activity between the women, Fanny ends up despising Phoebe (who also despises her lesbian self) begins to long for more solid food, i.e. a penis, and gets married. Is this story supposed to cheer lesbians up? Why is it featured so prominently on the front cover of a lesbian history book and given a full page illustration inside as well? What has it got to do with lesbians? What is new about the discussion of the novel? Well, yes, there's the rub, or nub, as it were. Faderman's much earlier analysis had pointed out Cleland's male agenda: his glee in presenting women as unable to satisfy each other sexually, turning against each other, the younger one becoming a wife, the older one consigned to frustrated oblivion. Faderman even pointed out that Cleland didn't even describe the 'lesbian' sex accurately:

> Cleland, with all this knowledge of sexual low life, seems to have had little idea of the role the clitoris played in female sexual response – her fingers are not long enough to effect her partner's orgasm or rupture the hymen. (Faderman 1989 p 28)

Donoghue makes some remarks about the anti-lesbian implications of the story but these are very brief and say little, if anything, that is new. She colludes with Cleland's male agenda in thinking it comical, because Cleland does, that the teenage Fanny, just arrived in London from the country, has been enticed into Mrs Brown's brothel and put into bed with Phoebe, to be warmed up for heterosex. Most of

Donoghue's commentary consists of a series of minute physical details of the female genital sex that takes place in the brothel, with the odd reference to heterosexual orgies. It reads like a bit of soft porn. Donoghue explains in her introduction that she has no space 'to follow some interesting tangents such as the links between lesbian culture and . . . *prostitution*' but has had 'to focus on the *lesbian content* of texts, making only brief reference to their *genres, authors* and *social contexts*.' She explains that her primary intention is 'to get the *stories* to the women.' (Donoghue 1993 p 11, my italics). Historians know that a story is never just a story. This approach seems to me to patronise women, too.

In this lesbian history book, there are several long summaries of nasty novels by men. Some of these men are very nasty men and some of the summaries are very long. Take the case of Diderot and *The Nun* (1797). Donoghue's commentary on this novel is an example of how lack of context and a concern with erotic storytelling can distort the meaning of a text. The summary takes up seven pages consisting mainly of very detailed accounts of lesbian sexual encounters. There is no mention, however, of the personal circumstances of Diderot's life at the time he wrote it, which do seem to have had a major effect on the novel. It is clear from his letters that he was obsessed by jealousy and suspicion about his wife's attachment to another woman whom he obviously saw as a lesbian, referring to 'that nun for whom she had such a passion'. Elsewhere, he writes, 'Oh, women, you are such extraordinary children!' Faderman contends that, to Diderot, 'the convent was a place where . . . the depraved led the innocent into depravity. It was the one French institution where women, who were, at best, incapable children, actually ruled.' (Faderman 1985 pp 44–5)

The relationship between literature and history is complex. The most that can be said about *The Nun* in terms of historical evidence is that, taken together with non-fictional sources such as letters, essays and information about contemporary lesbian fashion, it gives some impression of Diderot's attitudes to women, lesbians, lesbian sex and convents. Writing about eighteenth-century representations of lesbians in *Surpassing the Love of Men* Faderman argues that:

The most virulent depictions of lesbian . . . behaviour seem to have been rooted in the writer's anger at a particular woman's conduct in an area apart from the sexual. Her aggressive sexuality was used primarily as a metaphor. (Faderman 1985 p 46)

The story of *The Nun* revolves around Susan who is forced into convent life by her greedy mother. In a series of institutions, she falls prey to the power games of a number of nuns whom Diderot presents as sadistic, predatory and generally vicious lesbians. The Mother Superior is particularly sinister. In the end, Susan turns against the Mother Superior who by now is dying and flees the convent with the priest who has been her confessor. The priest then rapes her and leaves her destitute. End of story.

The characters in *The Nun* are creations of Diderot's imagination and necessarily reflect his attitudes and experiences but not necessarily the real attitudes or the real lives of the lesbians of that time. It is, after all, a novel. Donoghue focuses on the issue of Susan's knowledge or ignorance about same-sex desire. It is an interesting gloss on the novel from the point of view of literary criticism but the connection with lesbian history is difficult to see, except in the terms already outlined – the history of male representation of lesbianism in literary and other texts.

Donoghue's analysis of the evidence of cross-dressing follows predictable political lines and is influenced by her concern to validate the current fashion of 'playing with gender'. She asserts, without offering evidence, that cross-dressers have usually been explained before as women 'simply wanting to be men'. This is a way of attempting to dismiss radical lesbian feminist and other critiques of cross-dressing by caricaturing them. Donoghue's account of female cross-dressing is about 'women dipping in and out of masculine disguises, roles and styles and the ways in which this influenced erotic expression between them.' Early in this section she discusses *The Female Soldier* (anon. 1750). This is one of what seem to be several curious choices to illustrate the 'dipping in and out' theory. It is the story of Hannah Snell who, we are informed:

married a Dutch sailor, James Summs in 1774. He stole her possessions to finance his use of prostitutes and finally ran away, leaving her pregnant and facing his debts. After the death of her baby,

motivated by a mixture of love and hatred, Hannah followed Summs
to war. She cut her hair and used the name of her brother-in-law,
James Gray. (Donoghue 1993 pp 91–2)

It is difficult to believe that, given what happened to her, Hannah
Snell did all this in a mood of playful experimentation, going about
'dipping in and out of masculine disguises' playing with gender.
Given that the next crisis is the intended rape of a young woman by
Hannah's superior officer, which Hannah prevents by forewarning
her, it is not beyond the bounds of belief that Hannah, still not in a
playful mood exactly, stays dressed up as a man. This example lends
support to the radical lesbian-feminist analysis that women's reasons
for dressing up as men in the past were often for protection, freedom
of movement and the privileges of male power in a sexist society.
Interestingly, the reason why the young woman falls in love with
Hannah is because Hannah has shown her a kindness and support
unusual, the young woman thinks, in a soldier and not because of
Hannah's cross-dressing. A radical lesbian-feminist critique could
well envisage lesbian love and desire growing out of such a relationship but would not see the love and desire enabled by butch-femme
role-play.

This strange notion that 'playing with gender' somehow has revolutionary potential is one of the many tenets of the queer politics on
which Donoghue's account of lesbian history in this period is based.
The notion is deeply anti-feminist, seeming to arise out of a defeatist
acceptance that the radical feminist project of moving beyond gender
in the material world is impossible. So all we can do is play. Lesbians
can dress up as butch daddy-dykes and lesbian boys and enter the
fairyland of postmodern-speak. Only representation exists here. Male
power cannot survive in its rarified air. The trouble is that midnight
strikes sooner or later, calling all daddy-dykes and lesbian boys back
to the ultimately inescapable reality of their lives as women in a
society increasingly hostile to them. Oppression has to be faced again
and the dressing-up to play won't have changed a thing for the better.
On the contrary, these excursions into fairyland help to sharpen
everybody's sense of 'the feminine' and 'the masculine' and, of course,
the power differentials within those categories in the real world of
everyday living. This is very different indeed from the cross-dressing

that Hannah Snell did to survive in situations dangerous and possibly fatal to her as a woman.

Elsewhere in *Passions Between Women* Donoghue claims that bisexuality is part of lesbian history, 'woven right through our history', in fact. What this amounts to, as Kathy Miriam has pointed out, is the libertarian reversal of the radical lesbian-feminist philosophy that 'any woman can . . .'. (Miriam 1993 p 10) In these anti-feminist times, any woman can now sleep with a woman today, a man tomorrow. Donoghue does not see any political significance in a woman's choice to sleep either with women or with men. Some of the texts chosen to illustrate that bisexuality is woven right through lesbian history must be a bit depressing for bisexuals though, because, in several, either one or both women end up dead. Where there is a 'happy bisexual triangle' at the end, Donoghue rather inconsistently suggests that we should take them with a pinch of salt since 'women writers often used a heterosexual plot as a framework for a safe discussion of women's love for each other'. (Donoghue 1993 p 138)

In an attempt to give separatists a place in lesbian history, Donoghue offers an analysis of a play called *The Convent of Pleasure* (1668) by Margaret Cavendish, Duchess of Newcastle. It is presented as a literary example of a lesbian-feminist separatist community. The main character is an orphan who inherits great wealth on her father's death. To avoid the many men who want to marry her, she goes off with her female friends and sets up a women-only community: widows are allowed to visit but not wives. Lady Happy wants to avoid marriage because it will bore her, restrict her freedom and, on account of her husband's expected use of prostitutes, will ruin her health. Excluded men are furious and threaten violence. Eventually, a princess from a distant land hears about the community and is allowed in. She is described as 'a Princely brave woman truly, of a masculine presence.' Lady Happy falls in love with the princess. The princess is later found out to be a man. He agrees to leave on one condition: Lady Happy must marry him. This she does.

Marilyn Frye has written brilliantly on how women-only groups work as a fundamental challenge to male power. She argues that women take power by denial of access and that a declaration of autonomy names that power. That is why men find it so threatening. The story of *The Convent of Pleasure* is, in reality, the story of defeat for women in the most crucial battle of all. Yet Donoghue describes it as 'a lesbian romance' which she finds 'satisfying' because it shows passion between women generated by life in a separatist community. She makes no attempt to explain the ending of the story. (Donoghue 1993 p 232)

What seems to have happened in *Passions Between Women* is that the search for and detailed description of the erotic and the pornographic has taken precedence over all else. It is difficult to see the motivation for this search as anything but an attempt to validate every kind of sexual practice in the anti-feminist lesbian present, including lesbian sado–masochism. Despite Donoghue's awareness of Vicinus' warning (which she quotes) that lesbian historians should not 'ransack history to find women who fulfil current expectations' this is exactly what Donoghue seems to have done. The language of the book reverberates with the buzz words of the backlash: erotically charged/charged with danger/sado–masochistic intensity/erotic gaze/bisexuality/gender-bending/culture/variety/range/respect for love in all its forms/and so on.

Donoghue states that 'it should be possible, then, to broaden the meaning of lesbian history to include a variety of concepts *from previous centuries* without diluting it into a study of all forms of sisterly affection.' But whose concepts are these? The frequent lack of detailed context is alarming. One of several possible approaches in literary criticism is to regard the text as primary, that is, all that matters is the text itself. However, all text and no context in a study of history is problematical in the extreme. The connections made between history and literature in this book are neither clear nor consistent. Assertions like the fact that because 'something was not stated does not mean it was not known' might well be true but hardly amount to firm evidence.

One of her stated aims in writing this book has been to unite the lesbian 'community'. She writes in her introduction:

In the past few decades it has proved difficult to make connections across ideological barriers; perhaps we can make them across time instead. Celibate friends, sm dykes, women who get mistaken for men whether they like it or not, singles and couples and threesomes, separatists, prostitutes, in-your-face activists, respectable closet cases, those of us who also like orgies or weddings or study groups or men or domestic bliss; we can all find our origins here. If we take the long view, learning that we all have a share in the past and none of us can own it, perhaps we will not fight so bitterly over the present. (Donoghue 1993 p 24)

This is an aim embarrassing in its naivety. The existence of something in history does not necessarily justify its continued existence in the present: fascism or colonialism, for example. The idea also patronises radical lesbian feminists by its implication that their politics are of the kind that can be cast aside the minute someone 'discovers', yet again, Juvenal's description of a lesbian sex orgy or an account of a lesbian whipping-club in an eighteenth-century pornographic men's magazine. Even if there were proof that these things happened in reality in the past or even that women organised them, which there certainly isn't in this book, the point would remain. One thing being suggested here is that radical lesbian feminists 'give in', jump on the 'all in together, girls' bandwagon, keep quiet, lie back, enjoy it and stop challenging the backlash against lesbian feminism. Kathy Miriam has lucidly described the dangers of the kind of approach that Donoghue, Faderman and others are now advocating:

> ... abstention from political struggle under the name of creating lesbian culture serves to mystify predicaments of class, race and sex oppression that can hardly be challenged by culture ... alone. This rejection of politics in the name of culture mystifies, reinforces social inequalities among lesbians and thus idealises, in the worst sense, lesbian community. (Miriam, in Reti 1993 p 63)

Both *Odd Girls and Twilight Lovers* and *Passions Between Women* will no doubt be widely read and very influential. They will find a place in popular lesbian culture as well as in women's studies and lesbian studies classes. They present no challenge to the mainstream, which will remain unthreatened by any feminism in their pages and be pleased by the attempt of the one to caricature radical lesbian feminists out of existence, and of the other to coax them into compliance. Both books after all, in their different ways, centre on the idea that men had the right idea all the time. All that lesbians have to do is follow. These are tall stories that radical lesbian feminists must constantly challenge.

The section in this article on *Odd Girls and Twilight Lovers* is substantially based on an article written by Elaine Miller in *Trouble and Strife*, No 25, Winter 1992/3.

References

Donoghue, E, *Passions Between Women: British Lesbian Culture 1668–1801*, Scarlet Press, London, 1993.

Faderman, L, *Surpassing the Love of Men: Romantic Friendship and Love Between Women from the Renaissance to the Present*, The Women's Press, London, 1985.

Faderman, L, *Odd Girls and Twilight Lovers: A History of Lesbian Life in Twentieth-Century America*, Penguin Books, Harmondsworth, 1992.

Harne, L, *Contemporary Lesbian-Feminist History: the Politics of Lesbian Community*. An unpublished paper given at the Women's Studies Network Conference, Nottingham, 1994.

Jackson, M, *The Real Facts of Life: Feminism and the Politics of Sexuality 1850–1940*, Taylor & Francis, London, 1994.

Jeffreys, S, *The Spinster and Her Enemies: Feminism and Sexuality 1880–1930*, Pandora Press, London, 1985.

Jeffreys, S, *The Lesbian Heresy*, Spinifex, Melbourne, and The Women's Press, London, 1993.

Lesbian History Group, *Not a Passing Phase: Reclaiming Lesbians In History 1840–1985*, The Women's Press, London, 1989.

Miriam, K, in I Reti (ed), *Unleashing Feminism: Critiquing Lesbian Sadomasochism in the Gay Nineties* Herbooks, Santa Cruz CA, 1993.

Rich, A, *What Is found There*, W W Norton & Co., New York and London, 1993.

Taylor, M, *Miss Miles: A Tale of Yorkshire Life Sixty Years Ago*, Remington & Co., London, 1890, and OUP, Oxford, 1990.

THE FLIGHT OF THE FEMINIST

ELAINE HUTTON

'Look Elaine! I've got a fantastic new book just come in. You'll want to see it. It's such fun.' So spoke my friendly gay bookseller as he rushed to the table to present me with my first view of *The Penguin Book of Lesbian Short Stories*. I managed to fight down my uncontrollable rage as I looked at the cover – a full-frontal portrait of two women, one in collar, tie and jacket with her arm and gloved hand proprietorially around the waist of the other. The 'wife' had several strings of Victorian-style pearls dangling between her breasts and a little lacy bolero draped over her otherwise naked body; the 'Victorian patriarch' had an appropriately patriarchal expression – and was naked from the navel down. The photograph is, incidentally, cut off at upper-thigh level, by a dark background containing the title, so the eye is immediately drawn to the two women's genitals.

Just what is this cover meant to portray? That the lesbian community has reached a cultural maturity, as popular opinion now proclaims? That we can send ourselves up? Or that we are still being treated as sex objects, under the literature?

I did not find it 'fun' when the gay man handed me this book with the pornographic cover. I felt humiliated. After fighting for nearly two decades to eradicate images which degrade women and are an expression of male dominance over women, it is the ultimate in bad tricks to have this kind of image repackaged as lesbian camp, or Lesbian Chic: something for the girls, that the boys can have a laugh at as well. And if the girls don't? . . . Well, we're so humourless and uptight. Where have I heard this before? Couldn't have been the

1960s, could it? 'Relax babe. Be an ice–cool dyke.' (*Lip*, Summer 1994)

About eleven years ago, I and three other lesbian feminists walked into a fringe gallery and physically removed from the walls a whole pornographic art exhibition, arguing with the management that it degraded women. It was not put back up. The local press reported our stance relatively sympathetically, even printing statements from other women who agreed with us. This kind of action was not unusual in those days.

Lesbian feminism is a political identity. Being a lesbian feminist means being part of a movement that has set itself the task of systematically demolishing male power over women. In the recent past, a large number of women saw it as their life's work to dismantle the patriarchy, by creating a revolution of attitudes, by political action against anti–women legislation and media representation and by working together to deconstruct ideologies harmful to women.

Publications of the 1970s and early 1980s, whatever their faults and whatever our retrospective criticisms of them, tended to reflect the struggles, and debated relevant issues at great length. They were part of the dynamic of the Women's Movement. *Spare Rib*, the long-running feminist magazine, made the debates accessible to women up and down the country; the newsletter *Wires* practised collectivity by shifting editorial control to different groups of women throughout Britain; the crucial debate about political lesbianism, brought together in *Love Your Enemy?*, (Onlywomen Press 1981) was first aired in the pages of *Wires*; the *London Women's Liberation Newsletter*, however acrimonious at times, at least had a hotly debated editorial policy and gave the impression it had its un–latexed–clothed finger on the pulse of political debate (rather than parts of the body). It also served as an efficient means of communication; women knew what was going on and when, and could organise and attend meetings and actions at short notice. *Outwrite*, a feminist newspaper published in the 1980s, broadened the debates, in terms of demonstrating how racism and imperialism interact with the oppression of women. There was a burgeoning of brilliant pro–feminist humour, often in cartoon form, enhancing political articles in the magazines and newsletters or appearing in self-contained collections of their own. (Jackson 1984 *Wonder Wimbin* and 1986 *Visibly Vera*) These magazines and newsletters, integral to the political activist climate of the time, were produced by women for women. They were not exclusively for lesbians, as being/becoming a lesbian and the context that would encourage this was part of the political debate during that period. Ironically, the plethora of publications directed at lesbians now combine to undermine the lesbian–feminist project in a number of implicit and explicit ways.

In the examination of how this is done, I will focus on the *Pink Paper*, *Shebang*, *Diva* and *Lip*, with passing references to *Lesbian London*. The comments will deal with passing impressions and the 'drip, drip' effect of these publications: how they represent lesbians and misrepresent lesbian feminism. It must also be said that they do not all have the same effect. The *Pink Paper*, *Shebang* and *Diva* are qualitatively worse than the others, in the harm they wreak on radical lesbian–feminist ideas.

These magazines share a number of characteristics which contribute to undermining radical lesbian feminism. They are, broadly:

- Liberalism – an 'anything goes' policy.
- Erasing radical feminist viewpoints and perspectives.
- Ridiculing radical feminist lesbians.
- Co-opting/heterosexualising lesbians by creating a pervasive image of what the lesbian of today is, both through articles and pictorial representation.
- Promoting male interests at the expense of women's autonomy.
- Attacking radical feminism, and pretending it had held back the production of positive lesbian images.
- Reconstructing an image of a radical lesbian feminist which distorts historical truth.

In reality these characteristics cannot be separated out; they operate in different combinations to devastating effect. Because these are leisure-time fillers the 'dip in' becomes 'drip in' and so, I maintain, they are a powerful instrument of the backlash against lesbian feminism.

The *Pink Paper*, a free British weekly publication 'for lesbians and gay men' started in 1988, evinces most of these features and has had a considerable effect on subsequent publications. The agenda was set in the early years with the tedious page after page spread of male pornographic advertisements. Chat lines, date lines . . . Big boys doing it . . . spanking gays at it . . . chained and dominated . . . meat market . . . rear entry . . . power tool . . . rough trade . . . hung like a donkey. . . . Confronted by seven pages of this rubbish week after week it was hard to take the rest of the rag seriously. It was also difficult to see how this was a newspaper for lesbians. Because of a change in editorial policy, the pornographic advertisements decreased after 1992 but the representation of lesbian and particularly lesbian-feminist interests has remained minimal.

In fact, the promotion of male interests at the expense of women appears to be the policy of this paper. Over a recent three-year period extensive coverage, in lead articles, has been given to HIV and AIDS: government health policies on . . . discrimination because of . . . advertising campaigns involving . . . drug cure claims. Other topics covered were: discrimination against gay men (for instance the Spanner case, swoops on gay parties or saunas and the Age of Consent campaign); hunts for serial killers of gay men in London and New York; and male rape. On reading this, you would be excused for thinking that discrimination against women, let alone lesbians, did not exist.

Some examples of the way this operates are as follows. A lot of what is termed discrimination against men is, in actuality, about arguing for men's right to have unbridled sex, anywhere, everywhere, all the time. The second-wave women's movement, in common with the first wave, has been consistently critical of male sexuality and has consistently analysed how it is linked with male violence, predominantly manifested as control over women. Therefore, when the paper focuses on cases concerning male sex, the notion of what is discrimination against lesbians and gays, shifts subtly. For a start, lesbians are disappeared, subsumed into the category 'lesbianandgay'. Secondly, the feminist agenda is obscured, if not erased.

The erasure not only of feminist perspectives and achievements but of women altogether, is reinforced by a number of devices. The first of these is reversal. The proportion of serial killers killing men is minimal compared to attacks on and slaughter of women. Yet while the paper is silent on misogynist rape or murder, it screams headlines such as 'Two men strangled in their homes' and 'New York police hunt serial killer'. The most blatant example of this is the headline 'Serial killer: "Whole community under threat" warns police chief'. (Issue 283) It emerges that the police chief is talking about all gay men, not just those that are sado-masochist! Lesbians could be excused for feeling marginalised.

Another reversal is in the manner of reporting on legislation to make rape of men a crime in English law. (Issue 336) The last sentence of the report, presented almost as an afterthought, reads, 'Campaigners now hope that Rape Crisis Centres around the country will improve their service to male victims'. We note here that the campaigners are gender free, which is a clever device to end the report with an implicit attack on feminist activism and an expression of support for the erosion of services created by women, for women. Rape Crisis Centres were set up in the 1970s in Britain and were located very firmly in the context of an analysis of male violence and male power over women. Feminists spent a lot of time dispelling the myths of rape, for example that women ask for it, say no when they mean yes, or wear provocative clothing that leads men on. Most importantly, in common with their sisters in campaigns at the beginning of this century, they challenged the myth of the uncontrollable male urge. The Centres were run by women, a large number of whom were lesbians, to support victims because of the rape or sexual abuse they had endured, and against the system which was seen to rape them again if they reported the crime. They were unique in that they combined this function with mounting an ideological battle against the male presumption that men had the right to any woman's body at any time. Therefore, the throwaway sentence is much less innocent than it appears. Its anonymous 'campaigners' are either proposing mixed gender Rape Crisis Centres or women volunteers putting their energy into supporting men rather than women. Equal opportunities for men in rape erodes the analysis of rape as a crime used by men against women. This, then, is a good example of how supposedly neutral reportage in the *Pink Paper* undermines feminism, by ignoring past important campaigns and decontextualising events.

One very common practice under patriarchy is to get prominent women speaking against women's interests and supporting those of men. In the same report, Angela Mason, executive director of

Stonewall, says, 'This is a historic development. It marks the beginning of a new era, in which the criminal law will be concerned . . . with providing protection for all men and women against serious sexual assault.' The *Pink Paper*, by selective reporting in this instance, appears to support rape being viewed as a gender-free crime perpetrated on men and women alike.

When women's interests are reported, it is often in a second-hand or trivial manner. For instance, the case of the lesbian head teacher victimised by her local council and vilified by the tabloid press has received scant and sometimes inaccurate coverage, giving the impression that much of the coverage has been picked up from elsewhere. There has been no analysis at all of the anti-lesbian press coverage and the implications for other lesbians in education, again contributing to the impression that women's concerns are unimportant. The case of Alison Halford, (the police officer who took her employers to court for sex discrimination, and was subsequently victimised), is reported under the tabloid headline 'Underwear officer suspended again'. (Issue 209)

In the final issue of *Lesbian London* (June 1994) the front-page article makes the point that its collective could ill afford to compete with the glossy magazines marketed for lesbians, *Shebang, Diva* and *Lip*. It points out that *Shebang* and *Diva* are produced with male resources, the former connected with the *Pink Paper* and the latter 'under the auspices' of *Gay Times*. The male agenda is explicit in both papers, and is not absent from *Lip*, which presumably feels it needs to compete with the others. Ironically, *Lesbian London* itself, which began by saying it operated from a feminist perspective, expressed anti-feminist or liberal opinions at times, which perhaps shows how pervasive is the effect of a particular climate.

It is in the realm of image that these rags really come into their own. The *Pink Paper* starts the process of redefining what a lesbian is, both through photographic representation and comment. Concurrently, a stereotype of a radical lesbian feminist is constructed, which is historically inaccurate. This stereotype is then ridiculed or misrepresented in a number of ways. The fact that a spectre of radical lesbian feminism is set up, only to be knocked down as having 'no content *except* as a repressive "political correctness" ' (Miriam 1993 p 12) indicates that the attack on radical lesbians, the attempt at deconstruction and the creation of a 'new look', freshly packaged lesbian product, is quite deliberate.

The lesbian of today, according to *Shebang, Diva* and *Lip*, is young, scantily clad, obsessed with style and image, likes for the most part to have men around, is fun–loving (defined as dancing, clubbing, drinking, sex), likes and happily participates in, pornography. She sleeps with men from time to time.

Shebang's photographers specialise in Club Crawls (Puss Puss, Girl Bar, Venus Rising) where they find cocktail waitresses in fish–nets, bunny ears, corsets and not much more, and the clientele in an assortment of clothes, from body stockings and leathers, to cut–down ball gowns and thigh–length boots. All these are lovingly described, not surprisingly with the name of the supplier given. For example, shoes by Marco Polo, body stockings by Vivienne Westwood. (Issue 2) One of the photospreads, with more cleavages, lacy bras, nipples and fish–nets dispensed liberally, includes a survey entitled 'Women-only or mixed clubs – which do you prefer?'. Although some of the respondents reply 'women–only', there are a variety of replies that make one wonder if the Women's Movement ever happened . . . 'gay boys have fun energy' . . . 'women–only but not die–hards who won't tolerate different types of lesbians' . . . 'it's nice to mix' . . . 'I like men' . . . 'women–only as long as the women aren't boring' . . . 'women–only is a bit boring' . . . 'Mixed – women are too moody'. (Issue 5)

This creation of the modern lesbian, underlaid by the lurking killjoy, appeared in an earlier *Pink Paper* in the guise of a survey. The whole tone is intended to create a picture of lesbian identity that is solely about sex and femininity, combined with a trite attack on the supposed rigidity of lesbian feminism.

When I see a woman, I see her body. Only the most politically correct are able to disregard this and immediately see the inner being.

I am sick to death of lesbians being portrayed not just in the media, but in real life as short–haired butch women. If only people saw more of the lovely femme ones who are 100 per cent lesbian. I am only ever attracted to women who look like women, i.e. not cheap imitations of men. I understand the politics behind looking 'dykey' but why can't we grow out of this? (Issue 205)

The latter quotation shows a misunderstanding of the radical lesbian-feminist project, which aims ultimately to transcend the concept of gender and therefore leave behind butch and femme role-playing.

The male-approved lesbian is allowed to appear occasionally on the front page of the *Pink Paper*, if she is wearing lipstick (Issue 282), dancing half-naked, fishnetted and leathered (Issue 278), participating in a 'queer Carnival' organised by Outrage (Issue 265), or three-quarters naked as a 'dyke girl' being kissed by a 'gay boy'. (Issue 291) Her nubile, scantily-clad figure raves, pubs and clubs through the pages of the other magazines, participating in pornography, and using sex toys. For example, *Shebang* in Issue 6 has a double-page spread entitled 'Kinky boots' with images lifted directly from male pornography. Issue 10 has an article 'Toys'R'Us', which goes into great technical detail about the pros and cons of certain types of dildoes and harnesses. It also goes into some detail about sado-masochistic practices, and how particular 'toys' can facilitate these. The piece is accompanied by a visual display of studded harnesses and an array of dildoes, with a list of places they can be obtained, including *Shebang* Mail Order.

These images of sex and style and the promotion of pornography permeate all areas of the magazines. An especially offensive and insensitive example of the objectification of women's bodies occurs in *Shebang*, Issue 5, where an article on breast cancer is accompanied by a number of photographs of perfectly formed pairs of breasts, from various angles. A feature on fat women in *Diva*, Issue 2, is within the framework of pornography, as the accompanying photo is of a woman in bra, heavy chain around her neck, leather studded strap on her arm, dress open to below the navel, pouting seductively at the camera. The fact that it is presumably meant to be ironic doesn't negate this impression. An article about ageism, one of the few reminders in these publications that older women exist, is again in a framework of sex. Entitled 'Age vs Lust', it is about ageing and sex. It is not that this article should not be there, but there is nothing else in any of these magazines about the political consequences of being an older lesbian, for instance illness, or discrimination in housing or employment or pensions. Similarly, black women appear predominantly as sexy models in these magazines, thereby reinforcing male pornographic stereotypes of black women.

The 'lesbians who sleep with men' syndrome, the ground for which has been prepared so effectively by the promotion of the modern lesbian in these magazines, is treated quite matter-of-factly in *Lip*. In an undated issue, Lisa Power, counsellor at London Lighthouse, says she 'knows many lesbians who sleep with males'. This is taken up again in a later issue (Summer 1994), where we are informed, 'Lesbians have difficulty facing up to safe sex when sleeping with men'. This is in a news item, which concerns itself with the apparently increasing number of lesbians who are sleeping with men, and, in doing so, ignoring safe sex, which is a problem. However, this isn't really what the news item is about. It gives a lot of space to one of these women who defines herself as a lesbian but sleeps with men on a spontaneous basis. She 'sees herself as part of a new wave of sexual freedom' and is 'contemptuous of the old sexual boundaries'. These old sexual boundaries are, according to her, 'lesbians sticking to what they know'. Several more of her insights are, 'Gay men are gorgeous' and 'A lot of [lesbians] are frightened of the penis'. So the concerned news item on safer sex turns out to be yet another attack on outmoded, sexually repressed lesbians, by, it would seem, heterosexual women. The tone of the criticisms are remarkably reminiscent of those that have always been made against lesbians by men.

Attacks on radical lesbian feminists do not only occur in the form of the indirect, oppositional reconstructions already demonstrated. There are more overt manifestations.

A 'stereotype' of an ugly, humourless, fat dyke who finds offence in anything and would be 'appalled' by the sight of feminine sexy women having fun is created by Donna McPhail in Issue 2 of *Shebang*. Donna McPhail is described in *Shebang* as a 'comedienne'. It is significant that a lesbian comic now apparently gets her laughs from mocking feminist political commitment, lesbians who do not dress to please men, and women who are fat. All this is doing is recreating tabloid stereotypes of lesbian feminists from the 1970s and 1980s: there is nothing original or humorous about it. What she also does in her description is to trivialise and distort what feminist politics are about, which is the deconstruction of ideologies harmful to women and the creation of new ways of viewing. Further, she implies that anyone who cares about oppression is easily shockable and cannot have fun. Here, she misses the point; that it is possible to create a different kind of humour, that is not based, as patriarchal humour is, around mocking groups in society who do not hold power.

Diva 2 continues the attack on lesbian feminists by running an opinion poll in which young women talk of 'seventies dykes' as 'dogmatic . . . frumpy . . . bitter and twisted'.

Lesbian London, which started off saying it operated from a feminist perspective, gets in on the act in its later issues, by giving space to s-m views and objectives, and coming out with the same tired old attacks on 'judgmental' lesbian feminists who are 'shocked' at women describing their work as lesbian pornography. Issue 20 of *Lesbian London* gives over its front page to publicising *SH!* whose products it describes in detail (via an account of a forthcoming court case) as 'the only sex shop for women in Europe'. Issues 21 and 22 give space to lesbian s-m views. Issue 21 claims that it has 'an anti-SM policy'. A double-page spread entitled 'Dyke-otomies' (pp 4–5) purports to be opening up a debate. There is no debate; instead, there is an airing of views by a photographer, a pornographer whose work, we are told, has been featured in *Quim* and a *SH!* catalogue. The interviewer, while pretending to represent the views of lesbian feminists, structures the whole interview in a way that allows the interviewee to 'correct' these views and put the 'definitive' view: that lesbian feminists 'bring baggage' to their gaze, are dogmatic and have 'blocks'. So the stereotype is put in place: women who object to pornography are unreasonable, intimidating and forcing their views on creative and liberal women.

Issue 22 goes further. It has a double-page spread entitled 'Towards a Lesbian Erotica' (pp 4–5). It contains no analysis but merely reinforces the stereotyping of lesbian feminists as judgemental prudes. The most revealing feature of this article, however, is in the *Erratum* at the end, in which they reverse their claim in the previous issue to have an anti-SM policy and state that they really meant to say that: '. . . we have an anti-SM reputation.' This issue also features a page, plus a cover photo, of Beth and Margaret, the young romantic lesbians in *Brookside*, but instead of analysing how the lesbian relationship is portrayed, *Lesbian London* provides interviews with the two young heterosexual women who state that they can in no way identify with the lesbianism of the characters they play. Nevertheless, the lesbian magazine produces two glamorous photographs, reinforcing glamour and youth as ideals for lesbians, represented by heterosexual women!

In an interview with Mary Daly in Issue 5 of *Shebang*, the interviewer, Tanya Dewhurst, does not engage with Daly's ideas at all. She pretends Daly writes for an elite few, seems unaware of the influence her radical feminist ideas have had, and does not appear to understand that radical feminism has any connection with lesbianism. She concludes by saying, cheaply, that Daly's book *Outercourse* feels like a symbol of her oppression.

Dewhurst is not alone in appearing to be totally unaware that Mary Daly is very engaged with being fun, that she aims to spark an imaginative leap in women by being outrageous and by making lots of jokes. Yet the same elements of the media that accuse radical feminists of being dull, old-fashioned and out of touch with the avant-garde, accuse Daly of not being serious and not engaged enough with 'ordinary' women. It seems radical feminists cannot win either way.

Sheila Jeffreys is accorded the same kind of treatment as Mary Daly in *Lesbian London*, Issue 22. The supposed 'review' of *The Lesbian Heresy* becomes nothing more than personal speculation on the reviewer's part as to Jeffreys' motives in writing it. She says Jeffreys' 'handling' of the content of the book 'verges on the obsessive', (no inkling of what she means is offered). She then questions whether lesbian historians simply 'recreate past eras for their own glory'.

Thus the distortion of radical feminism is complete. Its ideas are not engaged with at all in these magazines, in comparison to the debates in earlier publications such as *Spare Rib* or *Outwrite*. Radical feminist critiques of current tendencies in the lesbian community are silenced, by the device of attributing a number of deficient and undesirable characteristics to the critics. Hence, lesbian feminists are not given credit for observing critically, but instead are constantly described, with no evidence whatsoever, as 'shocked'. This is a convenient device for pro-pornography writers. They over-simplify the opposition to pornography by linking it with prudery and the moral Right instead of engaging with the feminist critique. Lesbian feminists are also described as 'judgmental, dogmatic, intolerant, prudish, obsessive, oppressive, anti-sex, and bitter'. And just for good measure, they are also presented as 'old, fat, ugly and humourless'. And 'mannish'. And they like women and don't like men.

By contrast, the modern lesbian is . . . modern, attractive, feminine, sexy, and likes men.

So we have come full circle. The tabloid stereotype of lesbian feminists is now recreated perfectly in lesbian magazines such as *Shebang* and *Diva*, by no accident owned by men. The man-made woman, deconstructed as part of the feminist project, has been reassembled as a modern lesbian, complete with new corsets and silicone dildoes. Meanwhile, the *Pink Paper* often uses photographs of drag queens on its front cover, just to remind us that men have the power to mock what they have created.

It is not difficult to see why these conservative and anti-feminist messages and distortions of lesbian identity prevail. A community/movement of resisting women with an analysis of the patriarchy and a critique of male sexuality is extremely threatening to the male establishment. It is in the male interest to create the commodity lesbian – a vapid sex object who complements men in their campaigns and in bed. In addition, her participation in life-style lesbianism makes money for men, and some women, through the porn, fashion and entertainments industries.

A CRIME IS COMMITTED – ONE INVESTIGATION

The new lesbianandgay conservatism expressed in magazines intended for the consumption of lesbians has influenced different kinds of publications in a more subtle and insidious way. Lesbian detective fiction is very much a part of influential popular culture in the lesbian community. Unfortunately, some of the tendencies of the magazines are recreated in lesbian detective novels. Despite their portrayal of what are generally considered to be autonomous, independent lesbian characters, there is an increasing trend in these novels to embody conservative values and actively anti-feminist positions.

A particularly good example of this trend is Barbara Wilson, in whose fiction the evolution from a feminist perspective to an anti-feminist position can be traced quite clearly.

Wilson, in her essay *The Outside Edge: Lesbian Mysteries*, (Wilson 1994 pp 217–28), stated that her three Pam Nilsen novels are 'quite in tune with other overtly feminist crime novels of the 1980s'. This is certainly true of *Murder in the Collective* (1984) and *Sisters of the Road* (1986). *Murder in the Collective* deals directly, from a feminist perspective, with various concerns of the late 1970s and early 1980s, such as tensions between lesbians and leftist heterosexuals, women's friendships, collective working, lesbian custody, and pornography. It is solidly feminist, in that it contains a critique of male sexual behaviour; 'He forgot to look cute and spaced out and seemed almost angry.' (p 17) In the course of the novel the not-so-cute man is murdered by the woman he has mistreated to prevent him carrying out his pornographic fantasies on a lesbian he is about to blackmail. The three women who know this band together to protect the woman who has murdered the racist, sexist blackmailer. Similarly, *Sisters of the Road* tackles violence against women and prostitution, and we experience the solidarity between women in the face of male violence.

However, in the last of the Pam Nilsen novels, *The Dog Collar Murders* (1989), Barbara Wilson appears to have turned away from feminism. She has thrown in her lot firmly with the 'new lesbians' of post-feminism. She claims that her novels 'call into question some of the hypocrisy and rhetoric of the feminist movement.' (Wilson 1994) Nonetheless, it is difficult to read this particular novel as anything but a blatant attack on radical feminism and, more especially, on well-known anti-pornography campaigners.

The plot hinges around the murder of an anti-pornography campaigner and writer, Loie Marsh, strangled at a sexuality/pornography conference with a dog-collar. Pam Nilsen investigates the murder. There are a number of suspects, including women who practise s-m and make lesbian sex videos, and other women speakers at the conference, who do not think pornography and violence are central issues in women's oppression.

Throughout the novel there is a pseudo–debate about lesbian sexuality, pornography and erotica. There are odd, out-of-character incidents, such as the occasion when Pam and her lover Hadley go to a Fun Palace to watch a porn show featuring a woman they want to investigate. They find her dancing naked in high heels with two other women. They both admit to being turned on. The impression given is that women are just like men supposedly are; drowned in uncontrollable lust at the sight of a naked woman's body. Elsewhere in the novel queer politics are touched on, when Hadley and Pam have a discussion with two gay men about sex, and express envy about their sexual practices; Hadley saying 'There was never that sexual joy in the lesbian–feminist community.' (p 127) The implication is that lesbians would be happier if they embraced male sexual behaviour.

Paulina Palmer (Palmer 1994 pp 101–102) sees the novel as hinging on the controversy between anti-pornography activists led by Loie Marsh, and those opposed to censorship, represented by Gracie London. However, it is difficult to read the novel as anything but a diatribe against those representing the former view. Advocates of s–m practices and those who are pro–pornography are allowed to put their views at great length. They are presented sympathetically, as charming and vulnerable, or attractive, rational and wise, as are those who are confused (such as Pam), or who don't feel strongly either way. The characters who are opposed to pornography, on the other hand, are never really developed as characters. They are presented as faceless followers of Loie and are portrayed as brainwashed and illogical.

The central character around whom the plot revolves is hardly allowed to speak for herself, as she is killed off early in the novel, but she is discredited and attacked throughout. This clearly indicates where the author stands. Loie is caricatured as a charismatic leader in the male tradition, being described by Pam, for instance, as a 'commander of an insurgent army' (p 32), and later, 'She was the teacher, we the schoolgirls'. (p 33) After she is killed, the gossip among the lesbian community is that she was secretly into s–m. She was once 'more adventurous, but now makes – made – a living out of puritanism'. (p 68) Again, in common with the magazines, we have the speculation about personal motives, the implication being that it is impossible to be critically opposed to pornography; there must be some underlying personal reason such as sexual repression. Just for good measure, Loie is also depicted as a plagiarist and a muddled thinker. The ultimate impression of the book is that no–one really cared about Loie or regretted her death. She is made to seem inhuman and there is almost an implication that she deserved to die. It does not take much effort to read the book as a symbolic murder of radical feminism.

The series of characteristics which contribute to undermining radical lesbian feminism in the magazines are greatly in evidence here as well. For instance, the politics of radical feminism are misrepresented as essentialist and radical feminists are presented as despairing, over-emotional and sexually repressed. They are also portrayed as having no sense of community or common purpose, as there is very little sense in the book of a radical movement of women opposed to pornography and male violence, merely the creation of a fanatic who sways others.

By the time Wilson came to write *Gaudi Afternoon*, she stated in her essay (1994) that 'the pressure . . . to discuss the issues in the lesbian community was lifting, and [she] wanted to be . . . more frivolous and more sophisticated – to joke more and ponder less'. This comment is revealing. Again there are parallels with the coverage in the magazines. Politics is depicted as too serious and not fun. More emphasis on fun, style and modernity is called for. She admits, in an equally revealing comment, that the 'tone' of *Gaudi Afternoon* is very different. 'Transexualism, child custody, motherhood – all are treated in a much more light-hearted fashion.' 'In the character of Cassandra,' she maintains, 'I found a tolerant sense of humour that could respect many people's choices while still finding them amusing.'

The whole novel is an extended joke about illusion; shifting reality, shifting identities, shifting pronouns, and distinctly shifting politics. Cassandra Reilly, an amateur detective, is hired by Frankie Stevens to track down Frankie's husband Ben, who has vanished from San Francisco. When Cassandra arrives in Barcelona, she embarks on a series of false trails, as no-one is what they seem. For instance, Ben turns out to be a lesbian mother whose present girl-friend and ex-husband are both male-to-female transsexuals, one red-curled, high-heeled, short-skirted and flamboyant; the other voluptuous and gorgeous, decked out in flowing kaftans and silk scarves. In short, men turn out to be women and women turn out to be men and the small daughter of Ben keeps getting kidnapped by various of these characters while all the others rush around trying to find her.

Looking at it from a feminist perspective the plot is as follows:

two transsexuals snatch a child from a lesbian. Later, a gay man kidnaps the same child so that the lesbian and transsexual parent will be reconciled. The parents then agree to share custody, and to go into counselling together. Another lesbian and this same gay man decide to have a baby together. So in reality, the humour and farce conceal quite a nasty plot, the resolution of which is that the lesbian mother goes into what amounts to family therapy to accept transsexuality, with which we are told she had 'huge problems' (p 166) and shared custody. Although realities are suspended, they are there in the background. For instance, Frankie, the transsexual, who turned out to be Ben's husband, not wife, is a really unpleasant character who minces around wiggling his hips and wrinkling his nose – mannerisms which mock women. He tricks Cassandra, so that he can steal his daughter from her mother. At one point, when he lurks near Cassandra and follows his ex-wife Ben, he is a menacing man in shades, reminding us that he can revert to his male identity whenever he wishes and still has the power to threaten women.

Trouble in Transylvania is also a comedy. The lesbian characters seem to have learnt from Pam and Hadley in *The Dog Collar Murders*; their sexuality is set in a male framework. They all – Cassandra, Jack, Bree – are ready to 'lay' any female character they see, and in some cases do, no matter how improbable.

Wilson concluded her chapter by saying 'I find myself more comfortable [working at the outside edge]. However, if one pushes hard enough . . . the boundaries change and what was once outside is now inside. If we are looking for inclusion rather than marginalisation perhaps that's as it should be.' (Wilson 1994) There are problems with this perspective from a feminist point of view. The implication of what she is saying, based on the content of her later novels, is that, to be included, we should take on the values of the patriarchy. The shifting boundaries, again, seem to involve capitulating to male definitions. Meantime, the realities of the oppression of women, by men, have not gone away. We have to ask whether the subjects she chooses to treat as farce or slapstick, such as lesbian custody and motherhood, are appropriate ones to joke about. Given the prevalent ideologies surrounding the institution of the family, and the reaffirmation of patriarchal values, is it not a little dangerous?

DYKES WE NEED TO WATCH OUT FOR

The trend of representing resisting women negatively extends to many areas. A further vehicle for this tendency is the cartoon strip *Dykes To Watch Out For* by Alison Bechdel, available in booklets and calendars. This series, much read and loved by dykes, details the lives of a community of lesbians, and has all the qualities of a soap. Black women and women with disabilities are there as major characters. Amid the agonisings over relationships, monogamy, non-monogamy and commitment, there are political discussions and debates. Two of the characters decide to have a baby, and the birth occurs at the end of the 1993 book. A very amusing ongoing critique of therapy is provided. In short, a lot of aspects important to the lesbian-feminist community are covered. So what is the problem?

The problem is the representation of Mo. Mo, in her striped T-shirt and jeans, is the one and only character who expresses feminist values consistently: 'We were so excited, so radical, so committed to dismantling the patriarchy.' (*More Dykes To Watch Out For* p 38) On a Gay Pride march, she declaims that 'the whole thing is getting kind of conservative' as she and her friends watch the parade of gay and lesbian Catholics, lesbian investment bankers, topless women in tutus and boots, men dressed as penises. Her friends tell her to 'lighten up . . . you only see the things that support your depressing theories.' (pp 54–5) This is typical of the whole portrayal of Mo, throughout four books and as many calendars. She is presented as a very unsympathetic character, who 'whines', is self-obsessed, and lectures and rants all the time. She is also unfashionable, confused in her politics, unable to get a lover or keep one for very long (the implication being that it is because of her 'negative politics'), humourless, uptight and prudish. This carries a very powerful message through the medium of a cartoon. For instance, all the covers and lots of the drawings show Mo frowning, angry or disapproving, cut off from the other characters who are enjoying themselves. As this is humour, and supposedly affectionately showing the foibles of the lesbian community, it is insidious.

In the two later cartoon books, *Dykes . . . The Sequel*, and *Spawn of Dykes*, there are debates about queer politics. Most characters take a liberal stance, and indeed, seem to embrace queer, for instance, reading lesgay porn, videoing themselves having sex, going to 'Love Tunnels'. Mo is the only character who has a critique of queer politics, and predictably, she is derided. For instance, in one cartoon, she calls Madonna an 'opportunistic, anti-feminist entrepreneur' and her video 'cheap, sadomasochistic imagery', yet in the next frame she is shown as engrossed, with the implication from the context that she is sexually turned-on. (*Sequel* pp 54–5) At the beginning of *Spawn*, she is commenting on the plethora of lesgay publications; 'What shallow, pandering, consumer-driven tripe! You won't catch me wasting money on one of these slick new ad-ridden queer magazines!' The reply is, 'That's because you read 'em all here.'

The 1993 *Dykes To Watch Out For* calendar concludes by inadvertently encapsulating the phenomenon described throughout this chapter; the parodying of feminist values, the ridiculing of lesbian feminists and the co-option and heterosexualising of resisting lesbians. Like little girls playing with our very own dolls we can cut out and dress Mo in a new set of clothes! We can clothe her in fishnets, lycra skirt, black bra, corset and pornographic T-shirt. In other words, we are invited to collude in the remaking of a lesbian feminist. But do we want to participate in making over ourselves?

Papers and Magazines

Diva: the lesbian lifestyle magazine, Millivres Ltd, London
Lesbian London.
Lip, London.
The *Pink Paper: the National Newspaper for Lesbians and Gay Men*, Gay Community Press Ltd., London.
Shebang; The Dyke Active Ingredient, Gay Community Press Ltd., London.

Novels

Wilson, B, *Murder in the Collective*, The Women's Press, London, 1984.
Wilson, B, *Sisters of the Road*, The Women's Press, London, 1986.
Wilson, B, *The Dog Collar Murders*, Virago Crime, London, 1989.
Wilson, B, *Gaudi Afternoon*, Virago Crime, London, 1991.
Wilson, B, *Trouble in Transylvania*, Virago Crime, London, 1993.

Cartoons

Bechdel, A, *More Dykes To Watch Out For*, Firebrand Books, New York, 1988.
Bechdel, A, *Dykes To Watch Out For: the Sequel*, Firebrand Books, New York, 1992.
Bechdel, A, *Spawn Of Dykes To Watch Out For*, Firebrand Books, New York, 1993.
Bechdel, A, *Dykes To Watch Out For*. 1993 Calendar, Firebrand Books, New York.
Jackson, C, *Wonder Wimbin: Everyday Stories of Feminist Folk*, Battleaxe Books, Hounslow, 1984.
Jackson, C, *Visibly Vera*, The Women's Press, London, 1986.

References

Miriam, K, 'From Rage to All the Rage: Lesbian Feminism, Sadomasochism and the Politics of Memory', in I. Reti (ed), *Unleashing Feminism*, HerBooks, Santa Cruz CA, 1993.
Onlywomen Press Collective (eds), *Love Your Enemy? The debate between heterosexual feminism and political lesbianism*, Onlywomen Press, London, 1981.
Palmer, P, 'The Lesbian Thriller: Crimes, Clues and Contradictions', in G Griffin (ed), *Outwrite. Lesbianism and Popular Culture*, Pluto Press, London, 1993.
Reynolds, M (ed), *The Penguin Book of Lesbian Short Stories*, Viking, London, 1993.
Wilson, B, 'The Outside Edge: Lesbian Mysteries', in L Gibbs (ed), *Daring to Dissent*, Cassell, London, 1994.

NICOLA HUMBERSTONE

Lesbian representations on British television have increased substantially in the last few years, although they are still not a common phenomena. They are located in soap operas, 'alternative' programmes (such as the *OUT* series), documentaries, dramas and popular series such as *Between the Lines* and *Casualty*. On one level, this recent visibility of lesbians in the media is a radical change and is particularly innovative where soap operas have constructed narratives around lesbian characters and issues. Although lesbianism is not the predominant theme in such cases, the issue of lesbian sexuality has been placed in British popular culture in a way that is new for viewers.

ALTERNATIVE PROGRAMMES

Representations of lesbians in 'alternative' programming have become increasingly framed within lifestyle or 'bizarre' contexts where the construction of the 'exotic' is seen as a radical move with an emphasis on dressing up and shocking heterosexuals and feminists. The *OUT* programmes, which were weekly lesbian and gay documentary programmes produced by Channel Four and screened over a period of five years, were earlier concerned with issues such as lesbians and gays in Russia and Europe, AIDS, lesbian and gay parenting, sometimes introduced by men in drag and often conflated gender issues into 'gay' issues; constructing a gay identity which, however well-intentioned, took the feminism out of lesbianism and tended to allow gay men to set the agenda. Radical feminism was never given much of a voice because the emphasis has been on presenting a unified picture of lesbians and gay men and then giving gay men priority to set the agenda. The possibility of a radical feminist analysis of the issues was an unlikely prospect because criticism of men, masculinity, or patriarchy was unacceptable within this framework.

This earlier 'issue' focus gave way to a location of homosexuality within fashion, lifestyle, sado-masochism, transgression (men in drag), body piercing, and 'irony', for example in terms of using fascist symbols 'ironically', implying we don't really mean it; how silly to think what you see is really there.

A few exceptions are identifiable within 'alternative' programming; for example older lesbians in *Women Like Us* and *Women Like That* produced for *Out on Tuesday* by Clio Co-op, were seen positively by the film-makers, and some of the women represented explained their lesbianism as integral to feminist politics. In these films it was noticeable that older women were validated and given space to articulate their experiences and their own perceptions of why they were lesbians.

However, in general, lesbian representation in alternative programming has and continues to be portrayed within the 'ironic' framework reflecting the wider alternative media context. Most of the articles about lesbianism in the gay press, the Della Grace photographs of s-m dykes raping (ironically?) powerless women, articles by Cherry Smyth extolling the radical power of the dildo, re-construct 'radical' lesbianism as 'queer' and phallic, violent, cruel and shocking, in opposition to feminism or indeed any structural analysis of power relations. Feminist analysis is present in a negative way, constructed and dismissed as simplistic, morally oppressive and against sex, except in 'romantic' terms.

> Lesbians as drag queens, prostitutes and porn stars were not the kinds of lesbian radical feminists wanted in their club. (Smyth in Gibbs 1994 p 209)

The idea of the transgressive, inextricably linked to violent sexuality, as being positive, shocking and with the power to deconstruct and reconstruct lesbian sexuality is brought to lesbian film-making: 'These women delight in the romance of cruelty, take pleasure in humiliation, and fight among themselves as much as with the outside world.' (Smyth op. cit. p 210)

'Queer' sex is seen as a reaction and antidote to radical lesbian feminism, a desire to demolish 'vanilla' sex as the apparently prevailing view of lesbians, and focuses anger and criticism on to radical feminist politics, constructed as an all-powerful moralism bearing close resemblance to Mary Whitehouse and the 'new Right', rather than an honest analysis of feminist discourse, or a questioning of patriarchal structures in society.

That the structure of the 'new' sexuality bears a closer, if not identical, relationship to 'normal' heterosexuality, with masculinity representing power, than does, a radical critique, is rarely mentioned. Instead the 'bad girl' of queer becomes a self-evident ideal. It is this view which is presented as the norm by and within gay/queer culture, in spite of the attempts to persuade us that this is the cutting edge of sexuality.

An interesting development is the lesbian boy: instead of butch-femme there is seen to be a universal desire for masculinity, which makes lesbians like gay men, rather than being modelled on heterosexual dualism. The presence of 'femininity', for example by lipstick and girlie clothes, is less of an emphasis within gay culture, although dressing up has become an end in itself, reflecting the post-modernist view that nothing is what it seems and that appearances have no relation to an objective truth.

While this is a radical and interesting idea, which questions all essentialist ideologies, and focuses on the power of the media to construct entire realities, the result is an embracing of appearances and symbols as an end in itself. Structural power relationships have no place in this framework, because there is no political perspective to start with, or where there has been it disappears into a multi-faceted post-modernist reality, having no relation to cause and effect, and no validity as an explanation of cultural conditions.

'Camp' within this post-modernist perspective is seen as radical. The traditional pantomime man dressed as a woman with every negative stereotype exaggerated, becomes pastiche, irony, post-oppressive. Feminists who object 'have no sense of humour'. Camp is largely based on men humiliating women and where lesbians are present in camp productions they inevitably become pastiches themselves. For example, *Camp Christmas* (Channel Four 1993), a programme with a theme of gay men and lesbians spending Christmas together and with famous guests phoning in, was framed within this perspective so that everyone had to go over the top or appear embarrassingly naive. Of course, a title like *Camp Christmas* could mean nothing else, but where lesbians become incorporated into this framework they are so far removed from themselves that they appear like male transvestites, camping it up and using the same camp dialogue as the men. The 'real' lesbians in the programme, including Polly Perkins and Pam St. Clements, have scripts which are indistinguishable from the men's and they present themselves as ironical limp-wristed drag artists. They can't quite compete with the overall tone but come over as watered-down versions – not good enough to be really camp because only men can do it properly. These women are set up to fail because the joke doesn't work in this way. What woman could be as camp as Lily Savage? The 'jokes' are about appliances and the focus is drag and puns on gay male dialogue.

The 'queen's' speech is presented by an inevitably camp Queen Elizabeth – 'The arts have always relied upon the support of queens.' Pam St. Clements is the fairy on the Christmas tree: 'Alas, I'm getting old . . . nobody loves a fairy when she's forty.' Ageism is turned into a joke.

'Your fairy days are ending, when your wand is always bending,' she sings, completing the impression of a male drag artist. It is in fact increasingly difficult to see her as a woman as the programme progresses.

The 'Santa Claus' figure in the programme makes 'jokes' about 'drilling my young assistant', and 'surprising children in that way I have . . . sliding up and down shafts'. Is this funny or is it ageism and/or sexual abuse? A feminist perspective would be implicitly humourless in this context. We see the joke or we are moralistic with no sexual desires ourselves. Penises and appliances are ever-present.

Lea Delaria's remark, 'It's not that I don't like penises; I just don't like them on men,' inserts 'queer' politics and the 'lesbian boy' into the agenda, to give a 'transgressive' edge and construct lesbians with dildos as unquestionably radical. The universal desire for a prick is assumed, making feminist analysis ridiculous and redundant.

Where does this leave feminism? It is not only lesbian feminism which has been reconstructed in order to make it easier to attack, but feminism of any kind has been represented by a male-dominated media as a certain kind of moralistic, anti-sex, archaic viewpoint which has long lost its bite. At the same time feminism is linked inextricably to political correctness, made to seem all powerful and dangerous, and 'reasonable' people are appealed to to reject its hypnotic effect.

Lesbian feminism is seen not in terms of sexuality at all but as a bitter hatred (envy) of men; lesbian feminists are represented as ugly women who, because men have rejected them, can only have sex with others like themselves.

There is a fundamental ageism, too, in all this which negatively locates feminism to the 1960s and 1970s and fixes it into a time warp. Women who call themselves lesbian feminists can only be seen as transfixed by the past and unable to make useful points about women today.

The emphasis on representing young white women as the norm and the invisibility of women with disabilities is an issue to be addressed within lesbian feminism, as well as outside of it. The one good aspect of the *OUT* series is that it has included more representations of and interviews with lesbians of colour than popular television programming.

INTO THE MAINSTREAM

There have been lesbians in British mainstream series, for example in *Portrait of a Marriage* and *Oranges Are Not the Only Fruit*, which have brought the issue of lesbianism into popular culture. Other series have brought a particular theme into the narrative: for example *Between the Lines*, a drama about policing the police. *Casualty* (a hospital drama set in an accident and emergency ward) has built story-lines around it and *Roseanne*, the American cult comedy, has Sandra Bernhard's lesbianism as an exotic addition to the close-knit 'family' cast.

With such a motley collection of representations it is impossible to generalise: the only common context is that of the problematic.

This means that lesbianism is constructed as perverse in the first instance and is confronted by antagonism and disbelief. The narrative has to go in one of two ways: the issue must be resolved and to do this it must become acceptable and therefore 'normal' and unthreatening, or it will be pathologised and remain deviant, sometimes disappearing from the frame altogether. The status quo will be reformed or the issue becomes a problem indefinitely.

The individualisation of lesbianism removes any feminist perspective and makes it a personal matter, yet happiness is dependent on other's responses. It is not simply that dramas and soaps cannot relate to a wider context, because they clearly do this continually by constructing themes around current 'issues'. More significantly, it is inevitable that the unpopularity of feminism, particularly lesbian feminism, will be visible by its absence in these programmes, and the individualisation of 'sexual preference' fits completely into most of the genre. Therefore, lesbianism can be constructed as a sudden 'desire' for another woman, explained in terms of a normal response in a genderless analysis, where 'love' becomes the main factor and gender/patriarchal relations disappear. Choice in terms of feminism is not articulated, not because it is too complicated to explain, but because it is not an acceptable idea.

While it is useful to set dramas in a situation which illuminates prejudice and others' inability to understand or to be actively antagonistic, the continual negative responses of the heterosexual community can reinforce the 'abnormality' and the difficulties faced by lesbians, particularly for women who may be thinking about acting on lesbian sexuality or coming out.

Oranges Are Not The Only Fruit, a dramatised version of the novel by Jeanette Winterson (1985) was an undeniable success, due to good casting and a script which was funny, dramatic, and accurate in terms of a particular northern patriarchal religious community. The strong women characters and a placing of lesbianism in a realistically antagonistic setting made the triumph of the central character in escaping from it and still being a lesbian a powerful force and an unusual progression for mainstream television.

Casualty's portrayal of lesbian characters has until recently been wholly negative. One character, while visiting on the ward, attempts to force her lover to leave her husband and choose her, resulting in the 'patient' relinquishing both of them in an exasperated rage. Another character was apparently a motor-bike riding 'boy' until a medical examination proved otherwise. After some discussion she admitted she had to be thought of as male by her girlfriends, otherwise it just didn't work for her. Attempts by Charlie, the ever-understanding male charge nurse, to persuade her to join a lesbian support group were inevitably doomed to failure, because she couldn't be seen to be, or even think of herself as a woman.

While *Roseanne*, an American cult comedy series screened in Britain by Channel 4, has always been seen as 'alternative' and radical; the way the much-publicised 'lesbian kiss' episode was contextualised only reinforced anti-lesbian reactions. Roseanne's lesbian friends invite her to a lesbian club, and one of them kisses her. Roseanne is repelled, then takes it seriously and becomes concerned about the 'girlfriend' being betrayed. She is then moved to tell her husband, who is predictably turned on by it. Roseanne's proclamation , after sex, of her love for his 'masculinity' is said by some to be ironic, but there is too much of the traditional portrayals here for it to be seen as more that a flirtation with the taboo and an attempt to be fashionable.

Between the Lines provided a more sympathetic interpretation where one of the main characters became a lesbian, confronted the police prejudice and went to the police dance with her lover, dancing openly with her and later gaining grudging acceptance by the male characters. A parallel existed in *Prime Suspect 1*, a police drama about a psychopath tracked down by a woman detective inspector, where her (Helen Mirren's) *coup de grace* is to be applauded by previously aggressive and sexist men. The problem with this is the necessary pleasure we, the viewers, get from watching the triumph of the strong woman, but which is modified by the equally strong message that the ultimate achievement and accolade is to win male approval.

The idea that men will be reasonable in the end if confronted with enough rational evidence and that women need this male validation to be successful or happy, is neither true, nor, from a radical lesbian-feminist perspective, desirable.

SOAPS

Where soap operas have taken up the lesbian theme, the characters have been able to develop in a way that short sharp focuses don't allow. The structure of soaps can accommodate this; allowing for the characters to be a part of the main community.

Emmerdale is a soap set in an all-white farming community and has featured Zoe the vet as a young, white, middle-class apparently heterosexual woman. The theme started boldly – especially for a seven pm transmission – and had Zoe's realisation that she was a lesbian coming slowly to articulation after unsuccessful attempts at sex with Archie. The suspense was built up by not letting the viewer know why she didn't like it. He was a sympathetic, if odd (left-wing/anarchist) character and was quite smitten with her. His reaction was extreme when she eventually told him and she spent some time consoling him, while facing her father's anger and disgust, which finally gave way to acceptance. As with the dramas, the common theme of male acceptance indicates that this is a good thing.

The introducing of the 'lesbian and gay society' from university (and Archie's heroic behaviour in not telling anyone, even persuading her to meet other lesbians) allowed the theme to broaden and the gossip of the village lent dramatic content as they thought it was *Archie* who was gay, and he still didn't crack. While the construction of Archie as the hero took some of the focus off Zoe, the plot still allowed for development: Zoe has dinner with a lesbian she has met at the 'society' and her father assumes they will have sex. Zoe explains that just because she's a lesbian doesn't mean she wants to have sex with just anyone. This contradicts a common assumption: that lesbians are motivated by desperation and want to have sex, or have a relationship with anybody who comes along. Zoe also articulates this in terms of an analogy with heterosexuality – no one assumes they will be attracted to absolutely anybody. Equally radically, she states that she likes the woman and respects her.

Brookside, the Liverpool soap, took the issue up in a more serious way and Beth's attraction to Margaret was realistically portrayed. Of course the obvious tendency was for the viewer to see Beth's abuse by her father as a *cause* of her lesbianism; her mother, Mandy, immediately jumped to that conclusion. That he had raped both his daughters had been a large feature of the previous episodes, culminating in the mother and daughter killing him and burying him under the patio. The dialogue did develop in a way which made it seem much less straightforward than that, although this idea would probably have reinforced existing beliefs that lesbianism is always about a bad relationship with a man. The 'safety' of a relationship with a caring woman is often held up as a refusal to face the 'real world'.

The affair appeared to be progressing satisfactorily, but Beth, who was doing a university course, met another lesbian and was attracted to her. The 'older woman' lecturer was initially seen as a spoiler of their relationship, 'taking Beth away' from Margaret, but became more three-dimensional in that her work was foregrounded. It was, however, purely set in the 'problematic' as a dramatic device. Mandy Jordash, Beth's mother, threatened to 'out' her to her colleagues and expose her 'unprofessional' relationship with one of her students.

Ageism has also been entwined in the theme, as Beth's lover was seen first as older and manipulative, and an older neighbour, Jean Crosby, admitted to being attracted to a woman in her youth. This probably shocked more viewers than the Jordash theme because her age and 'grandmotherly' persona had become constructed around a non-sexual and caring role; the idea of her past lesbian sexuality, ambiguous though it might have been, was at odds with the character's expected development. However, the fact that it was grounded very much in the past and was not actually acted upon, can reinforce ideas about lesbian 'phases'; acceptable in girls but to be grown out of. The strongest scenes were concerned with her husband's reaction to it – wounded, angry, betrayed and bigoted.

However, the way this issue reverberated through the rest of the cast could be seen to be positive: to isolate it and contain it would not have been realistic, and the reactions of the other characters were interesting in themselves. The bigoted responses were seen to be just that, and there was a bonding between the women characters in her defence. However, Beth's mother, Mandy was not so enamoured of the idea, and the daughter of Jean was threatened more by her mother's sexuality when she confessed to once being attracted to another woman, than she was by Beth's.

On the other hand the lesbian-feminist perspective that becoming a lesbian is a positive choice has been totally missing in *Brookside*.

The double radical insertion of the theme, focusing initially on a partly established character (Margaret) and not an 'outsider' (like Zoe, in *Emmerdale* or Della and Binny in *Eastenders*) who was straight and became sexually attracted to Beth, is outweighed by the way it was explained through the characters as an *inexplicable* desire. They continually expressed the fact that they had both fancied men (we have seen this), and there was no reason, within this context, to expect that they would not again. It all really looks like an argument for bisexuality rather than lesbianism, especially when Margaret leaves to join her ex-fiancé Derek once again.

Eastenders, a BBC 1 soap, has also taken up the lesbian theme. Two characters, Della and Binny, the former black, the latter white, had an affair/relationship which caused puzzlement, fury, and animosity to Steve, a black friend, who had hopes of an affair himself. Della is presented as in a trauma about whether she can cope with homophobia, and Binny is presented as aggressive and belligerent, snogging in the pub and daring Sharon (the pub owner) to throw them out. However, there are well-made points about how lesbians are expected to behave in public and Sharon is made to look inadequate in her defence of trying to make their sexuality invisible.

Because Steve is a constant in the series, and also because we know much more about him, the perspective is his, and the viewer is asked to question with him why a woman to whom he is attracted should prefer another woman. The past 'Steve', who treated his lover (Hattie) badly, has been subsumed into a nicer character who cannot understand why he can't have what he wants.

The issue of Della's 'coming out' very much focused on her mother's apparent naivety and prejudice; her refusal to see what to the viewer was obvious, is irritating and reinforces stereotypes of homophobic black communities. Della is represented in a vacuum with no evident black friends to support her, although Steve alternates between fury and a kind of irritated attraction/liking.

THE WIDER CONTEXT

Lesbianism as a fashion accessory

The structure of soaps – whereby everything is individualised – makes it very easy to de-politicise issues and the current 'fashion' for lesbian affairs adds to the confusion of representations and removes lesbianism from its social context. This inevitably takes lesbianism far away from any feminist perspective and constructs it as a chic accessory which enhances women's attraction to men. There is no analysis of ideologies/social constructions of sexuality and no questioning of gender roles, merely a focus on dress and appearance.

> With or without their lipstick, lesbians wonder if their image in the media will ever be more than a silly-season filler that's over when Martina leaves London and wends her way back to Aspen. When their fifteen minutes of fame are up, they will still be dealing with discrimination. (Grant 1994)

All representations of lesbians are confined by the unpopularity of feminism, which is seen as one dimensional, out-moded and bitter. This image of the lesbian feminist affects the representation of lesbians, whether fictionally or in a dramatic context. No positive image is allowed where feminism is a dominant force, so lesbians are not portrayed as feminists. Current fashionable images of lesbians remain closely tied to the femme-butch stereotypes that were constructed at the beginning of this century. (Jeffreys this volume)

On the one hand, there is the lipstick lesbian:

> in the words of Harper & Queen, those 'beautiful things, waifs straying across the sexual divide with no hint of the butch about them. They are subtle seductresses, alive to a light touch or glance at a party, soft skin and perfumed silk.' In other words, a six-stone weakling with no mouth or attitude, who won't give any trouble when homophobia is back in fashion. (Grant, Ibid. 1994)

On the other hand we have the butch image of k. d. lang, expressing a desire for a penis and looking like a man. The potential for positive imagery and a questioning of sexuality as a social construction is superficially there, combined with queer culture's obsession with dressing up and shocking; but the debate remains set within patriarchal norms, refusing to go beyond statements about fashion and the supposed radical power of transgression. The media is incapable of presenting a sympathetic picture of lesbian feminism, because it has constructed its own demon and shot it down.

The reality of lesbian-feminist politics was grounded in a realisation that heterosexuality is a form of male control and that 'masculinity' and 'femininity' are constructed. This understanding, combined with a clear awareness that to choose to relate to women was a political act, not 'non-sexual', as has been repeatedly claimed: most women who saw the possibility of choosing to be a lesbian did not suddenly robot-like force themselves to fancy women. However, this reality has not been portrayed reasonably and lesbians who are represented are removed from any feminist analysis of gender; rather these representations reinforce conservative and essentialist ideas about masculinity and femininity and about gender difference. Thus the only images we end up with are lipstick lesbians or lesbian boys.

The wider context cannot be ignored because it has had an effect on television's taking up of lesbian themes. Male reactions to lesbian representations are often, beneath the knee-jerk sneering, or sexual excitement, that of a threatened class. If the fashion for lesbian visibility were to be more long-lasting than it appears, then men may be right to feel threatened. However, without a feminist perspective, lesbian representations can be easily assimilated by patriarchal ideologies as the above discussion shows. As such, these representations pose little threat to patriarchal structures in our society as a whole.

FUTURE POTENTIAL?

If lesbian visibility within television is not merely transitory there remains the potential for more radical media representation in the form of girls and women seeing an alternative to heterosexuality. Soaps currently have the edge in more 'positive' representation, over alternative and queer productions where lesbians are often subsumed into gay male life-styles or don't appear at all. There is a certain irony here!

There is more character development and discussion within the soap genre and the added advantage of bringing the issue firmly into popular television, and initiating discussion in a wider forum. Characters must be contextualised, and this has to take into account the reactions of the community to lesbianism. At the moment, this is largely negative, but if soaps are to be at all realistic anti-lesbianism will have to be a component. It is the way anti-lesbianism is dealt with and challenged that is crucial to the potential for the linking up of feminist ideas with lesbianism in an implicit way.

Debates about lesbianism have resounded throughout the scripts and scenarios of soaps and both *Brookside* and *Eastenders* have tried to deal with this at a serious dramatic level. However, the soap lesbians would never call themselves feminist, because feminism is not a positive term, and they are not constructed as negative characters. This has nothing to do with the structure of soaps but the appropriation of feminist sexual politics by the media into a wholly negative phenomenon.

A further problem with soaps is that they tend to drop the lesbian story lines (as has happened in *EastEnders* and *Brookside*); and leave the issues unresolved or they are resolved in an anti-feminist way. This is the disadvantage of the genre: themes can be taken up and dropped if the producer/TV company/and male controlled institutions decide it is not important or is too controversial and a vast number of episodes can be negated by a single act. We the viewers, however, are not so forgetful, or stupid. The portrayal of lesbianism in soaps has had the effect of being discussed and taken up by a lot of people who regularly watch them, and this must have some positive effect.

In general the current portrayal of lesbianism within lifestyle contexts in both soaps and alternative programming either individualises and normalises the issue, or, with the focus on sex and appearance, attempts to shock people rather than to challenge them. While there are shifts in visibility and lesbianism may be presented as a possible option, there is little awareness that being a lesbian may produce violent reactions from men, or the need for visible systems of support. The emphasis on fashionable lipstick lesbianism as unthreatening to men, masks the realities which many lesbians, including lesbian mothers, experience in terms of male hostility.

One way forward is to present a range of representations of lesbians; this would have much more feminist impact and challenge widely held beliefs that lesbianism is a white middle-class indulgence, or that it is merely about lifestylism, adopting butch or femme roles, or about old lesbian feminists who cannot get a man.

If we are not to be always confronted by images of young, white, slim lesbians the issues of ageism and racism have to be faced and acted upon. Women of all cultures, races, ages and classes, disabled and non-disabled, are lesbians, not only the ones we currently see on television and in the magazines and newspapers.

Ageism in particular is an issue that has not been addressed well even within lesbian-feminist analysises. *Look Me in the Eye* (Macdonald and Rich 1984), a book about ageism in the lesbian-feminist community in the US, is a significant exception to this. Ageism is a powerful institution which, while it affects everyone, disempowers women much more extremely and in every sphere: appearance, work, sexuality, poverty, and so on. There are class and cultural variances but ageism is not withstanding a gender issue. We will not have positive representations of older women, and older lesbians from all communities and with all abilities, until we bring these issues into the open and disentangle social constructions of age from biological ageing.

Finally, for lesbian feminism to be represented positively at all within the media, feminism has to be reconstructed positively and there has to be a rejection of all the negative connotations of the word itself. Currently post-feminist ideology either marginalises, destroys or disappears radical feminism. This will involve ongoing feminist intervention in media representations and a challenge to the untruthful reconstruction of feminist history.

References

Television productions
Between the Lines BBC 1.
Brookside Channel 4.
Camp Christmas Channel 4. 1993
Casuality BBC 1.

Eastenders BBC 1.
Emmerdale ITV.
OUT Channel 4.
Women Like Us and *Women Like That*, Clio Co-op for *Out on Tuesday*, Channel Four. *Women Like Us* was made into a book by Suzanne Neild and Rosalind Pearson, The Women's Press, 1992.

Text references
Grant, L, 'Women in Love: More than Just a Fashion Statement' *Sunday Independent*, 3 July 1994.
Macdonald, B, and Cynthia Rich, *Look Me in the Eye: Old Women, Aging and Ageism*, The Women's Press, London, 1984.
Smyth, C, 'Beyond Queer Cinema: It's in Her Kiss' in L Gibbs (ed), *Daring to Dissent: Lesbian Culture from Margin to Mainstream*, Cassell, London, 1994.
Winterson, J, *Oranges Are Not the Only Fruit*, Pandora, London, 1985.

section four

LESBIAN FEMINISM AND ACADEMENTIA

This section is opened by *Jill Radford*, who places the backlash against lesbian feminism in the broader context of a global anti-feminist movement. She argues that a radical lesbian-feminist perspective has never been accepted by the Women's Studies establishment. Rather, this establishment has colluded in post-feminist analyses that remove the material realities of male power, racism, heterosexism and capitalism from the agenda altogether. She proposes that Women's Studies and Lesbian Studies should focus on the material realities of women's lives and should do so in a way that actively resists these conditions of oppression.

Rosemary Auchmuty's article focuses specifically on Lesbian Studies and demonstrates how their current acceptability within certain sections of academia has been made possible by a rejection of feminist constructions of lesbian identity. She traces the history of the setting up of Lesbian Studies in London and shows how they were originally located in adult education and taught from a lesbian-feminist perspective. She concludes that Lesbian Studies should be taught from a feminist perspective and that queer and other perspectives should be critiqued from a lesbian-feminist standpoint.

BACKLASH: OR NEW VARIATIONS ON AN OLD EXCLUSIONARY THEME

Looking for Lesbian Feminism in Academic Women's Studies

JILL RADFORD

'Backlash' is a broad and political phenomenon, as Egyptian feminist, Nawal el Sa'adawi (1994), has pointed out. It is occurring at a global level, as post-modern capitalism has increasingly mobilised and organised transnational markets, backed up by aggressive forces of militarism, as US feminist, Catharine MacKinnon (1993), has described in her analysis of 'post-modern genocide' in former Yugoslavia. Nawal El Saadawi argues that these economic, political and military shifts have generated a global revival of religious fundamentalism, including Hindu and Sikh fundamentalism in India and Sri Lanka as well as the better-documented growth in Christian, Jewish and Muslim fundamentalisms. The interaction of post-modern capitalism with fundamentalism, she suggests, is responsible in a major way for the 'backlash'; political and economic attacks against women, black communities, the poor, Asians and Latin Americans are justified in the names of 'religion', 'human rights', 'democracy' and 'free-market economies'. She identified post-modern capitalism and religious fundamentalism as 'two faces of the same coin': both actively involved in the domination, control and exploitation of women and women's bodies.

Nawal el Sa'adawi adds to the voices of feminists calling for the development of a global feminism to counter these growing forces of reaction. Globalist visions, networking and organisation, at the local, national and international level, are necessary to resist this harnessing of powerful transnational forces. Last year at the Women's Studies

Network (UK) Conference, I also argued that there was a crucial role for the Women's Studies academy in the development of global feminism, defined as a:

transformed, inclusive, explicitly anti–oppressive, anti–racist, anti–heterosexist, loud liberatory women's movement . . . with a globalist vision. (Radford 1994 pp 40–41)

A reason for offering a definition was to distinguish it from a potential and worrying possibility of its being mistaken for an elitist, 'first world' 'globetrotters' feminism, as Chandra Malpede Mohanty (1994) put it, in the context of US Women's Studies.

The struggle against backlash needs a radical–feminist materialist understanding of the nature of the oppressive forces confronting us. In the context of Women's Studies, and indeed more widely, the 'backlash' has been portrayed in a rather simplistic liberal way. Some writings assume that in the 1960s and 1970s, and early 1980s, clear progress was won by feminists which brought progressive benefits to women. Then, suddenly, surprisingly, inexplicably in the 1990s, patriarchal forces co–ordinated a protective retrenchment and 'back-lash', aimed at undermining any gains to shore-up patriarchal power. Susan Faludi's analysis sees the backlash as representing a 'powerful counter-assault on women's rights,' an attempt to undermine:

the handful of small and hard won victories that the feminist movement did win for women. (Faludi 1992 p 12)

This liberal representation recognises that the gains achieved by feminism were small, bringing progressive changes for a minority of women, and, as such, the backlash is a response, not to women having achieved full equality, but to the possibility that we might; 'a pre-emptive strike.' (Faludi p 14)

The limitations of this analysis can be seen in the liberal focus on rights and reforms. Susan Faludi does recognise that the 'backlash' is more than:

. . . just a continuation of Western society's long-standing resistance to women's rights. But if fear and loathing of feminism is a sort of perpetual viral condition in our culture, it is not always in an acute stage; its symptoms subside and resurface periodically. And it is these episodes of resurgence, such as the one we face now, that can accurately be termed the backlash. (Faludi 1992 p 13)

However, this use of a medical model fails to identify the forces of reaction as resistance to any challenge to male interests and power. Consequently it is presented as irrational and emotional. Many of the 'gains' secured by feminism were reforms, not transformations: for example, in relation to British campaigns against male violence, limited rights to protection and redress for women have been achieved in relation to law and policing, but sufficient refuge provision has not been made available, and we certainly have not ended men's use of sexual violence in the subordination of women either on the 'home front' or in international conflicts.[1]

Many reforms were partial and divisive, in that they benefited some white, heterosexual, middle-class women, but retained racist, heterosexist and economist exclusions. Gains secured were precarious, won through struggle and continually resisted, as illustrated by the number of times feminists had actively to defend the limited rights secured in relation to fertility control and abortion, for example the campaigns against the Benyon Bill, the Corrie Bill, James White's Bill and provisions in the Human Fertility and Embryology Bill. Today, having to take protective action to resist fundamentalist direct actions against clinics, adds a frightening dimension of terror. This threat has not arisen suddenly out of nowhere, but can be seen as a new dimension of a continuing patriarchal resistance to women's right to control our own bodies (see Mary Lou Greenberg 1993).

In the context of 'backlash' against feminism and lesbian feminism within Women's Studies, a model suggesting that the growth of Women's Studies in the 1970s represented an acceptance by the patriarchy of a feminist field of study, is too simplistic to be helpful. What is in danger of being lost is any acknowledgment that the history of Women's Studies was itself a history of struggle against active resistance and that feminism, particularly radical feminism and

---

[1]See Liz Kelly, Hilary McCollum and Jill Radford (1994).

lesbian feminism, has continually had to struggle for a presence within it.

A clearer understanding of these developments may be facilitated by a historical perspective. Audre Lorde's discussion of the importance of history and specifically her reference to a generation gap has particular salience in the context of what is currently happening in UK Women's Studies.

> By ignoring the past we are encouraged to repeat its mistakes . . . The generation gap is an important social tool for any repressive society. (Lorde 1984 *Sister Outsider* p 171)

In her own particular way, Mary Daly also talks of the importance of making connections across generations:

> It is essential to know that all of the Spiral Galaxies are interconnected, that all of the moments implicate each other. Herein lies the hope for resolving miscommunication arising from 'generation gaps' and time warps experienced by women in the Age of Dismemberment. (Daly 1993 p 10)

Making links across the generations is vital to the project of feminist history. The future of feminism will be shaped by our effectiveness in doing this. The extent to which future feminists will have to spend time 're-inventing wheels', as opposed to building on insights from the present past and developing the more complicated crafts needed for the 'next wave', may depend on these connections. Generation gaps disrupt the feminist project and are indicative of our failures to work across differences in age and experience. Problems of miscommunication currently abound in Women's Studies. Rather than attributing backlash solely to the powerful role of the media and the social, political, and economic transformations of post-modern capitalism, I am suggesting it is also necessary to acknowledge how the Women's Studies establishment is also implicated.

Current developments in Women's Studies illustrate a crisis in generational shifts. Those of us with a history of activism in 1960s and 1970s women's liberation, have now achieved our 'middle' years. With our understanding of stereotyping and representation, we should be aware of the hard work needed to spark respect from young women. In media representation we may lose out to queer in image terms unless we remember, and make space for, a spirit of excitement, energy and fun demanded by young lesbians and feminists.

Working across generational shifts is a challenge in Women's Studies classrooms, as increasing numbers of students enrolling on courses have no direct knowledge or experience of feminism and consequently are highly reliant on media and academic representations. In an earlier paper, I suggested that the issue of how feminism is represented in Women's Studies has:

> acquired a heightened salience, now we can no longer assume the presence of 'memory bearing' women in our classrooms, women who can mediate . . . received her-stories/heracies. (Radford 1994 p 42)

The expectations of today's students, as expressed in 'what is and why, Women's Studies?' discussions, strike me as being increasingly more mixed. While some students continue to make links with feminism, others seem attracted to courses for more instrumental and institutional reasons, linked to completing degrees or getting good grades in an 'easy' subject. If Women's Studies is perceived as just another field of study by some of our students, it is not surprising that their expectations will be shaped by those prevalent generally in academia. They may expect polished scholarship rather than provisional and contested knowledge; authoritative and definitive texts, rather than engagement in continuing debates; formal lectures as opposed to facilitated shared learning; and to be consumers of rather than contributors to the course. At a time of consumer sovereignty and contract culture, feminism in Women's Studies practice is threatened by these pressures.

The generational transition is not confined to students. As I look around staff rooms, and scan the biographical blurbs on book covers, it seems that many of our contemporary scholars and teachers are themselves reliant solely on received histories of feminism. Given the omissions and exclusions which characterise representations of feminism constructed by and acceptable to academia, the heritage of feminism is likely to be partial, unless something is done about it

– pdq. The tenuous status of academic Women's Studies has produced its own history of censorship, operating through college-appointment procedures, syllabus design and curriculum development, production of reading lists and contracts with publishers, in short, through the basic decisions made regarding what counts as knowledge:

> today's reading list, for a teaching session on 'feminisms', reflected theoretical omissions with surprising clarity: Liberal Feminism: readings 3, 6, 9, 12 . . . (ie lots) . . . Major Textbook; Socialist Feminism: readings 2, 7, 11 . . . (lots again) . . . Major Textbook; Radical Feminism – nothing in the course books, try *Trouble and Strife*; . . . Postmodern Feminism . . . (lots more); Global Feminism – no mention. (*JR journal entry, summer 1994*)

Referring to feminist academics who have chosen to adopt the protection of the malestream, Somer Brodribb comments:

> All feminist work faces a reality of exceptional hostility masked by a self-satisfied ideology of acceptance by institutions, some of which currently consume Women's Studies, like a prestige item. Radical work is perceived as dangerous, and discomforts those who have made more stable arrangements within patriarchal systems. (Brodribb p xxiii)

'Memory bearing'[2] women know that Women's Studies has been situated precariously in academia and consequently its survival a matter of struggle. Women's Studies course leaders, although now beginning to win academic respectability including professorial status, have frequently expressed anguish or despair about funding, institutionalised constraints on Women's Studies processes, and fear of being re-structured out of existence. Concern over being consumed by the contemporary contract-culture of post-modern capitalism may be the present site of contradiction, struggle and compromise. Rather than something completely new, I see the 'post-it' face of

[2]From Mary Daly (1993)
. . . those who have Moved for some Time on the Be-Dazzling Voyage and those who therefore can have an overview of its Spiralling Paths. These women are the Memory-Bearing Group – those who have 'been around' and can Re-Call earlier Moments, and can *bear* the memories and knowledge of destruction. Ibid. p 10.

'backlash' as having continuities and connections to the complex history of struggle and compromise within Women's Studies and academia.

If by Women's Studies we limit our vision to form academic courses, it may appear to be characterised by growth, as MA courses and undergraduate options are now up and running in many universities, particularly the new ones. If we extend our vision to community Women's Studies the picture is different. In all the talk of validations, I have heard little comment on the disappearing adult education and community Women's Studies classes. These were spaces where a degree of autonomy from patriarchal institutions enabled *some* quite radical feminist work, particularly in relation to black and working-class Women's Studies and Lesbian Studies. The potential contribution of community education Women's Studies to a global feminist project of thinking globally, acting locally, could be considerable. In a global context, women's education is community education. It is, perhaps, more than coincidence that the Women's Studies community in the UK, in its rush for status and respectability, is allowing these forums to become major casualties.

Lesbian Studies, while unusual, did have a presence in community women's studies in the 1980s. However, as the Taking Liberties Collective (1989) documented, they were very much a casualty of Clause 28, one of the earliest manifestations of 'backlash' in the UK. (see Auchmuty this volume)

The process of establishing Women's Studies as an academic field of study in polytechnics and universities was fraught with contradiction and struggle, negotiation and compromises. Consequently, its success has been necessarily partial, and to that extent divisive, empowering for some but excluding of others. In retrospect the high cost paid for our partial success in terms of sacrifice is becoming apparent. Among these costs as I have argued elsewhere[3] are: loss of feminist process in institutionalised Women's Studies; the threat to and appropriation of feminist theory; exclusions in our texts, our research agendas and our classrooms; and increasing inaccessibility of academic Women's Studies. It may well be that it is in the gaps

---

[3] See Jill Radford, 1994.

and divisions left by compromise and omissions that the backlash found its foothold.

If the concept 'backlash' is to be useful, it needs to go beyond liberal formulations which dis-connect it from histories of oppression and resistance, whether at a global or local level, or from struggles over and within Women's Studies. The power relations of 'backlash' also need naming in the same way as the power relations of patriarchy, which includes racism, heterosexism and economic oppression. Similarly, it is important to identify responses to oppression include collaboration, collusion and accommodation, as well as feminist challenges and resistance. This holds as much in the Women's Studies academy as in any other context.

In the context of Women's Studies, the present face of 'backlash' is represented in the trendy growth of non-materialist theory, the 'post-' theories: post-structuralism, post-modernism, post-feminism and queer. Brenda Polan has written:

> Any movement or philosophy which defines itself as post whatever came before it is bound to be reactive. In most cases it is also reactionary. (Polan, cited in Faludi 1992 p 15)

As reactionary theories, a central aim is to disparage, disrespect, dismiss and 'deconstruct' – 'diss' – theories which came before it. In Women's Studies, 'post-it' theories target all forms of materialist feminism, whether socialist feminism, radical feminism, black feminism or lesbian feminism. They label as 'essentialist' any feminist politics which holds on to beliefs that women exist, women are oppressed and that it matters enough to develop political strategies for change and resistance. As anti-materialist theories they have nothing to say about making change in the real world, a real world in which the condition of the majority of women is one of absolute poverty and starvation. Whereas materialist theory recognises and explores the nature of oppression in women's lives, as a precondition for making changes, 'post-it' theory operates at the level of ideas and representations. So a lot of time is spent watching TV – deconstructing or 'dissin' dominant representations, subverting or transforming them, not with spray paint, but through complex and elitist theory, which includes very long words. 'Post-it' theories can demon-

strate amazing levels of academic arrogance, inaccessibility and inco-
herence in language.

> Plato answered the question of Being by awarding true reality to
> the realm of ideas; the sensible world possesses only the appearance
> of reality. Post modernism is no less metaphysical: here too the
> idea absorbs and denies all presence in the world. (Brodribb 1992
> p xvi)

> In today's discussion of assessing auto/biographical writing, – a
> required element of course work – the tutor team was questioning
> the acceptability of factional/fictional subjects, as a strategy to
> avoid 'uncomfortable' aspects of women's oppression: racism,
> sexual violence, lesbian oppression . . . which characterise so many
> women's lives. The consensus seemed to be that for assessment, it
> didn't much matter whether the subjects were real or imagined
> women. How close is this to saying that it is the narrative text, not
> women's lives, that matters in contemporary Women's Studies?
> (*JR's journal, July 94*)

As a white lesbian feminist with a commitment to, and history in
Women's Studies, including community women's studies, I have concerns about the increasingly tense and conditional relationship
between Women's Studies feminism and the marginalisation of lesbian
feminism. Rather than attributing the 'backlash' to outside forces
alone, I suggest that it may also be connected to the processes of
exclusion and inclusion operating within Women Studies, processes
which have marginalised feminism and, even more so, lesbian
feminism.

Women's Studies grew out of the wider feminist project of understanding the nature of women's oppression with a view to changing
it. My earliest experience of Women's Studies was in the context of
community education on a course planned and run collectively by
women in the local women's liberation group and funded by a
Worker's Education Association, which allowed us absolute autonomy,
provided we attracted enough students. As I remember it, our motiv-
ations in setting up the course included promoting women's liberation; reaching more women; and developing feminism by learning

more about women's oppression and developing visions and strategies for change.

Such a radical agenda for change inevitably posed problems in higher education. There, feminists – students and tutors –, who struggled for recognition of feminism as a legitimate theoretical perspective, and Women's Studies as a field of knowledge, encountered fierce resistance, as Mary Evans documented. Writing in 1982, she identified the development of academic Women's Studies as one of the most obvious results of contemporary feminism, explaining

> None of the courses can be said to have been welcomed with wild enthusiasm by the male academic establishment, at best a benign tolerance has allowed academics to teach courses about half the population, which has generally been invisible in much of traditional scholarship. (Evans 1982 p 61)

Frequently heard arguments against Women Studies put forward by male academics turned on apparently rational issues like staffing levels, lack of academic literature and potential controversy with funding authorities. Mary Evans also noted:

> many feminists . . . may suspect that behind every rational argument about the availability of books . . . lurks an irrational beast that is longing to say that it can't stand women . . . but the rules of the game make it impossible for the beast to voice such prejudices explicitly. We might hope to lure him from his cover of rationality and respectability by tantalizing offerings called 'The Study of Sexuality' or 'The Lesbian Experience' but that exercise always contains the danger of the beast devouring the bait and avoiding the trap. (Evans 1982 p 62)

Women's Studies addressed theories of feminism, but broke a fundamental feminist link between theory and activism. Academics, tempted by careerism, are required to reject, or are allowed little time for, activism. As has been argued elsewhere (Kelly, Radford and Scanlon 1992), the loss of connection with activism had a profound impact on Women's Studies, shifting its focus to the abstract theorising more acceptable to malestream academia. This in part facilitated theoretical interest in post-structuralist academic theories.

Historically, the development of Women's Studies in Higher Education coincided with the rise of identity politics within feminist activism, growing out of unresolved tensions within feminism around class, race and sexuality. It was reflected in the growth of self-defining, autonomous groups based on oppression and recognition of differences between women as defined by these oppressive structures. Many black feminists, working-class feminists and lesbian feminists who experienced marginalisation in the women's liberation movement, saw autonomous groups as a valuable space to develop frameworks for understanding complexities in the interaction of gender oppression with racism, classism and heterosexism. However, some white, middle-class, heterosexual women with no specific identity other than being women, seemed to feel threatened, excluded or guilt-tripped by some forms of identity politics. This led some to announce the end of feminism and the arrival of a post-feminist era. Others, pursuing identity at a personal level as a resolution to the contradictions of patriarchy, were attracted by psychoanalysis, as reworked in post-structuralism.

While some forms of identity politics were valuable in leading to an increased political awareness of issues of race, class and heterosexism within feminist analysis, other forms were problematic as identity, outside a political framework, cannot provide a basis for shared political organising. (McNeill this volume)

In the context of sexuality, post-structural deconstructionism serves to hide or negate lesbian-feminist recognitions of the power relations of heterosexism. Instead it re-presents a sexualised definition of sexuality in terms of difference, preference, or orientation. Such sexualised representations of sexuality have indeed become 'bait' as Mary Evans anticipated, and are being happily and voyeuristically devoured by the male gaze and deconstructed by queer. No respect is accorded to what feminists in the 1980s referred to as 'political correctness'. dianne post and olivia free-woman (1994) have reminded us of that earlier meaning:

Then it meant, and still does for some of us, that we were personally responsible for our words and deeds. It meant that we were considerate of people beyond ourselves, people whose culture and traditions were not our own. It meant that we must seek to be inclusive rather than exclusive and . . . white women (had a responsibility) to learn about others and act on what we learned.

When lesbians ridicule 'pc' they are agreeing with the mainstream that we do not need to be ethical in our behaviours. Because we ourselves have been the recipients of . . . discrimination we know the price of oppression and should reject it for ourselves and in our relationships with others. (dianne post and olivia free-woman 1994 p 13)

The shift towards post-modernism and queer in Women's Studies and Lesbian Studies can be seen as part of a continuing struggle against radical feminism and lesbian feminism. However, it is important in developing an understanding of these shifts, to recognise them as part of a longer history of unease around the relationship of feminism and Women's Studies. Mary Evans' (1982) contribution to the 'Women's Studies versus Feminist Studies' debate, was to suggest it was a spurious one. She argued it is impossible to imagine that researching women's lived reality would not produce feminist theory or analysis, particularly given the broad range of feminist positions. What this argument did not anticipate was the rise of anti-materialist theory which, rather than taking women's material realities and experiences of oppression as its subject, denied the existence of women through analysis of ideas, discourse and representations.

An understanding of the shift to queer may be facilitated by recognising the absences created by marginalising lesbian feminism within academia. One way of addressing lesbian experience in a non-challenging way, as Mary Evans recognised, was representing lesbians in terms of sexuality alone. A sexualised definition of lesbianism reduces it to issues of sexual preference located in privatised bedroom politics, and fails to take on board lesbian-feminist critiques of patriarchy, lesbian oppression and analyses of compulsory heterosexuality. However, in the early years of Women's Studies, lesbian feminism was silenced more directly through a denial of lesbian existence.

Reflecting on their own experiences as lesbian tutors and students on Women's Studies courses, contributors to the *Taking Liberties Collective* volume expressed this:

> The voices of black and working-class women are excluded from the books on the shelf called Women's Studies. For all those women, Women's Studies, as taught in malestream colleges, is just another academic subject . . . academic in the sense of being irrelevant to our lives. (p 133)

> As a lesbian I teach lesbian students, but there are few lesbian voices in the books. Actually it's worse than this. Many of the writers are lesbian, but they are not writing as lesbians. The message then, I'm offering students in referring them to these books is not a strengthening one. (p 133)

> If feminism was threatening, lesbianism was completely off limits. (p 135)

It was not only gaps on the library shelves and omissions in syllabi which troubled lesbian feminists on Women's Studies courses,' concerns were also expressed in the *Taking Liberties Collective* about the failure of feminist processes in Women's Studies classrooms, failures which further marginalised black and lesbian students:

> I spent 2 years doing a diploma in Women's Studies – the only lesbian in the group, so far as I know . . . I felt completely invisible in that group and was reduced to silence – even during the two sessions (on lesbian issues) they decided to discuss me. (p 151)

> we were talking about the ways in which lesbians are stigmatised in ways that, as well as being personally damaging, are used against us in custody battles and barring us from jobs . . . One woman said she'd never allow lesbians or gays to baby sit her children just in case . . . (p 151)

The exclusion of lesbian existence was challenged by Sue Sanders in a paper presented at the 1984 National Women's Studies conference at the University of Bradford. She acknowledged the work and commitment of feminist teachers and feminist students in making

Women's Studies acceptable in universities and colleges, while arguing that Women's Studies must be broadened out to include lesbian feminism. In questioning lesbian invisibility in Women's Studies, she identified various forms of censorship operating in academic Women's Studies:

> It is time perhaps to ask ourselves what has contributed to the charge that Women's Studies has so far only concerned itself with the reclaiming and rediscovery of white heterosexual middle-class women. (Sanders 1984)

In a discussion at the workshop, lesbians, both students and tutors, commented on the exclusion and marginalisation of lesbian existence, lesbian feminism and analyses of heterosexuality as a compulsory and coercive institution. Many lesbians reported a serious lack of feminist support in all forms of education around heterosexism. It was also noted that the dominance of white heterosexual middle-class women as teachers and students clearly shaped inclusions and exclusions in Women's Studies courses.

Susan Hemmings (1988) made a similar argument in a review of lesbian history. She commented on the limited commitment on the part of the Women's Studies establishment to British radical feminism, particularly lesbian-feminist critiques of heterosexuality. She suggested that these theories might have had a stronger presence had radical and lesbian feminists been appointed to academic posts in the 1970s in the same numbers as socialist feminists. One consequence of this exclusionary practice is that radical and lesbian feminist thought has not only had a very marginal presence in Women's Studies, but that, when addressed at all, they are represented by women outside who are critical of these perspectives. As such, lesbian feminist thought:

> [has] consistently been represented as intellectually unsound and unsuitable for an academic setting. (Hemmings 1988 p xii)

In a recent paper, Liz Kelly and I also voiced our discomfort with the way early radical feminist ideas are being represented in academic Women's Studies. By revisiting some key texts we challenged widely reproduced claims that: radical feminism was essentialist; and failed to engage with issues of race and class; that sexual violence, sexual objectification, pornography and heterosexuality were not critiqued; and that questions of what non-oppressive sex and sexuality might be like were not explored by radical feminism in the early days of women's liberation. We argued that the teaching of radical feminist theory has been subject to omissions and distortion:

> All too often, in Women's Studies texts, selected extracts are taken out of context, and accompanied by notes or instructions on how to 'read' them, and by implication the particular writers' work or the perspective she represents as a whole. It sometimes seems as if the extracts are selected more for ease of 'deconstruction' or trashing, than with respect for their authenticity and context. While some of these distortions have been repeated in ignorance, other misrepresentations are arguably deliberate, or used to justify or reinforce a particular definition of the past and present. (Kelly and Radford – unpublished paper 1993)

In 1985, Sue Sanders developed her critique of the censoring of lesbian feminism in Women's Studies by calling for the recognition of Lesbian Studies:

> I want to know how and why other lesbians lived their everyday and extraordinary lives. We cannot expect anyone else but lesbians to do this work and I wouldn't trust anyone else but lesbians to do it. As lesbians we have invented many different life styles and come from every class and race background, but it seems to me no accident that the few lesbians patriarchy has let through . . . are white, privileged, non political women. (Sanders 1985)

Recognising the troubled history of radical feminism and lesbian feminism in universities, she cautioned:

> We do not have to start Lesbian Studies in universities and colleges although there might be a place for it, taught by lesbians, in the future. If Lesbian Studies has anything to offer to us or to women

in general, we need to study all lesbian lives and learn from the omissions and problems in Women's Studies. (Sanders 1985)

Sue Sanders' intervention played a significant role in putting lesbian feminism on agendas in community women's studies. Her question about whether universities were the most appropriate context for this work does not seem to be have been followed up. Questions arising out of working around lesbian issues or from a lesbian-feminist perspective with mixed, lesbian and heterosexual, Women's Studies classes, and in Women's Studies classes containing male students, remain unexplored.

As a lesbian feminist teaching Women's Studies in university contexts, I am completely supportive of demands from lesbian students that space for theorising about lesbian oppression is made available. Yet experience has shown that addressing heterosexism and lesbian existence can generate serious levels of anti-lesbianism in mixed (lesbian and heterosexual) classes. Dealing with this is part of the necessary process, but this does not mean it is easy. Specifically I have found that when lesbians are in a minority among the staff and student groups, careful strategies need developing to ensure this is neither an undermining nor voyeuristic experience. All too often, lesbians present have to give more time to educating heterosexual women than to exploring lesbian–feminist analysis and discussion.

Tutoring for the Open University, I regularly attend Women's Studies Summer Schools and am one of a group of lesbian-feminist tutors committed to facilitating optional space for addressing lesbian-feminist theory. Traditionally we draw on the Adrienne Rich paper 'Compulsory Heterosexuality and Lesbian Existence' (1980) as a route into the issues. This approach facilitates making connections between the oppression of women and lesbian oppression specifically, through exploring the compulsory nature of heterosexuality. The argument that until women are free to become lesbians, heterosexuality can not be freely chosen, is a powerful one. We usually engage with both strands of Rich's thesis: that heterosexuality, as a social institution, is imposed by force, in societies where sexual violence is prevalent and permitted, by the failure of the legal system to act effectively against it; and the denial of lesbian existence, culture and history, through silence and pathological representations of lesbians as sick, misguided and inadequate. We also make space for discussion of lesbian existence, and present it as a positive choice for women while recognising lesbian oppression.

In presenting this session, our aim is to make up for silences and omissions and to make networking among lesbians possible to avoid the isolation lesbian students could otherwise experience during the week. Liz Kelly, in discussion with other summer school tutors, explains further:

> Some of the lesbians on the course weren't happy with the emphasis of the session on heterosexuality; they didn't wish to hear hetero-sexual women asking silly questions. But there were other lesbians who thought it was the best thing they'd done for years, because these things were being said rather than whispered in corners; there was a space for a dialogue to take place.

> Women came to the session for a whole host of different reasons; some were lesbians wanting to meet other lesbians, some women had questions around sexuality, but couldn't articulate them; a few, I have absolutely no doubt, came for voyeuristic reasons, wanting to see what a real lesbian looked like. And I think these women were quite shocked when we turned the question round and started talking about the compulsory heterosexuality argument.

> Some of the questions were hostile; others genuinely arose out of ignorance and interest. A lot of the women there had no idea about lesbian oppression. I've been in sessions where women have cried hearing accounts of what happened in lesbian custody cases, or what its like to be spat at in the street because you are holding hands with another woman. (*Trouble and Strife* 24 1992 p 49)

As this account reflects, and as we know from hearing from many students, this session has been a personally significant crossroads in the life journeys of many women. For some women it helped connect being lesbian with feminism, for others it opened new possibilities.

However, as Liz Kelly described, facilitating such sessions can involve risks. We have learned from collective experience over the years and attempted to anticipate and develop strategies for dealing with problem issues, with differing degrees of success. We always run the session in a women-only context, even though this means repeating it later in the week in a mixed (women and men) context. We suggest a confidentiality rule, asking students to respect the confidentiality of personal contributions, while taking the ideas wherever they want. The value of this lies as much in acknowledging risks lesbians may face in 'coming out', as in expecting all students to honour it fully, when sometimes there have been as many as eighty students attending. It alerts students to the limitations as well as possibilities of making some lesbian space in the context of Women's Studies.

Another strategy is planning and presenting the session collectively, usually by three or four 'out' lesbian-feminist tutors. Collective presentation makes for a degree of safety for the tutors, as it avoids any one of us being isolated during the rest of the summer school; it allows students to appreciate differences and commonalities in lesbian experience, by introducing a range of lived experiences and circumstances; it enables us to introduce a breadth of lesbian-feminist scholarship and interests, drawing on lesbian history, arts, culture and creativity, relationships to law, understandings of sexuality; relationships to motherhood; in a micro-cosmic way it illustrates the importance of lesbian friendship and community; and practically it helps with facilitating the meeting, enabling us to be sensitive to contributions and silences, to pick up threads in danger of being lost, and spot danger points, as discussion wanders back and forwards. We conclude the formal session early enough to make less formal space available for unfinished conversations. We have learned by experience of the need to be sensitive to possible 'fall-out' in the following days. We have come to recognise the dangers and strange working of heterosexism in the context of a summer school. One year, for example, a peculiar, yet not unfamiliar, chain of events resulted in the meeting being cited in the national press, mis-labelled 'compulsive heterosexuality'!

It is my experience that working politically and supportively around lesbian issues is only possible within a feminist framework, one which defines lesbianism in its political, social and historical contexts, rather than in terms of a solely sexualised identity – 'preference' or 'orientation'. The contemporary trends of post-structuralism and queer, while coming from different places, both promote sexualised definitions; post-structuralism, through its deconstruction of power relations and with them the material realities which frame lesbian existence, and queer, which attempts to subsume lesbian experience with that of gay men.

Queer is most likely to intrude into Women's Studies in the area of sexuality and in the context of Lesbian Studies. (Auchmuty this volume) If its explicitly anti-feminist politic is recognised, then the task of constructing critiques may be clearer. Reports from the US, however, suggest that this might not be easy. At a workshop on the issue of lesbian-feminism within Lesbian/Gay Studies, Bonnie Zimmerman of San Diego University identified and deplored the current situation there, where lesbian feminism is being silenced and lesbian-feminist ideas are selectively appropriated without any recognition as the queer movement deliberately misrepresents the past and refuses even to read lesbian-feminist work. At the same workshop, Vivienne Ng identified the racism of queer:

> Queer studies is Women's Studies going backwards. Where are race, gender and class in Queer Studies – look at who is who in Queer Studies. How many of them are people of colour?

These speakers were supported by lesbian feminists present in the workshop who endorsed this analysis. One student reported that it was made clear to lesbians on her programme that they had to know queer theory and were discouraged from reading lesbian-feminist work. Others stated that they had been marked down in examination for discussing lesbian-feminist theory. Bette Tallen argued that because queer addresses sexual identity rather than gender as its subject and because it draws on a reformist liberal-rights model rather than a transformative model for change, its proponents buy into rather than challenge elitist scholarship and so perpetuate its sexism, racism and classism. Like other contributors cited here, she called for a re-assertion of feminism in Lesbian Studies and Women's Studies.

If both queer and post-modernism represent faces of backlash against feminism, both in the media and in academic Women's Studies, the narrative here demonstrates that the marginalisation of feminism and specifically radical feminism and lesbian feminism is not something new. I suggest, rather, that the disregard and distortions which have characterised Women's Studies in the West created a space which was appropriated by these movements. To that extent, the backlash, while linked to wider political change in global politics, cannot be solely explained by 'outside forces'; it is also a product of developments within Women's Studies itself.

Unavoidable questions exist about why, at a time of global crisis when a need for global feminism is clearly pressing, are the academics of Women's Studies so preoccupied by deconstruction and anti-materialist theories? Post-structuralism, reacting against the feminist project of constructing Women's Studies as a legitimate field of study, represents itself as an exciting and progressive development today. But it is rooted in psychobabble, existentialism, libertarianism, individualism, and free marketism and as such is fully grounded in traditional anti-feminist thought. It is dismissive of all materialist theories, including materialist feminism, by defining them as 'essentialist and outmoded'. Despite this rejection of feminism, post-structuralism and post-modernism are built on insights from feminism and other modernist and structuralist theories, whose ideas they have appropriated, corrupted and re-presented as new. For example they claim to own the idea that knowledge can never be impartial, objective or universally valid, but always situated – context-bound and historically specific. These ideas are in fact central to feminist (and marxist) critiques of malestream (bourgeois) knowledge claims. It was feminism, for example, which demystified malestream claims to holding objective and universal truths, revealing them as partial, reflective of an elitist, white, and male supremacist standpoint. Feminist identity politics, for example, centred on standpoint, developed the recognition that who we are and where we are coming from – in relation to structures of power and privilege – shapes how we see, know, understand and act in the world.

Somer Brodribb (1992) has produced a major feminist critique of post-modernism and post-structuralism which identifies the fundamentally masculinist, hierarchal and mystificatory and confusing nature of this theory. Engaging closely with their texts, she points out, that as well as appropriating ideas of progressive thinkers, these theories are centrally based on the work of profoundly misogynous writers: Foucault, Derrida, Lacan, Nietzsche and Freud – 'the masters of Postmodern discourse'. Their work, she suggests, is not harmless or sexist by default, but so intensely so as to be beyond redemption. The 'death of woman', she argues, is central to notions of transgression and liberation, central to the post-modern consciousness:

> The Masters of Discourse have . . . said that it requires a great deal of sophistication to speak like a woman, clearly it's best left to men. Their texts play with and parade a hysterical femininity, in our best interests of course, to help us transcend the category of woman we somehow got into, and the neurotic idea that we can tell the truth. Or that we know when they are lying. Talking, writing, telling stories out of school, this is what is forbidden. The Master wants to keep the narrative to himself, and he's willing to explode the whole structure of discourse if we start to talk. They don't want to hear our stories: listening to women's stories of incest and rape almost cost Sigmund Freud his career before he decided these were simply female fantasies of desire for the father . . . And he told us: it didn't happen, you made it up, you wanted it, or brought it on yourself. What is the Master narrative? That we can't tell the truth, we can't tell the difference between our rights and their wrongs. (Brodribb 1993 p xviii)

Post-modernism is problematic, in part, because it sets out to deconstruct theories which feminists have struggled hard to develop and express, always against active opposition. It has appropriated, transformed and is attempting to use feminist thought to deconstruct feminist politics. It has attempted to negate feminist research, methodology, and knowledge that feminist activists have used and are continuing to use in the project of creating changes that matter in the lives of women and children: for example feminist campaigning, policy and support work around sexual violence, at local, national and global levels. It seeks to fragment the tentative alliances some feminist activists are attempting to build across differences of power and privilege. It undermines feminist process and praxis, through a denial of women's lived reality. Given that all that counts is the 'text' or narrative, if nothing is real, then, as Somer Brobribb has said, 'Nothing Mat(t)ers' and political activism becomes redundant.

It is significant that this is occurring at a time when feminists who experienced marginalisation in the early years of women's liberation are 'breaking the silence', with the development of black-feminist and lesbian-feminist thought. It is significant that a retreat into an elitist and often comfortable world of representation is taking place at a time when women are under attack. In the UK women are under attack from a government attempting to scapegoat single parents, including lesbian mothers, for the consequences of Thatcherite Majorism. Women as mothers, as paid workers, and as claimants are blamed for: unemployment; rising crime; drugs; poverty; crises in the housing, education, health, welfare and benefits systems; declining standards; collapse of the family; and the crisis in masculinity. There is an urgent need for feminist analysis to inform resistance to, and survival strategies for, the multi-layered attacks on women by patriarchal, post-modern capitalism: the introduction of 'pro-family' 'pro-father' policies which re-assert the patriarchal (ie white, middle class, heterosexist) family values of Victorian life; an authoritarian criminal code which criminalises travellers and political protests and direct actions like Greenham, while offering nothing to address the problem of male sexual violence; the state control of education in the name of 'choice'; the active promotion of racist immigration policies; and an increase in militarism.

It is a problem that post-structuralism has been allowed success in diverting and absorbing women's time and energy by attempting to force feminists to engage with dense, misogynous theory and convoluted word games, making this a requirement of academic credibility even within Women's Studies. Theory which places weight on texts and narratives is prioritised above theories rooted in the reality of women's oppression and resistance; it seems Women's Studies, as well as feminism, is at risk of being deconstructed. Without a reinstatement of a materialist feminism, which is committed to understanding women's experiences of oppression within a patriarchy structured by racism, economic oppression and heterosexism, and which acts on this understanding to create progressive change, then Somer Brodribb's title 'Nothing Mat(t)ers' may become as applicable to Women's Studies including Lesbian Studies as it is within post-structuralism.

Women's Studies and Lesbian Studies need feminist theory, process and activism to survive and to sustain any level of commitment to women. To survive and to make a difference in women's lives, Women's Studies and feminism need to be well-grounded in the material world. To survive and make a difference feminism also needs to be re-asserted outside as well as inside Women's Studies academia. It also needs to include a feminist praxis which acts and thinks globally, locally and in personal practice.

References

Brodribb, Somer, *Nothing Mat(t)ers: A Feminist Critique of Post-modernism*, Spinifex, Melbourne, 1992.

Evans, M, *In Praise of Theory: the Case for Women's Studies*, Feminist Review 10, Spring 1982 pp 61–74.

Daly, M, *Outercourse: The Be-Dazzling Voyage*, The Women's Press, London, 1993.

Faludi, S, *Backlash: the Undeclared War Against Women*, Chatto and Windus, London, 1992.

Greenberg, Mary L, *Clinics under the Gun: Blockades, Firebombs and Murder*, On the Issue, Fall 1993, Canada.

Hemmings, S, *Radical Records: 30 years of Lesbian and Gay History*, Bob Cant and Susan Hemmings (eds), Routledge, London, 1988.

Kelly, L, Radford, Jill and Scanlon, Joan, *Feminism/Feminisms: Fighting Back for Women's Liberation*, unpublished, presentation at The Open University, Women's Studies Summer School, 1992.

Jackson, C, 'School for Scandal: Tutors and Students talk to Cath Jackson about U221 – the first Open University Women's Studies course', *Trouble and Strife* 24 1992 pp 49.

Kelly, L, McCollum, Hilary and Radford, Jill, 'Wars Against Women', *Trouble and Strife* 28 1994 pp 12–18.

Kelly, L and Radford, Jill, *Minimising Dominance, Maximising Difference: the inversion and denial of feminist challenges to the sexualisation of women and children*, unpublished paper at the British Sociology Conference, Preston, 1994.

Lorde, A, 'Age, Race, Class and Sex: Women Redefining Difference', in *Sister Outsider: Essays and Speeches*, The Crossing Press, Freedom California, 1984.

Mohanty, C M, at National Women's Studies Conference, Aimes, Iowa, 1994, as reported in *off our backs*, Aug/Sept 1994, p 13.

MacKinnon, C, 'Turning Rape into Pornography: Postmodern Genocide', *Ms* magazine vol 4 no 1 July/August 1993.

post, d and free-woman, o, *off our backs* Aug/Sept 1994 p 20.

Radford, J, 'A History of the Women's Liberation Movement in Britain: a Reflective Personal History', in *Stirring It: Challenges for Feminism*, Griffin, Gabriele, et al (eds), Women's Studies Network UK, Taylor & Francis, London 1994.

Rich, A, 'Compulsory Heterosexuality and Lesbian Existence', *Signs, Journal of Women in Culture and Society*, Summer 1980.

el Sa'adawi, N, *Thinking and Acting: The Challenge of Global Feminism*, keynote speech Women's Studies Network UK Annual Conference 1994, University of Portsmouth, and also keynote speech at National Women's Studies Conference (USA) at Ames, Iowa, as reported by karla mantilla in *off our backs*, Aug/Sept 1994 pp 8–9.

Sanders, S, *Why are lesbians invisible in Women's Studies?*, unpublished paper at the 1984 Women's Studies Conference in Bradford, UK.

Sanders, S, 'Was She a Dyke?: Proposing Lesbian Studies', *Radical and Revolutionary Feminist Newspaper* 1985.

Spender, D, *Women of Ideas and What Men Have Done To Them: From Aphra Behn to Adrienne Rich*, Ark, London, 1983.

Taking Liberties Collective, *Learning the Hard Way: Women's Oppression in Men's Education*, Macmillan, London, 1989.

LESBIAN STUDIES: POLITICS OR LIFESTYLE?

ROSEMARY AUCHMUTY

At the annual Women's Studies Network Conference in July 1994, held in the UK at the University of Portsmouth, Patsy Staddon of the University of Bristol led a well-attended workshop on the teaching of Lesbian Studies (Staddon 1994). Lesbian Studies has been around in Britain for some years now, but mostly in adult education, and in focusing (partly, at least) on higher education, the workshop seemed to me to be a significant landmark. In the discussion which followed Patsy's paper, it became clear that, while Lesbian Studies is not yet by any means an integral part of the fast-multiplying Women's Studies provision in British universities, it is beginning to secure a foothold. In my own university, for example, a Lesbian Studies module is included in our MA in Women's Studies. That is surely something to celebrate.

Lesbian Studies seems to me to stand today at approximately the state of representation in higher education that Women's Studies occupied about twenty years ago; that is to say, there is the odd module here and there, but no general acceptance – yet. Where it *has* found a footing, however, it seems to have done so with considerably less difficulty and opposition than Women's Studies faced in the 1970s and 1980s. For this we should perhaps be grateful, but I can't help feeling a certain uneasiness: *why* should Lesbian Studies have fared better than Women's Studies? Part of the answer must lie in the recognition of the battles already fought and won by the pioneers of Women's Studies, now finally accepted as a legitimate field of study in higher education. But part is due, I think, to the fact that Lesbian

Studies appears to present less of a threat to the academic establishment than does Women's Studies; for while outsiders perceive the latter to have an explicitly feminist agenda, they do not seem to have the same idea about the former. And they may be right.

WELCOMING LESBIAN STUDIES

Before I attempt to explain why this might be so, I want to stop and consider what an achievement it is to have Lesbian Studies in academia at all. Such a presence would have seemed a miracle to the lesbian feminists of twenty – even ten – years ago. When Women's Studies was establishing itself as an academic discipline, a lesbian focus was rarely present. Lesbian experience, lesbian theory, if mentioned at all, occupied only the odd session; a heterosexual perspective was almost universally assumed – and still is – on most Women's Studies courses and in much feminist scholarship. Though many of those teaching and writing in the area of Women's Studies were themselves lesbians, they often felt it necessary to soft-pedal or hide their sexuality and politics altogether so as not to alienate their students or employers. As one member of the Taking Liberties Collective put it:

> [I]f you want to have any credibility as a 'serious academic feminist' you should try to avoid looking anything like a feminist at all and especially not like a dyke. Forget the spiky hair and dungarees. Never go to important meetings wearing trousers – and remember 'the smattering of lipstick' to fend off any suggestion that you're queer (Taking Liberties Collective 1989 p 137).

Although this rather overstates the position – personally, I have always worn trousers to meetings, and have never needed to call upon the smattering of lipstick – certainly many people felt that Women's Studies might not be taken seriously as an academic subject if a teacher was known to be a lesbian (read: man-hater and extremist). We had to reach 'ordinary women' who were, by definition, heterosexual and homophobic; we also had to win over hostile colleagues and superiors.

Though post-modernism tends to claim the credit for introducing the notion of 'difference' to feminist analysis, it was in fact the radical feminists of the mid-1970s who made it possible for lesbian and also black, working-class and other voices to be heard within feminism and Women's Studies, by pointing out that they had been excluded from analyses of white, middle-class, heterosexual women and that their situation, in some respects similar, was in other respects quite different. In the United States, lesbian caucuses were formed within the academic disciplines and, in 1977, within the National Women's Studies Association (Stimpson 1992 pp 377–8). Feminist theorists wrote books and essays, much discussed within Women's Studies, which took lesbian experience as their starting-point.[1] Lesbian pioneers set the record straight about lesbian life and chronicled lesbian liberation.[2]

This work was welcomed in Britain, and the necessity for feminism to be available to *all* women, and for Women's Studies to consider the situation of *all* women, became established as a principle by the late 1970s. Within this framework, a session on race, a session on class, a session on sexuality, and so on, became the mark of the typical 'progressive' Women's Studies class, in an effort to be truly inclusive. But, of course, a couple of hours spent under the spotlight did not necessarily make Women's Studies an empowering – or even a comfortable – experience for black or working-class or lesbian students.

The advent of Lesbian Studies thus represented a tremendous step forward. For the first time it was possible to study a whole course or module from a lesbian perspective, with lesbian experience rather than heterosexuality taken as the norm and starting-point. (Feedback from the courses I have taught indicates that this is the single most positive factor in students' learning experience.) To find themselves at the centre of their analysis, their lives not simply tolerated but validated, has been a strengthening situation for many lesbian students on Lesbian Studies courses, who also derive support (and sometimes rather more) from fellow-students with whom they have so much in

[1] For example, the work of Ti-Grace Atkinson, Mary Daly, Marilyn Frye, Jill Johnson, Janice Raymond and Adrienne Rich.
[2] For example, Atkinson, Ti-Grace, *Amazon Odyssey*, Kinks Books, New York, 1974; Abbott, Sydney and Love, Barbara, *Sappho Was a Right-On Woman*, New York, Stein & Day 1972; Martin, Del and Lyon, Phyllis, *Lesbian/Woman*, Morrow, New York, 1974.

common. Lesbian Studies has the potential to be uniquely empowering for lesbian students, whose perspectives and experiences are so often denied in other areas of their lives and studies. It offers women an opportunity to reclaim and validate lesbian experience, and to develop lesbian-feminist strategies to challenge heterosexism and homophobia.

SETTING THE RECORD STRAIGHT: THE RISE OF LESBIAN STUDIES IN BRITAIN

Adult education has been the site of some of the most innovative and exciting learning in Britain. (That is doubtless one reason why the Conservative Government has spent the last fifteen years trying to dismantle it.) Women's Studies began in adult education in the very early 1970s, before moving slowly into the institutions of higher education. Likewise, it was out of adult education that Lesbian Studies emerged, a decade later.

A number of factors combined to make the educational recognition of Lesbian Studies in Britain possible. The writings of radical and lesbian feminists both in Britain and the United States had been circulating through the women's liberation movement throughout the 1970s. Some of these were picked up by the new feminist presses in Britain, particularly Onlywomen (an explicitly lesbian-feminist enterprise), Virago and The Women's Press, and eagerly discussed in consciousness-raising and Women's Studies groups. Among the most influential were Onlywomen's *Love Your Enemy?* (1981), which contained in one volume the Leeds Revolutionary Feminists' Political Lesbian paper of 1979 and a range of responses, positive and negative, to its thesis that every women not only could but *should* be a lesbian; Adrienne Rich's classic essay 'Compulsory Heterosexuality and Lesbian Existence' (also reprinted by Onlywomen in 1981); and Lillian Faderman's pioneering study in lesbian history, *Surpassing the Love of Men* (1981). These, and The Women's Press's collection *On the Problem of Men* (edited by Scarlet Friedman and Elizabeth Sarah, 1981), papers from two feminist conferences, demonstrated that heterosexuality was being problematised within the women's movement and Women's Studies, and paved the way for the arrival of Lesbian Studies.

Those of us who were teaching Women's Studies in Britain at this time were excited to realise, from reading American books like Margaret Cruikshank's *Lesbian Studies Present and Future* (1982), that such courses existed on the other side of the Atlantic; but we were slow to see the need for them in the UK. This timidity was born of fear of rejection (after all, there was no general acceptance of Women's Studies yet), a residual impression that it might not be a 'valid' field of study (we had all been educated in a patriarchal system, and old prejudices die hard) and also some debate over whether Lesbian Studies was just a subject area, or a different way of looking at things. Even then we were concerned that the students who came to a Lesbian Studies course might not all be feminists, and some of us felt that we might find teaching or attending a Women's Studies class, where all the students were (in those days) avowedly feminist though some might be straight, more rewarding than one where all the students were lesbians but some a–political.

At that time, there was still very little Women's Studies going on in higher education, and what few full-time jobs existed were occupied almost exclusively by socialist feminists. Radical feminists were not then welcome in the universities and polytechnics[3] and, with a few exceptions, their work was rarely accepted by the prestige publishing houses and journals.[4] In the 1990s things changed with the expansion of Women's Studies, particularly in the 'new' universities (the former polytechnics) which were less hidebound than the universities and, because they were often setting up Women's Studies from scratch, happily ignorant of the differences of opinion among feminists, or actually open to radical feminists. The existence by then of journals with a radical–feminist perspective, and the eagerness of publishing houses to get into the new and lucrative Women's Studies market, made it a little easier for some radical feminists to get published and so secure academic jobs. But there are still very few lesbian feminists with secure jobs in higher education.

[3] This was one reason why such a distinguished scholar as Sheila Jeffreys had to emigrate to Australia to get a full-time job in higher education.
[4] Exceptions included Di Leonard at the Institute of Education and Margaret Jackson at Goldsmith's College, both in the University of London. Dale Spender edited the Women's Studies International Forum and several of her books were published by Pandora Press.

A number of Adult Education Institutes in London were staffed by feminists and lesbians working within progressive local authorities dedicated to the development of Equal Opportunities. At Fulham-Chelsea AEI, Jayne Nelson defied Section 28 of the Local Government Act 1988, which prohibited the 'promotion' of homosexuality within local-authority funded bodies, and continued to run what was probably the most extensive Lesbian Studies programme outside the Extra-Mural Department of London University,[5] with classes in history, literature and 'issues'.

One final factor important in the rise of Lesbian Studies in London was the market demand, which today plays a greater role than it did in the mid-1980s. Adult education provision was influenced to some extent by the fact that students paid their own way and classes had to have a 'viable' enrolment in order to continue. The Extra-Mural Department and the WEA – Workers Education Association – were always ready to support classes in pioneering subjects in their first year or two, to enable them to get established; Lesbian Studies, however, always recruited well. We targeted our advertising carefully and were able to demonstrate, by reference to attendance figures at the South London Women's Studies Group's classes, the existence of a large audience of lesbian feminists keen to enrol on Lesbian Studies courses. Further up the administrative ladder, and in some other institutions, doubt was sometimes expressed – surely very few people would wish to study such an esoteric subject? – but the success of the lesbian history courses, which were quickly followed by literature, film, creative writing, sexuality, health and 'issues' courses, soon put paid to that form of opposition.

The high point of Lesbian Studies in adult education in London – and in some respects the low point, for the political disagreements which marked this occasion were a foretaste of battles to come (see also McNeill this volume) – was the Lesbian Studies Summer School organised by the Lesbian Archive at the London Women's Centre in July 1988. Lesbians came from all over Britain and abroad to study parallel courses in lesbian history, film, literature, creative writing

---

[5] Feminists owe a debt of gratitude to Mary Kennedy, the then Women's Studies organiser within the Extra-Mural Department (now the Centre for Extra-Mural Studies, Birkbeck College), for pioneering both Women's Studies and Lesbian Studies in Adult Education, making a home for feminism long before the conventional parts of the university would have anything to do with it.

and other fields over a packed long weekend. Here a public row blew up when lesbian feminists objected to the film which was shown to the whole summer school, *She Must Be Seeing Things*, which the film tutors did not present in the context of a lesbian-feminist critique. This indicated the emergence of a new direction in Lesbian Studies, one which was to become a dominant mode of analysis in media studies and cultural studies, but was also to have a profound effect on every aspect of the subject. No longer would Lesbian Studies be the exclusive domain of the lesbian feminist.

'LESBIANANDGAY' STUDIES, QUEER POLITICS, POST-MODERNISM – AND FEMINISM

It is clear that Lesbian Studies in Britain and America owed its existence to the women's movement of the 1970s, and that it was an offshoot of Women's Studies. However, once Lesbian Studies was firmly established within Adult Education, other, non-feminist perspectives – such as gay men's studies and queer politics – muscled in. Many factors have contributed to the anti-feminist backlash of the 1990s, but in Lesbian Studies the single most destructive factor has been the rise (or resurgence) of non-feminist politics and theories around sexuality, which have mounted a powerful challenge to the lesbian-feminist analysis which gave rise to the subject in the first place. These new approaches include 'Lesbianandgay' Studies (Jeffreys 1994a p 97), queer politics, and the so-called post-modernist feminism, which many feel is not feminist at all.

Jeffreys has shown how any form of analysis which links lesbians and gay men, as do both 'Lesbianandgay' Studies and queer politics, is hostile to feminism. This is inevitable, because such an analysis is premised on an identity of interest between lesbians and gay men, whereas the starting-point of feminism is the different power positions occupied by men and women. The feminist agenda, in fact, sets out to challenge (and ultimately to destroy) male power. Simply being gay does not give a man any reason to be critical of the institutions of patriarchy which benefit him as a man. It may not even make him critical of heterosexuality, which lesbian-feminists see as a major site of women's oppression. He may only wish to share in its privileges.

By advocating a deliberate playing around with gender roles, the advocates of queer theory also claim to challenge dominant notions of sexuality. Such roles will cease to hold their power, they contend, when all their limits are transcended and boundaries blurred. Once lesbians, for example, are seen to dress in ultra-feminine modes, to imitate men, even to sleep with men, then how (and for what) can lesbians be discriminated against? One problem with this strategy is the difficulty of distinguishing a lesbian who is pretending to be heterosexual from the real heterosexual woman who is simply fulfilling society's expectations of her. More seriously, feminists argue that playing around with gender roles and 'sexualities' does not challenge patriarchal structures because masculinity and femininity are not equally valued gender roles in our society, nor are heterosexuality and homosexuality equally valued sexualities. At bottom 'gender-bending' merely reinforces existing gender norms by uncritically adopting imagery and behaviour which demonstrate, often in exaggerated form, society's institutionalised power relations between men and women, heterosexuality and homosexuality. Playing at being a man or a heterosexual woman does not alter the way society views (and treats) women generally and lesbians in particular.

Many courses in 'Lesbianandgay' Studies (sometimes called 'Sexuality') have sprung up in recent years, generally as part of undergraduate degrees, although it is possible to study for an MA in Lesbian and Gay Studies at the University of Sussex. A typical example of an undergraduate module is the course in Gay and Lesbian Literature offered as part of a degree in English Literature at Cambridge University, which is taught by a man and heavily dominated by men's writing. Lesbianism is represented by, among others, Pat Califia and Joan Nestle (known for their advocacy of sado-masochism and butch and femme respectively),[6] but no lesbian feminists. On such courses lesbian experience tends to be included only where it fits comfortably into male gay models, culture and politics. It would be hard to introduce a feminist analysis of, say, sado-masochism or paedophilia, practices favoured by many gay men but seen by feminists as abuses of power. Indeed, lesbian experience on these courses

---

[6] See, for example, Califia, Pat *Sapphistry. The Book of Lesbian Sexuality*, Naiad Press, Florida, 1983; and Nestle, Joan, *A Restricted Country*, Sheba, London, 1988.

(and in 'Lesbianandgay' Studies writing) is often measured against gay men's experience and found wanting, and lesbians are castigated for their inferior range of sexual practices (Auchmuty, Jeffreys and Miller 1992).

Twenty years ago feminists fought for Women's Studies out of the despair and anger they felt at always being ignored and looked down on in the traditional courses of the patriarchal academy. But now, the experience of a lesbian in a 'Lesbianandgay' Studies class is of the same sort of exclusion and marginalisation. 'Lesbianandgay' Studies does nothing to challenge her second-class status; it simply reinforces it.

queer Post-modernism, too, is antagonistic to radical and lesbian feminism. Like the socialist feminists before them, post-modernists together with 'Lesbianandgay' Studies and queer theorists regard radical- and lesbian-feminist critiques of male sexual practices as 'anti-sex', prudish and prescriptive. Of course, they are wrong; but the accusation has gained currency in both popular and academic discourses. What radical feminism actually did for women was to *open* doors, not close them – it made it possible for some of us to sleep with women, for a start – but it did say that our sexuality, and our sexual practices, were socially constructed, not innate, and that we should examine and (if necessary) change our sexual behaviour, in our pursuit of genuine equality in relationships in *all* areas of our lives.

Where radical feminists have published a huge body of literature analysing practices such as sado-masochism, pornography, paedophilia, prostitution and heterosexuality itself in terms of reinforcing power relations,[7] an increasing scholarly literature has now emerged which defends all these examples of sexual abuse in the name of liberalism (anti-censorship), sexual liberation, and even feminism. These books are written by respected academics and authorities and published by reputable publishing houses, and they appear on the

---

[7] See, for example, Itzin, Catherine (ed), *Pornography: Women, Violence and Civil Liberties*, Oxford University Press, 1993; Jeffreys, Sheila, *Anticlimax: a feminist perspective on the sexual revolution*, The Women's Press, London, 1990; Douglas, Carol Anne, *Love & Politics: Radical Feminist and Lesbian Theories*, Ism Press San Francisco, CA, 1990; Linden, Robin Ruth et al (eds), *Against Sadomasochism*, Frog in the Well East Palo Alto, CA, 1982; the six numbers of *Gossip: a journal of lesbian feminist ethics*, Onlywomen London 1986–8; and *Trouble & Strife: the radical feminist magazine*, 1984 to date.

reading lists of courses in 'Lesbianandgay' Studies, 'Sexuality', and even Women's Studies.[8]

The end result is that it has become very difficult to teach Lesbian Studies from a lesbian-feminist perspective. Though born of radical-feminist theorising and lesbian-feminist activism within Women's Studies, Lesbian Studies has been co-opted by the male input of 'Lesbianandgay' Studies and the backlash politics of queer and post-modernism, both of which enjoy greater acceptance and prestige than lesbian feminism ever had. Of course lesbian feminists like myself do teach Lesbian Studies and we teach it within Women's Studies. But our students come to us widely influenced by other perspectives, which are glamourised and supported by the academy and the outside world.

LESBIAN STUDIES IN THE CLASSROOM: PROBLEMS AND STRATEGIES

In the early 1980s, students who came to Women's Studies classes were, for the most part, feminist in outlook, however embryonically; even the lesbians who came to my Lesbian Studies classes in adult education in the late 1980s *expected* a lesbian-feminist perspective to underpin the course, even though some were 'lifestyle' lesbians who came on courses mainly to meet other lesbians. Today it is still true that many of the women who come on Women's Studies courses are feminists. But on degree courses, we are beginning to see students who are more concerned to collect a qualification in an academic discipline than to explore the reality of women's position and apply feminist theories to their own lives. Many are too young to have experienced the women's movement, and others have not come to Women's Studies through feminism. Some have absorbed society's hostile view of feminism. For all these students, feminist ideas and analyses need to be introduced, discussed, justified. The teacher has

[8] For example, Assiter, Alison & Carol, Avedon, *Bad Girls and Dirty Pictures*, Pluto London, 1993; Gibson, Pamela Church & Gibson, Roma (eds), *Dirty Looks: Women, Pornography, Power*. bfi, London, 1993; Abelove, Henry, Barale, Michele Aina & Halperin, David M, *The Lesbian and Gay Studies Reader*, Routledge, New York, 1993.

to be prepared for feminism to` be criticised; perhaps for it to be rejected.

A further difficulty arises out of the essentially personal nature of the subject matter of Lesbian Studies. Lesbians who are happy to study women in the abstract may find it hard when the spotlight is turned on areas of their own lives. For feminists, the personal has always been seen to be political, but the dominant view in the wider society today is that one's sexuality and sexual practice are private matters. Since Lesbian Studies must by its very nature subject sexuality and sexual practice to critical analysis, much grief and distress may result.

One lesson – perhaps the only one – that the current generation has taken from feminism is that we should be accepting of all women and the choices they have made. But this concept means something quite different today from what it meant to the women's movement. Then, it enabled us to analyse and attack society's structures and institutions without denigrating individual women caught up in them. So, for example, whatever critique we might have of prostitution as a system, we would always support individual prostitutes as sisters. But in the subsequent anti-feminist backlash, this policy became transmuted into an uncritical acceptance of any and all behaviours. The political dimension was lost; all choices became equal and all okay. To criticise patriarchal power relations came to be seen as an attack on the actual women who took part in them – hence 'unfeminist'.

This shift in understanding may also affect the classroom. Lesbian students who choose to adopt butch or femme identities or engage in sado-masochistic practices may strongly resist any attempt to give space to a feminist analysis of these phenomena, and other students may equally feel that such a discussion constitutes a lack of respect for women's choices; at best an invasion of their privacy and at worst a personal attack. Suppose, for example, a student decided to give a presentation on lesbian sado-masochism, in the course of which she made it clear she was herself in a sado-masochistic relationship. Such a student would obviously feel more comfortable with a queer or a 'hands off' analysis of her lifestyle than with a feminist one, and with strong scholarly backing for such a view, might choose to present her seminar in such a way as to favour this and disparage a lesbian-feminist critique.

Many lesbians do not see their sexuality as a choice, let alone a political statement. Many 'believe' they were born different from heterosexual women. Academic studies, however, can hardly leave beliefs to be accepted at face value, but for feminists to have to go over the whole essentialism versus social constructionism debate yet again is dispiriting. Feminism was premised on the recognition that sexuality was socially constructed, and for twenty years this view needed no defence. Since the advent of 'Lesbianandgay' Studies, however, the essentialism versus social constructionism debate has become a matter of opinion. There is now academic support for the view, common among gay men and much aired during the campaigns against Clause 28, that homosexuals are born, not made – an idea which has no substance at all in lesbian-feminist theory and which simply does not fit the facts of many of our lives.[9] These women who saw themselves as heterosexual, married, bore children and lived conventionally for years, before deciding to become lesbians at some point in their thirties or forties or fifties or later, find it puzzling to be told that they were lesbians all along. No research has ever proved a biological difference between heterosexual and lesbian women, and lesbian feminists regard the search as profoundly dangerous. We don't want toleration and acceptance of our difference, à la Radclyffe Hall; we want to transform sexual relations in our society.

In these days of 'student-centred' learning, the content of a Lesbian Studies course will be negotiated among students and teachers. Students will naturally wish to look at the most current issues and controversies in the field, and the teacher has to be on top of the latest debates and literature. On a Lesbian Studies syllabus today students would certainly expect to see a consideration of queer theory, sexual practice, media representations and (probably) 'transgenderism; (formerly called transsexualism). The difficulty for the feminist teacher with such a syllabus is to ensure that, particularly in a short module of 12 to 15 weeks, lesbian-feminism is not squeezed out. This is not as easy as might be thought, when so much of the

[9] See Alderson, Lynn & Wistrich, Harriet 'Clause 29 [sic]: radical feminist perspectives', *Trouble & Strife*, 1988 13, p 3.

classwork is actually done by the students themselves, and when whole volumes on these topics to which they will turn for their research either ignore the lesbian-feminist viewpoint or trash it. At the same time, the lesbian-feminist theories and analysis that the teacher might like to spotlight on her Lesbian Studies course may seem old-fashioned and 'irrelevant' to some of her students, who have seen them discredited by post-modernists and queer theorists in the books they have read. How does she ensure that these receive the attention she feels they deserve?

As well as incorporating feminist content, feminist teachers will want to use feminist teaching and learning methods on their Lesbian Studies courses. A great deal of energy has been expended by the women's movement on critiquing patriarchal education and devising feminist modes of learning. Many feminists were (and are) deeply suspicious of attempts to conduct feminist education at all within the male-dominated academy, and some have rejected the possibility altogether. Those who do try to teach Women's Studies in the universities tend to espouse a participatory approach, on the grounds that students have relevant knowledge and experience to contribute to the learning process, and this is certainly preferred by most students.

These feminist debates over pedagogical issues have, however, bypassed many teachers of 'Lesbianandgay' Studies. Patsy Staddon noted that in one university:

> in the course module 'Lesbian and Gay Sexualities: Sociological and Political Perspectives', teaching methods are to consist of lectures and seminars, and assessment techniques will consist of coursework and an examination. (Staddon 1994 p 4)

Such methods make it even more difficult for lesbian feminists to make a contribution.

So, how is the feminist teacher to try to ensure that lesbian feminism is *not* squeezed out of Lesbian Studies? She could start by placing feminism on the agenda from the outset. Lesbian Studies should ideally be located within Women's Studies, whose basis in feminist scholarship needs to be asserted and continually reiterated. The different theories of Lesbian Studies should be explored and critiqued in the light of each of the others. This will ensure that all receive a feminist analysis. Clearly it will entail some sort of historical overview, which will demonstrate to students how lesbian feminism has been ignored and distorted by received scholarship in the past. The record is now being set straight, and a body of academic work is building up to counter the 'Lesbianandgay' and queer and post-modern approaches, and the teacher of Lesbian Studies should soon be in a position to offer her students a balanced view *on the reading list*. This is important because whatever the teacher *says* in class can always be put down to her *personal bias*; what is in a published book *always* carries more weight with students.

Students must always be free to form their own views and develop their own political analysis. But so long as feminism is present within a Lesbian Studies course, so long as its theories are considered and in a correct version, not the distortions of our opponents, students will be properly equipped to come to their own reasoned conclusions. The real struggle is for us to keep feminism on the agenda of *all* Lesbian Studies courses amid the torrent of backlash literature. This book is a contribution to that goal.

References

Auchmuty, R, Jeffreys, S, and Miller, E, 'Lesbian History and Gay Studies: Keeping a Feminist Perspective', *Women's History Review*, 1992 1/1, pp 89–108.

Cruickshanks, M, *Lesbian Studies Present and Future*, The Feminist Press, Old Westbury, New York, 1982.

Faderman, L, *Surpassing the Love of Men*, The Women's Press, London, 1981.

Friedman, S, and, Elizabeth, S (eds), *On the Problem of Men*, The Women's Press, London, 1981.

Jeffreys, S, *The Lesbian Heresy: A Feminist Perspective on the Lesbian Sexual Revolution*, The Women's Press, London, 1994a.

Jeffreys, S, 'The Queer Disappearance of Lesbians: Sexuality in the Academy', *Women's Studies International Forum* 1994b, 17/5 pp 459–472.

Onlywomen Press, *Love Your Enemy?*, Onlywomen, London, 1981.

Purvis, J, *Writing Women's History*, paper delivered to the Women's Studies Network Conference, 10 July 1994.

Rich, A, *Compulsory Heterosexuality and Lesbian Existence*, Onlywomen, London, 1981.

Staddon, P, *Lesbian Studies: an opportunity not to be missed*, paper delivered at the Women's Studies Network Conference, University of Portsmouth, 9 July 1994.

Stimpson, C R, 'Afterword: Lesbian Studies in the 1990s', in C Jay and J Glasgow (eds), *Lesbian Texts and Contexts: Radical Revision*, Onlywomen, London, 1992.

Taking Liberties Collective, *Learning the Hard Way: Women's Oppression in Men's Education*, Macmillan, Basingstoke 1989.

section five
MOVING FORWARD

This section demonstrates above all else that radical lesbian feminism has a promising future. The individual chapters are written by lesbians spanning two generations. Together, they offer a combination of lesbian-feminist vision and practical strategies for radical feminist struggles today.

Audre Lorde, in this ground-breaking article first published in 1984, looks at how differences based on age, race and sexuality have been used to create 'insurmountable barriers' between women and to reinforce structures of oppression. She names the generation gap as a powerful tool manufactured by oppressive regimes to separate generations of women from each other. She argues that our future depends on our ability to recognise our differences and to use them creatively within a framework of equality to enrich our visions and joint struggles. We reprint this article here because we believe it still contains the only hope for women to be able to work across differences to bring about change.

The piece by *Janice Raymond* is an extract from an inspirational address that she first gave to the Lesbian Summer School at Wesley House in London in July 1988. The Summer School was a political watershed for lesbian politics and community in London. Organised by the London Lesbian Archive, initially as a fundraising event, it proved to be the site of a bitter struggle between lesbian pornographers and radical lesbian feminists, where pornography and sado-masochism began to gain the ascendancy in lesbian politics.

In this extract, Raymond poses a vision of lesbian sexuality connected to imagination and lesbian-feminist reality; a vision that moves beyond imitations of heterosexual constructions of sexuality. She argues that sexuality cannot be disconnected from other aspects of women's lives and that feminism needs to be put back into sexual politics.

The concluding two articles address how radical lesbian feminism is moving forward in this decade. They stress that it is a politics that is both self-reflective and responsive to changes in social conditions. They demonstrate that the generation gap is not inevitable and that it is possible to learn from history.

The series of interviews with young lesbians clearly show that younger women are still being drawn to radical lesbian feminism because of its potential to make sense of their experience and change their lives. Many of these younger women initially found radical feminism through books, because of the lack of visible women's liberation groups in the late 1980s. However, they had gone on to find and to initiate different forms of radical feminist activism relevant to the changing conditions of today and to develop an increasing awareness of the need for feminist organising on a global scale.

In the concluding article, *Julie Bindel* addresses some practical strategies for the way forward. After an incisive critique of some of the negative effects of identity politics in the women's liberation movement in the UK, she puts the case for principled coalitions based on common ground between feminists in the present context. She cites examples of black and white feminists successfully working together around male violence against women. She stresses the importance and illustrates the possibility of holding fast to a radical feminist agenda while working within broad-based coalitions, and emphasises that there are many different ways of being a radical feminist activist in the current period.

AGE, RACE, CLASS AND SEX: WOMEN REDEFINING DIFFERENCE

AUDRE LORDE

Much of Western European history conditions us to see human differences in simplistic opposition to each other: dominant/subordinate, good/bad, up/down, superior/inferior. In a society where the good is defined in terms of profit rather than in terms of human need, there must always be some group of people who, through systematised oppression, can be made to feel surplus, to occupy the place of the dehumanised inferior. Within this society, that group is made up of Black and Third–World people, working–class people, older people and women.

As a forty–nine–year–old black lesbian feminist socialist mother of two, including one boy, and a member of an inter–racial couple, I usually find myself part of some group defined as other, deviant, inferior, or just plain wrong. Traditionally, in American society, it is the members of oppressed, objectified groups who are expected to stretch out and bridge the gap between the actualities of our lives and the consciousness of our oppressor. For in order to survive, those of us for whom oppression is as American as apple pie have always had to be watchers, to become familiar with the language and manners of the oppressor, even sometimes adopting them for some illusion of protection. Whenever the need for some pretence of communication arises, those who profit from our oppression call upon us to share our knowledge with them. In other words, it is the responsibility of the oppressed to teach the oppressors their mistakes. I am responsible for educating teachers who dismiss my children's culture in school.

Black and third-world people are expected to educate white people as to our humanity. Women are expected to educate men. Lesbians and gay men are expected to educate the heterosexual world. The oppressors maintain their position and evade responsibility for their own actions. There is a constant drain of energy which might be better used in redefining ourselves and devising realistic scenarios for altering the present and constructing the future.

Institutionalised rejection of difference is an absolute necessity in a profit economy which needs outsiders as surplus people. As members of such an economy, we have *all* been programmed to respond to the human differences between us with fear and loathing and to handle that difference in one of three ways: ignore it, and if that is not possible, copy it if we think it is dominant, or destroy it if we think it is subordinate. But we have no patterns for relating across our human differences as equals. As a result, those differences have been misnamed and misused in the service of separation and confusion.

Certainly there are very real differences between us of race, age and sex. But it is not those differences between us that are separating us. It is rather our refusal to recognise those differences, and to examine the distortions which result from our misnaming them and their effects upon human behaviour and expectation.

Racism, the belief in the inherent superiority of one race over all others and thereby the right to dominance. Sexism, the belief in the inherent superiority of one sex over the other and thereby the right to dominance. Ageism. Heterosexism. Elitism. Classism.

It is a lifetime pursuit for each one of us to extract these distortions from our living at the same time as we recognise, reclaim and define those differences upon which they are imposed. For we have all been raised in a society where those distortions were endemic within our living. Too often, we pour the energy needed for recognising and exploring difference into pretending those differences are insurmountable barriers, or that they do not exist at all. This results in a voluntary isolation, or false and treacherous connections. Either way, we do not develop tools for using human difference as a springboard for creative change within our lives. We speak not of human difference, but of human deviance.

Somewhere, on the edge of consciousness, there is what I call a *mythical norm*, which each one of us within our hearts knows 'that is not me'. In America, this norm is usually defined as white, thin, male, young, heterosexual, Christian, and financially secure. It is with this mythical norm that the trappings of power reside within American society. Those of us who stand outside that power often identify one way in which we are different, and we assume that to be the primary cause of all oppression, forgetting other distortions around difference, some of which we ourselves may be practising. By and large within the women's movement today, white women focus upon their oppression as women and ignore differences of race, sexual preference, class and age. There is a pretence to a homogeneity of experience covered by the word *sisterhood* that does not in fact exist.

Unacknowledged class differences rob women of each others, energy and creative insight. Recently a women's magazine collective made the decision for one issue to print only prose, saying poetry was a less 'rigorous' or 'serious' art form. Yet even the form our creativity takes is often a class issue. Of all the art forms, poetry is the most economical. It is the one which is the most secret, which requires the least physical labour, the least material, and the one which can be done between shifts, in the hospital pantry, on the subway, and on scraps of surplus paper. Over the last few years, writing a novel on tight finances, I came to appreciate the enormous differences in the material demands between poetry and prose. As we reclaim our literature, poetry has been the major voice of poor, working-class and Colored women. A room of one's own may be a necessity for writing prose, but so are reams of paper, a typewriter, and plenty of time. The actual requirements to produce the visual arts also help determine, along class lines, whose art is whose. In this day of inflated prices for material, who are our sculptors, our painters, our photographers? When we speak of a broadly based women's culture, we need to be aware of the effect of class and economic differences on the supplies available for producing art.

As we move toward creating a society within which we can each flourish, ageism is another distortion of relationship which interferes without vision. By ignoring the past, we are encouraged to repeat its mistakes. The 'generation gap' is an important social tool for any repressive society. If the younger members of a community view the older members as contemptible or suspect or excess, they will never be able to join hands and examine the living memories of the community, nor ask the all-important question, 'Why?'. This gives rise to a historical amnesia that keeps us working to invent the wheel every time we have to go to the store for bread.

We find ourselves having to repeat and re-learn the same old lessons over and over that our mothers did because we do not pass on what we have learned, or because we are unable to listen. For instance, how many times has this all been said before? For another, who would have believed that once again our daughters are allowing their bodies to be hampered and purgatoried by girdles and high heels and hobble skirts?

Ignoring the differences of race between women and the implications of those differences presents the most serious threat to the mobilisation of women's joint power.

As white women ignore their built-in privilege of whiteness and define *woman* in terms of their own experience alone, then women of Color become 'other', the outsider whose experience and tradition is too 'alien' to comprehend. An example of this is the signal absence of the experience of women of Color as a resource for women's studies courses. The literature of women of Color is seldom included in women's literature courses and almost never in other literature courses, nor in women's studies as a whole. All too often, the excuse given is that the literatures of women of Color can only be taught by Colored women, or that they are too difficult to understand, or that classes cannot 'get into' them because they come out of experiences that are 'too different'. I have heard this argument presented by white women of otherwise quite clear intelligence, women who seem to have no trouble at all teaching and reviewing work that comes out of the vastly different experiences of Shakespeare, Molière, Dostoyevsky and Aristophanes. Surely there must be some other explanation.

This is a very complex question, but I believe one of the reasons white women have such difficulty reading Black women's work is because of their reluctance to see Black women as women and different from themselves. To examine Black women's literature effectively requires that we be seen as whole people in our actual complexities – as individuals, as women, as human – rather than as one of those problematic but familiar stereotypes provided in this society in place of genuine images of Black women. And I believe this holds true for the literatures of other women of Color who are not Black.

The literatures of all women of Color recreate the textures of our lives, and many white women are heavily invested in ignoring the real differences. For as long as any difference between us means one of us must be inferior, then the recognition of any difference must be fraught with guilt. To allow women of Color to step out of stereotypes is too guilt-provoking, for it threatens the complacency of those women who view oppression only in terms of sex.

Refusing to recognise difference makes it impossible to see the different problems and pitfalls facing us as women.

Thus, in a patriarchal power system where whiteskin privilege is a major prop, the entrapments used to neutralise Black women and white women are not the same. For example, it is easy for Black women to be used by the power structure against Black men, not because they are men, but because they are Black. Therefore, for Black women, it is necessary at all times to separate the needs of the oppressor from our own legitimate conflicts within our communities. This same problem does not exist for white women. Black women and men have shared racist oppression and still share it, although in different ways. Out of that shared oppression we have developed joint defences and joint vulnerabilities to each other that are not duplicated in the white community, with the exception of the relationship between Jewish women and Jewish men.

On the other hand, white women face the pitfall of being seduced into joining the oppressor under the pretence of sharing power. This possibility does not exist in the same way for women of Color. The tokenism that is sometimes extended to us is not an invitation to join power; our racial 'otherness' is a visible reality that makes that quite clear. For white women there is a wider range of pretended choices and rewards for identifying with patriarchal power and its tools.

Today, with the defeat of ERA, the tightening economy, and increased conservatism, it is easier once again for white women to believe the dangerous fantasy that if you are good enough, pretty enough, sweet enough, quiet enough, teach the children to behave, hate the right people, and marry the right men, then you will be allowed to co-exist with patriarchy in relative peace, at least until a man needs your job or the neighbourhood rapist happens along. And true, unless one lives and loves in the trenches it is difficult to remember that the war against dehumanisation is ceaseless.

But Black women and our children know the fabric of our lives is stitched with violence and with hatred, that there is no rest. We do not deal with it only on the picket lines, or in dark midnight alleys, or in the places where we dare to verbalise our resistance. For us, increasingly, violence weaves through the daily tissues of our living – in the supermarket, in the classroom, in the elevator, in the clinic and the schoolyard, from the plumber, the baker, the saleswoman, the bus driver, the bank teller, the waitress who does not serve us.

Some problems we share as women, some we do not. You fear your children will grow up to join the patriarchy and testify against you, we fear our children will be dragged from a car and shot down in the street, and you will turn your backs upon the reasons they are dying.

The threat of difference has been no less blinding to people of Color. Those of us who are Black must see that the reality of our lives and our struggle does not make us immune to the errors of ignoring and misnaming difference. Within Black communities where racism is a living reality, differences among us often seem dangerous and suspect. The need for unity is often misnamed as a need for homogeneity, and a Black-feminist vision mistaken for betrayal of our common interests as a people. Because of the continuous battle against racial erasure that Black women and Black men share, some Black women still refuse to recognise that we are also oppressed as women, and that sexual hostility against Black women is practised not only by the white racist society, but implemented within our Black communities as well. It is a disease striking the heart of Black nationhood, and silence will not make it disappear. Exacerbated by racism and the pressures of powerlessness, violence against Black women and children often becomes a standard without our communities, one by which manliness can be measured. But these women-hating acts are rarely discussed as crimes against Black women.

As a group, women of Color are the lowest paid wage-earners in America. We are the primary targets of abortion and sterilisation abuse, here and abroad. In certain parts of Africa, small girls are still being sewed shut between their legs to keep them docile and for men's pleasure. This is known as female circumcision, and it is not a cultural affair as the late Jomo Kenyatta insisted, it is a crime against Black women.

Black women's literature is full of the pain of frequent assault, not only by a racist patriarchy, but also by Black men. Yet the necessity for and history of shared battle have made us, Black women, particularly vulnerable to the false accusation that anti-sexist is anti-Black. Meanwhile, woman-hating as a recourse of the powerless is sapping strength from Black communities, and our very lives. Rape is on the increase, reported and unreported, and rape is not aggressive sexuality, it is sexualised aggression. As Kalamu ya Salaam, a Black male writer points out, 'As long as male domination exists, rape will exist. Only women revolting and men made conscious of their responsibility to fight sexism can collectively stop rape.' (1980).

Differences between ourselves as Black women are also being misnamed and used to separate us from one another. As a Black lesbian feminist comfortable with the many different ingredients of my identity, and a woman committed to racial and sexual freedom from oppression, I find I am constantly being encouraged to pluck out some one aspect of myself and present this as the meaningful whole, eclipsing or denying the other parts of self. But this is a destructive and fragmenting way to live. My fullest concentration of energy is available to me only when I integrate all the parts of who I am, openly, allowing power from particular sources of my living to flow back and forth freely through all my different selves, without restrictions of externally imposed definition. Only then can I bring myself and my energies as a whole to the service of those struggles which I embrace as part of my living.

A fear of lesbians, or of being accused of being a lesbian, has led many Black women into testifying against themselves. It has led some of us into destructive alliances, and others into despair and isolation. In the white women's communities, heterosexism is sometimes a result of identifying with the white patriarchy, a rejection of that interdependence between women-identified women which allows the self to be, rather than to be used in the service of men. Sometimes it reflects a die-hard belief in the protective colouration of heterosexual relationships, sometimes a self-hate which all women have to fight against, taught us from birth.

Although elements of these attitudes exist for all women, there are particular resonances of heterosexism and homophobia among Black women. Despite the fact that woman-bonding has a long and honourable history in the African and African-American communities, and despite the knowledge and accomplishments of many strong and creative women-identified Black women in the political, social and cultural fields, heterosexual Black women often tend to ignore or discount the existence and work of Black lesbians. Part of this attitude has come from an understandable terror of Black male attack within the close confines of Black society, where the punishment for any female self-assertion is still to be accused of being a lesbian and therefore unworthy of the attention or support of the scarce Black male. But part of this need to misname and ignore Black lesbians comes from a very real fear that openly women-identified Black women who are no longer dependent upon men for their self-definition may well reorder our whole concept of social relationships.

Black women who once insisted that lesbianism was a white woman's problem now insist that Black lesbians are a threat to Black nationhood, are consorting with the enemy, are basically un-Black. These accusations, coming from the very women to whom we look for deep and real understanding, have served to keep many Black lesbians in hiding, caught between the racism of white women and the homophobia of their sisters. Often, their work has been ignored, trivialised or misnamed, as with the work of Angelina Grimke, Alice Dunbar-Nelson, Lorraine Hansberry. Yet women-bonded women have always been some part of the power of Black communities, from our unmarried aunts to the amazons of Dahomey.

And it is certainly not Black lesbians who are assaulting women and raping children and grandmothers on the streets of our communities.

Across America, as in Boston during the spring of 1979 following the unsolved murders of twelve Black women, Black lesbians are spearheading movements against violence against Black women.

What are the particular details within each of our lives that can be scrutinised and altered to help bring about change? How do we redefine difference for all women? It is not our differences which separate women, but our reluctance to recognise those differences and to deal effectively with the distortions which have resulted from the ignoring and misnaming of those differences.

As a tool of social control, women have been encouraged to recognise only one area of human difference as legitimate, those differences which exist between women and men. And we have learned to deal across those differences with the urgency of all oppressed subordinates. All of us have had to learn to live or work or co-exist with men, from our fathers on. We have recognised and negotiated these differences, even when this recognition only continued the old dominant/subordinate mode of human relationship, where the oppressed must recognise the masters' difference in order to survive.

But our future survival is predicated upon our ability to relate within equality. As women, we must root out internalised patterns of oppression within ourselves if we are to move beyond the most superficial aspects of social change. Now we must recognise differences among women who are our equals, neither inferior nor superior, and devise ways to use each others' difference to enrich our visions and our joint struggles.

The future of our earth may depend upon the ability of all women to identify and develop new definitions of power and new patterns of relating across difference. The old definitions have not served us, nor the earth that supports us. The old patterns, no matter how cleverly rearranged to imitate progress, still condemn us to cosmetically altered repetitions of the same old exchanges, the same old guilt, hatred, recrimination, lamentation and suspicion.

For we have, built into all of us, old blueprints of expectation and response, old structures of oppression, and these must be altered at the same time as we alter the living conditions which are a result of those structures. For the master's tools will never dismantle the master's house.

As Paulo Freire shows so well in *The Pedagogy of the Oppressed*, the true focus of revolutionary change is never merely the oppressive situations which we seek to escape, but that piece of the oppressor which is planted deep within each of us, and which knows only the oppressors' tactics, the oppressors' relationships.

Change means growth, and growth can be painful. But we sharpen self-definition by exposing the self in work and struggle together with those whom we define as different from ourselves, although sharing the same goals. For Black and white, old and young, lesbian and heterosexual women alike, this can mean new paths to our survival.

We have chosen each other
and the edge of each others battles
the war is the same
if we lose
someday women's blood will congeal
upon a dead planet
if we win
there is no telling
we seek beyond history
for a new and more possible meeting.

(From 'Outlines', unpublished poem.)

'Age, Race, Sex and Class: Women Redefining Difference' originally appeared in *Sister Outsider*, The Crossing Press, Freedom, Ca. USA. Copyright © 1984 Audre Lorde

References

Freire, P, *The Pedagogy of the Oppressed*, Seabury Press, New York, 1970.
Salaam, K ya, 'Rape: A Radical Analysis, An African-American Perspective', *Black Books Bulletin*, vol 6 no 4, 1980.

A VISION OF LESBIAN SEXUALITY

JANICE RAYMOND

Mary Daly has outlined several elements of radical feminism. (Daly 1984 pp 397–8; Daly 1987 p 75) In a similar fashion I would highlight several commonly-held values of lesbian feminism that allow us to say *we* again. If we are lesbian feminists, we have clear and present knowledge that the boys, and some of the girls, are not going to like us and that we just might run into trouble along the way.

If we are lesbian feminists, we are radically different from what the hetero-society wants us to be. It is not a fake difference, but a real difference. For example, lesbian sexuality is *different*, rooted in the lesbian imagination. It is not the same old sexuality that women must submit to in hetero-reality. It is not pornography, it is not butch and femme, and it is not bondage and domination. It is for one thing, a sexuality that is imagination rooted in reality. As Andrea Dworkin has written, 'Imagination is not a synonym for sexual fantasy . . .' Fantasy can only conjure up a scripted bag of tricks that are an endless repetition of heterosexual conformist practices. 'Imagination finds new meanings, new forms; values and acts. The person with imagination is pushed forward by it into a world of possibility and risk, a distinct world of meaning and choice.' (Dworkin 1987 p 48); not into the heterosexual junkyard of lesbian libertarian and lifestyle activities that get re-cycled to women as fantastic goods. Lesbian lifestylism puts fantasy in place of imagination. Have you ever noticed how everyone talks about their fantasies and not about imagination?

If we are lesbian feminists, we feel and act on behalf of women as women. Lesbian feminism is not a one issue movement. It makes connections between all issues that affect women – not only what affects this particular group, class, nationality, and not only what affects lesbians. We feel and act for all women because we are women, and even if we were the last ones to profess this, we would still be there for women.

If we are lesbian feminists, we keep going. even when it's not popular. Even when it's not rewarded. Not just yesterday. Not just today. Not just a couple of hours on the weekend. Lesbian feminism is a way of life, a way of living for our deepest Selves and for other women.

And those who think that the objectification, subordination and violation of women is acceptable just as long as you call it lesbian erotica or lesbian sado-masochism – they're not lesbian feminists. And those who think that it's acceptable in the privacy of their own bedrooms, where they enjoy it, where they get off on it – especially sexually – they're not lesbian feminists either. As Mary Daly has said, they're lesbians 'from the waist down.'

And to those who say, how dare we define what feminism means, I say – if we don't define what feminism means, what does feminism mean?

For years, we fought against the depiction of lesbians in hetero-pornography. We said, 'that's not us in those poses of butch and femme role-playing. That's not the way we make love. That's not us treating each other as sadists or as masochists. That's not us bound by those chains, with those whips, and in those male fantasies of what women do with other women. That's a male wet dream of what a lesbian is and what lesbians do,' we said. And we didn't only say it. We fought it. So now what happens. We have lesbian pornography appearing in US 'women's' porn mags such as *Bad Attitude* and *On Our Backs*. And we have the *FACT* Brief. And all of this 'feminist and lesbian literature' tells us that straight pornography, that hetero-pornography, is right. We are butches and femmes, we are sadists and masochists, and we do get off on doing violence to each other. We've come full circle – unfortunately back to the same negative starting point.

So I want to end by talking about a vision and a context for lesbian sexuality. For those who want how-to-do-it guidelines, this ending will be a great disappointment. I want to suggest what sexuality might look like rooted in lesbian imagination, not in the hetero-fantasies of lesbian pornography. This is a vision, a context, an end note that is really a beginning.

This vision of sexuality includes the 'ability to touch and be touched'. But more, a touch that makes contact, as James Baldwin has phrased it. Andrea Dworkin, building on these words of Baldwin, writes about sexuality as the act, the point of connection, where touch makes contact if self-knowledge is present. It is also the act, the point of connection, where the inability of touch to make contact is revealed and where the results may be devastating. In sexuality, intimacy is always possible, as much as we say that sex is sex – that is, simple pleasure. In sexuality, a range of emotions about life get expressed, however casual or impersonal the intercourse – feelings of betrayal, rage, isolation, and bitterness as well as hope, joy, tenderness, love, and communion. (Dworkin 1987 pp 47–61) All, although not all together, reside in this passion we call sexuality. Sexuality is where these emotions become accessible or anesthetised. A whole human life does not stand still in sex.

Libertarian and lesbian lifestylism simplifies the complexity of that whole human life that is present in the sex act. Abandoning that totality – that history, those feelings, those thoughts – allows for wildfire but not for passion. 'All touch but no contact . . .' (Baldwin 1962 p 82).

Passion, of course, allows for love. Its possibility, not its inevitability. Passion is a passage between two people. Love is an extension of that passage. Passion can become love, but not without the openness to it. Sex as passion, and perhaps as love, not merely as wildfire is a radical experience of being and becoming, of excavating possibilities within the self surely, and within another perhaps, that have been unknown.

I began this talk by stating that, although the lesbian lifestylers talk about sex constantly, they are speechless about its connection to a whole human life, and, therefore, they are speechless about sex itself. The presence of a whole human life in the act of sexuality negates any reductionistic view of sex as good or bad, sheer pleasure or sheer perversion. Dworkin reminds us that when sex is getting even, when sex is hatred, when sex is utility, when sex is indifferent, then sex is the destroying of a human being, another person perhaps, assuredly one's self. Sex is a whole human life rooted in passion, in flesh. This whole human life is at stake always.

This extract is taken from *Putting the Politics Back into Lesbianism* which was originally a talk given at the Lesbian Summer School at Wesley House, London, July 1988. It was later published in *Women's Studies International Forum*, Vol 12, No 2, pp 149–56, USA 1989.

References

Baldwin, J, *Giovanni's room*, Penguin, London, 1990.

Daly, M, *Pure lust: Elemental feminist philosophy*, The Women's Press, London, 1984.

Daly, M, in cahoots with Jane Caputi, *Websters' First New Intergalactic Wickedary*, The Women's Press, London, 1988.

Dworkin, A, *Intercourse*, Secker & Warburg, London, 1987.

FACT (Feminist Anti-Censorship Taskforce et al), *Brief Amici Curiae*, no 84–3147 1985. In the US Court of Appeals, 7th Circuit, Southern District of Indiana.

VALUING WOMEN: YOUNG LESBIANS TALK

LYNNE HARNE

One of the myths that has been created by the patriarchal backlash is that radical lesbian feminism is old-fashioned and no longer relevant to younger women. While the political context has changed and feminism is much less visible nowadays, the following interviews with younger lesbian feminists speak for themselves in showing that radical feminism is alive and well and actively moving forward.

In these accounts there is a sense of political confidence and a belief in the rightness of challenging male sexual violence and patriarchal states on an international level; of getting on with what's important and not being diverted by the arguments of queer, identity politics and post-structuralism; of valuing women and radical feminist solidarity. There is a sense of optimism, which, while tempered with an understanding of the considerable forces of patriarchal resistance and global capitalism in the current historical period, is based on the knowledge that radical feminist struggle will continue.

In the first part of this chapter, Helen and Rowan (in two separate interviews) talk about becoming radical lesbian feminists in the early 1990s. They talk about the activism they are involved in, in campaigning against pornography and within the women's peace movement and their thoughts on the future. Both are aged 25. Helen until recently lived in London and Rowan in Cambridge.

In the second part, four women Sarah, Joy, Simone and Louise, who were active in the London group of the Campaign against Pornography and other campaigns against male sexual violence, reflect on their experiences of becoming radical lesbian feminists between the mid 1980s and early 1990s and discuss the current state of radical feminism. Their ages range from 24 to 30.

Lynne: Can you say how you first became a lesbian feminist?

Helen: I came out as bisexual and then as a lesbian at college. There was a lesbian and gay and bi-sexual group there, but I didn't get very involved. It was a-political in that there was a strong emphasis on people saying they were born that way. I never felt I was born a lesbian, I didn't feel I was born heterosexual either. I felt that heterosexuality had been socially imposed on me. I remember gay men saying they were really glad about the 'gay gene', because it meant they were born homosexual and this meant that they couldn't help it and people would be more sympathetic. In the same article [in which the gay gene was reported] it said that most lesbians laughed at the idea, but there wasn't much publicity about that.

To me, it was a choice to become a lesbian, and feminist politics were an important part of coming out. I was involved in the joint CAP/NUS Women's Campaign against pornography in 1989–1990 called 'Off the Shelf'. I also discovered Sisterwrite bookshop in London and it made a tremendous difference to me finding books to read about radical lesbian feminism. These included Lillian Faderman's *Surpassing the Love of Men*, Sheila Jeffreys' *Anti-Climax* and Janice Raymond's *A Passion for Friends* – books written with a radical lesbian-feminist analysis.

Lynne: What sort of activism are you involved in now?

Helen: After I left college in 1992 I came to London and I wanted to get involved in lesbian-feminist activism and it was really hard to find anything. After a bit I became involved in the Campaign against Pornography (CAP) and that was really good because I found a network of other lesbian feminists. At the moment I am more involved with the women's peace movement.

At college I had been involved in mixed green and peace politics, but since I've left I've mostly been active in the women's peace movement. There are lots of lesbian feminists involved, but I still have doubts about whether I should focus on lesbian-feminist activism more specifically. Lesbian feminism isn't directly addressed within the movement, but it comes through in the way things are done, in the way we think about actions and newsletters. You spend your time with lots of women and women are prioritised. Going on actions is important, and it's important that women are supportive and come to your aid if needed – having been involved in the mixed peace movement, this is a real difference. You get such a contrast at women's peace camps with the police on one side, who become so obviously the symbol of capitalist patriarchy, and this contrast gives you a sense of solidarity and at the same time these situations can be very humorous.

I think it's important to make the connections between war, male violence and pornography. Two years ago at the International Women's Day action at Faslane Peace Camp, in the morning we did a blockade outside the base and in the evening we went on a reclaim-the-night march in Alexandria. One of the speakers at the march made the connections between violence against women on the street and in the home and pornography and how it is sent out on nuclear submarines. This connection is so obvious once you recognise it. This year when we had been arrested after taking action at Faslane peace camp, we found pornography at the police station in the room where we were being held. The women tore it to shreds!

There is still a very strong women's peace movement, which is very separate from the mixed one. There is still a permanant camp at Greenham and a new permanent camp at Menwith Hill US spy base, as well as regular weekend camps at Aldermaston and Sellafield. There's always women's actions for International Women's Day (8 March) such as the one at Faslane.

The Women's nuclear test ban network was behind the Buckingham Palace action last year, when fifteen women put up ladders and stormed the palace gardens to draw attention to British nuclear testing which violated the land rights and sovereignty of the people of Western Shoshone.[1] There are several groups making connections with women against war in the former Yugoslavia; for example with Women in Black in Belgrade, and there are also groups that are collecting aid and driving it out to former Yugoslavia themselves.

Lynne: What does being a radical lesbian feminist mean to you?

Helen: It means being active in feminist campaigns and groups which is where I feel more at home. Feeling that I've got a feminist philo-

---

[1] Western Shoshone is located in Nevada, USA and belongs to the Native American Western Shoshone people.

sophy and politics and being involved in direct action in the women's peace and green movements, in opposing the way men are destroying the world, and for me, that's part of radical lesbian-feminist politics.

I get very angry and feel totally alienated at what is represented as the prevailing lesbian culture. For example, I went to see the film 'Go Fish' and I felt angry at the way that film was presenting lesbians to the mainstream world. There was a complete lack of politics and it made out that lesbian life was all about match-making which is not what my life is about. A lot of lesbians are not happy around the politics of s-m, yet this film was making jokes about it, that makes it seem acceptable. There was one scene in the film where this lesbian had slept with a man, and is surrounded by other lesbians, who are represented as the lesbian-feminist 'thought police'. This was a direct attack on lesbian feminism, and equated us with the police making homophobic attacks.

There is also the lesbian club scene which is represented by the gay media as the be-all and end-all of lesbian life. When I first came out I went to one or two of these clubs. At Venus Rising most women don't dress in s-m gear but the club has semi-pornographic projections on the walls. When I was there, there was also a corner with a women's sex stall selling dildoes, harnesses and s-m gear. This is what young lesbians are being told being a lesbian is all about. You are told you have to accept it; its part of the lesbian community and if you object, you are just labelled a prude. The media, including the gay media, is totally controlled by money and the people who've got the money are the ones who are pro s-m and pro-porn so it's a complete stitch up. I came out to my mother recently, but I can't show her just anything about what it means being a lesbian. I don't want to take her to a film like *Go Fish* or show her a copy of *Shebang* – they don't show what being a lesbian means to me.

Lynne: What is the way forward, then?

Helen: We live in a world where we are conditioned to treat people in a sado-masochistic way, but just saying 'well that is the way the world is, and let's get on with doing it more' is not the way to change it. We have to talk about constructing relationships differently. Lesbian feminists need to be more connected with each other and more visible. It was really important to me finding other lesbian feminists. I attended a lesbian-line conference recently in Glasgow and there was a very large workshop on lesbian feminism, but there was not a great awareness of the need for a visible lesbian-feminist community or for visible lesbian-feminist campaigns.

Lynne: What are the benefits of being a radical lesbian feminist?

Helen: You can understand and make sense of the world and work out why things are as they are. Being in a feminist campaign like the women's peace movement you develop a sense of power among women you can trust and an amazing sense of solidarity. I get a lot of strength from that.

Lynne: How did you become a radical lesbian feminist?

Rowan: I know that there is a radical feminist critique of therapy, but I was introduced to radical feminism initially through therapy. I first became mentally ill at 13 and was diagnosed as anorexic, schizophrenic and temporarily epileptic. I was depressed and had visionary and sensory hallucinations. I didn't socially interact with other girls at school, I just read books. At the same time I knew I wanted to be a mathematician, and my first awareness of feminism was very individualistic; as a woman I was going to get to the top. I could see barriers, but I thought I could break through them.

When I got to university I slept with a lot of men; that was my idea of social interaction. I had a lot of women friends but no friends who were men.

As far as lesbianism was concerned I just thought you were born one. It also wasn't a possible option. My father said he would kill any of his children who were 'homosexual'.

At university I was in therapy and I would talk about specific incidents which I couldn't make sense of from my own perspective. For example, my work would always be given a low grade and initially I couldn't understand it. I then realised it was because I was a woman, but in some way I still thought I could escape my gender. My therapist made suggestions which enabled me to develop a wider perspective. Then I went out and bought some books – I remember Dale Spender's *Women of Ideas* just lit up light bulbs in my head.

All this was being supported by my therapist and no-one else I knew. I remember a woman friend in the mathematics department telling me that if I went around saying 'the personal is political' people would think I was crazy. I thought, well people have been calling me crazy for all the wrong reasons, so they might as well call me crazy for the right ones.

This was when I began to define myself as a radical feminist and began questioning my own heterosexuality. I could see that all the trappings of heterosexuality were constructed, but I thought, there's a problem here, I don't fancy women. (I think this is where Germaine Greer is still stuck.) It took me a while to realise that 'fancying' is also just a construct. I went along to the university lesbian and gay group, but it wasn't very supportive – they said go away and come back when you want to come out, but I wanted support then. Also it wasn't feminist. It was the sort of group which if you said you objected to s-m they said you can't object. I said read my lips, I am objecting.

I started working around women's issues mostly in my work and I started thinking, what's stopping me? I read Rich's article about the lesbian continuum and I started thinking it's this total focus on genital sex, which of course is a mind-numbing fantasy of the heteropatriarchy. Being a lesbian feminist for me, is working with women and being for women and if I happen to be in a sexual relationship that's just part of it.

Lynne: How did you start getting involved in radical-feminist activism?

Rowan: After doing all this reading, I had come to an understanding of the systematic nature of women's oppression, but all these ideas were just in my head. So I searched for a women's group, a feminist group, but I couldn't find one. So with a friend, we decided to set up a group and we advertised it. It was a group of about ten women, all of whom were lesbian or bi-sexual. We didn't have an agenda – anyone could bring an issue or an action they wanted to talk about. After a time, two women in the group said they were very angry because I constantly took an anti-porn position and this was how our group was perceived. Naively, I had assumed that if you were in a feminist group, you must be against pornography. I hadn't appreciated the backlash that was going on about queer, and s-m. These women said they agreed with Feminists against Censorship. A number of us didn't want to be in a group that didn't actively oppose pornography. So the group split and we set up the Cambridge Campaign Against Pornography.

I am also involved in Yellow Gate women's peace camp at Greenham Common. At Yellow Gate, we see nuclear weapons as one of the most destructive aspects of partriarchy and we challenge the patriarchal state, mainly through direct action.

Lynne: What do you get from being involved in radical feminist politics?

Rowan: In Cambridge CAP we've done a lot of consciousness-raising about how pornography has affected our own lives. This helped me get over some masochistic sexual practices I'd been involved in when heterosexual and about which I'd been having nightmares. When I was 18, I saw 'Jagged Edge': a film which shows a woman being tied up, mutilated and killed by her male partner. I'd found this film absolutely terrifying and had started screaming in the cinema. At the time I was told by my psychiatrist that I was displaying socially unacceptable behaviour. It was shortly after seeing this film that I got involved in sado–masochistic sexual practices. Talking through this with other radical feminists has helped me understand and get over that experience and be able to oppose pornography and s–m.

I've also started doing public speaking against pornography to schools and women's groups. I've really benefited from doing that, as it's something I've always been frightened of. I was involved in a court case around taking action at Greenham and I defended myself in court, supported by other women, and I felt I was directly confronting the state. I wouldn't have done that four years ago.

When I first became a radical feminist and contacted London CAP I felt I didn't have the feminist language and I was frightened of getting things wrong. I felt that there were all these older women involved, who were far more experienced than me. In the Cambridge group, we are all about 25 or 26 and learning together. Actually once I'd got to know the women in CAP I found out it wasn't the case at all, and it was my own projection.

Lynne: What do you think the way forward is for radical feminism?

Rowan: Feminist language is difficult and I think it can act as a barrier to women getting involved. Mary Daly is an exception to this as she defines what language she is creating as she goes along. In order to discover radical feminism, I had to do it through books since if there is a radical lesbian-feminist community in Cambridge, I still haven't found it.

Lynne: Do you think that younger women need to create their own radical–feminist groups as you did?

Rowan: Yes, but there is a problem with this, because you have to keep re-inventing the wheel. If each generation has to go through the same level of consciousness–raising then we are going to lose out. One thing I love about Greenham is that women are extremely diverse in age. I was in a court case where the women involved represented every decade from twenty to ninety. You can learn a great deal from older women if they have the time to share the experience. The connection between theory and practice is essential to radical feminism, but as individuals our experience is going to be limited. We need radical–feminist groups which are diverse.

Lynne: Are you optimistic about the future?

Rowan: I am optimistic and the reason is that I know we are right – not in the sense that I think 'right will out', but because we are right we will not stop fighting. It's an optimism that stems from the knowledge that where there is patriarchy there will always be radical-feminist resistance.

I don't feel specifically optimistic about the current state of feminism, as the backlash is very strong. I just think that we will have to keep working away.

* * * *

Lynne: Can you say how you became lesbian feminists?

Sarah: I was a lesbian first. At university there seemed to be very few lesbians, but a lot of gay men. I discovered Mary Daly and made contacts outside the university with lesbians in Lesbian Line. I initially got involved in struggles against sado–masochism, and was involved in the whole sexuality debate about s-m, that was going on in the mid-1980s. It connected up with my own history and experience, the way men control things, and the aping of gay male culture. I went on the last lesbian strength march, where S & Mers tried to take it over. They weren't offering anything interesting or radical but were just doing what men were doing. It was the same old shit.

Simone: I became politically active when I was 13, mostly in CND and around peace issues, and I considered myself a socialist. Feminism, though, didn't touch my life really apart from all the traditional stereotypes in the media and I had really no idea what you had to do to be called a feminist.

Although I'd had doubts to some extent about my sexuality, I genuinely believed for quite a long time that you couldn't be a lesbian unless you lived in London! My perceptions gradually changed and by the time I was 18 and went away to university I realised I probably was a feminist and I knew for sure that I was a lesbian. I decided to come out (selectively). My first relationship was abusive and really quite damaging and I knew in my mind that wasn't how things should be. Talking to other women and reading a lot of feminist stuff made me aware of how connected feminism had to be with lesbianism for it to make sense.

Sarah: My experience was similar. The first lesbian relationship I was in was abusive and at the same time I was reading Mary Daly and it helped me connect lesbianism and feminism, when before I had seen them as something separate.

Louise: There was no separation for me between lesbianism and feminism. I got to find out about feminism when I was 14, when someone told me about *Spare Rib*. I was reading about radical feminism in books that aren't even available now. At Cambridge there was a lesbian scene which was very pro s-m and had no place for radical feminism. I did some work at a hostel for incest survivors and in Women's Aid, but there was no independent activism. I was sustained by some lesbian feminist friends at a women's college.

Joy: I come from a fiercely pro-union, vaguely socialist background. I felt lesbianism didn't have anything to do with me, it was something you were born with. You were 'normal' or you were 'abnormal'. Because I felt I was 'normal' therefore I wasn't a lesbian. I called myself a feminist when I was 15 and I applied to work in a women's building, but I was a liberal feminist in a lefty sort of way. I thought rape was an individual thing – what individual men did to individual women and that pornography was an individual right. I could see things going on which I didn't agree with but I didn't have a framework apart from an individualised one in which to understand it. When I came to England I began to read feminist theory. I wanted to get involved in activism around male violence which had become a focus for me. I went along to this group called November Women's Action, which was a coalition of women's groups organising a march for an International Day to End Violence against Women in London. It was in this group that I was exposed to ideas like compulsory heterosexuality. It was the first time that I'd come across the idea that heterosexuality is not natural; that it's something which is inculculated into women for particular reasons and that it underpins patriarchy.

It was a very liberating experience becoming a lesbian feminist, because finally everything fitted into place in my mind – all the doubts, all my previous history and my growing radical feminism.

Lynne: Why do you think you were able to become lesbian feminists and others got into what would now be called queer politics?

Louise: I think the backlash hadn't taken such a hold as it has now. There wasn't this 'queer' critique of radical feminism which said 'that's what we were into, but it's all over now', which has had quite a big influence.

Sarah: It was hard enough finding radical feminists in the mid-1980s, but once you had found a few, you found a whole lot more, but now when there's this whole idea that there isn't feminism, it's that much harder.

Louise: I don't know that it's worse now, it just seems worse. When I first started calling myself a feminist, everyone thought I was completely mad and it meant being absolutely isolated.

Joy: I didn't get into queer politics, because it is just an extrapolation of the politics I had had and was finding increasingly problematic. I think the whole idea of queer politics fits in with the current liberal context and it's why it's so prevalent in the liberal environment of universities. They are not going to be challenging patriarchal structures.

Sarah: What has gone is the idea of sexuality being constructed, that we have chosen to be lesbians. On the whole, the influence of gay men on young lesbians has been catastrophic and young lesbians these days are more likely to meet gay men than radical feminists.

Louise: I also think it's about what we've got to say as radical feminists which is difficult, in the way that what gay men say is not difficult. I think that saying you're a radical feminist, what it means is massive. What we are basically about is recognising that we live in a horrific world and facing up to that and wanting to change it – that's frightening.

Simone: I think it's possible to underestimate the terrible effects of all those years of Thatcherism. This has been an immensely demoralising thing, particularly for young people who really haven't had much of a glimpse of any alternatives. It's not surprising they want to escape from the world and get out of their heads on Ecstasy and stuff and young lesbians are by no means immune to this.

Lynne: What do you think the benefits are of being lesbian feminists?

Joy: One of the key differences between being a lesbian feminist and being a lesbian is the idea that as a lesbian feminist, you value women. For me it was mind-boggling, the idea that you take women seriously and that going out to a women-only group is time well spent. You are trained to think that the only people worth valuing are men and that men's lives and activities are the important ones – ideas which are essential to compulsory heterosexuality.

Sarah: Yes, we take what women say seriously. But that's also the difference between not only lesbians and lesbian feminists, but between lesbian feminists and heterosexual feminists, who continue to put a whole lot of energy into men. There is that whole contradiction that you can never see putting energy into men as bringing about women's emancipation. It just can't.

Joy: A heterosexual friend of mine was telling me that she had been out with some women friends and I asked her if she had had a nice time. She said, 'Oh you know what women are like together.' What she meant was that women in a group are incomplete. For me, once I'd found radical lesbian feminism I wasn't going to give it up. When I first went along to November Women's Action it challenged a whole load of assumptions I had, like every political action should include men, or should have the possibility of including men. In my early twenties radical feminism was demonised by the culture around me; I didn't know what it was, all I knew was that it was bad.

Louise: The major benefit for me of being a radical lesbian feminist is that it makes sense. From that point it begins to change your life and a lot of the confusion and contradictions and unhappiness really move. Because you can read what's gone on in your own life and in the lives of people around you in a different way. It moves you away from all the lies you tell yourself in order to make life more bearable and I think that's one of the major benefits, but it's scary as well. On a much broader level, it helps you to understand what's going on in the entire system. Things start to fit into place and that gives you a lot of control over your life and a grip on it, in a way that being confused doesn't.

Sarah: One of the advantages is being around other lesbian feminists who are interesting women.

Louise: I think that part of the reason you come into radical politics in the first place is the absolute boredom and emptiness in people's lives, and you don't want the options that are on offer, but it also means that you are a world away from most of the population.

Lynne: What about a sense of lesbian-feminist community – is that a benefit?

Sarah: I think that lesbian feminists look out for each other. I don't think you could say that there's a sense of *lesbian* community in London anymore. There's a lesbian scene where the attitude is, 'fuck em, suck em and leave them'. It may be different out of London.

Lynne: Is activism an important part of radical lesbian feminism?

Sarah: Yes and that's one of its benefits, that there's somewhere to channel your anger. There's somewhere for it to go constructively instead of the navel gazing and individualism of therapy for example. I think activism is intrinsic to radical lesbian feminism and it's what it's got going for it, that you can go out and do something about the way women get fucked over.

Louise: It's crucial to the theory of radical feminism. It makes links between fighting patriarchy and compulsory heterosexuality. It's a whole politics.

Lynne: What sort of activism are you all involved in?

All: Activism around the whole issue of male violence and male sexuality, which is about controlling women; that includes domestic violence, campaigning against pornography, but also specific work around rape, sex tourism and sex trafficking on an international level; Justice for Women, which is a campaign for justice for women who have killed violent men; challenging false memory syndrome, which denies that girls have been sexually abused.

Lynne: What's the way forward for radical feminism?

Louise: I think there are elements of the backlash which have always been there. There has always been an attack on feminism. Radical feminism got very bogged down with it, but now we are just getting on with our campaigns, realising we are still fighting the same enemy and we are on the attack again and controlling our own agendas.

Sarah: I think Justice for Women and CAP have made a difference. Justice for Women has managed to achieve some real change and I think radical feminism has gone back to its roots, which is about activism.

Lynne: There doesn't seem to be the same mass movement against male violence and compulsory heterosexuality as there was in the late 1970s and early 1980s . . . ?

Louise: The situation has changed; there isn't such a powerful feminist movement as there was (if there ever was). I think there was a massive backlash and I think that was inevitable, but a lot of women were taken by surprise by it.

Joy: I think as far as the 'backlash' is concerned, it took a long time for patriarchy to realise what the implications of radical feminism were. That it is about challenging powerful men. A strong message started to come through that rape is about male power and that heterosexual sex is about male power and the two messages came together in an analysis of male sexual violence.

Louise: Yes, and that's because once we began to raise the issues of sexual harassment and child sexual abuse, it began to hit men's own self interests at a particular level and I think that's why there has been such a big backlash against date rape.

Sarah: There isn't a mass movement. But if you look at the response to the Zero Tolerance campaign in Edinburgh, they had 160 women come to their first meeting and had hundreds of women phoning up saying they wanted to do something, and CAP has 1500 members. I also think that radical feminist organisations have learnt from being infiltrated by groups like Wages for Housework and Militant. We have learnt about structures and all this nonsense that you have to listen to everybody and give equal weight to what they are saying. London Justice for Women initially set up a hierarchical structure so that it would not be infiltrated and so it could be opened wider. If people don't agree with our agenda, then they can just get lost, because we haven't got the time to waste on them.

Louise: CAP went through a whole period of instability, but now women who are active in London CAP have a very strong line about where CAP is going, and though we might have some minor disagreements about what we should be doing, we have learnt to protect our organisation and there isn't space to start trouble anymore.

Sarah: I think it's still difficult to find radical-feminist activism. CAP is an activist organisation, but there are a lot of feminist organisations that have gone into band-aid feminism such as Rape Crisis and Women's Aid, where they are nursing a particular individual back to life. They didn't start off like that, but they have lost sight of the fact that you've got to change the whole patriarchal structure.

Lynne: What about coalitions?

Louise: I think its important to have links with other women's groups, not necessarily coalitions. I think coalitions can be important strategically when groups working around the same issues converge. This happened with the Justice for Women Campaign and Southall Black Sisters (SBS) who were both working around the same issue of women who killed violent men. But coalitions can take up an enormous amount of energy and are not necessarily effective.

Joy: CAP works jointly with other groups such as Rape Crisis and Women's Aid on particular issues, but you couldn't be in coalition with a group with totally different politics such as Feminists Against Censorship (FAC).

Simone: I think it's really important that radical feminism begins to readdress socialism. We need to take on a very strong anti-capitalist line.

Louise: I think there are women who are involved in radical feminism that haven't thought about socialism, it's important and it's up to us to raise those issues.

Simone: I'm not saying that we should get side-tracked off into socialist feminism. But many radical feminists have failed to tackle issues of class politics and we need to stress the connections with economic oppression – they're also an enormous part of patriarchal society. In terms of coalitions of women, it would really increase our potential to link with other struggles.

Lynne: There have also been massive attacks on single mothers and lesbian mothers; particularly in terms of recent legislation such as the Child Support Act, which is forcing women back into financial dependence on men and is affecting women who want to get away from violent men.

Louise: I think radical feminists need to work in other campaigns – the ground on the family has really been lost and we do need to work more broadly on this and bring in the radical-feminist agenda.

Lynne: There's also the danger of co-option. For example, we don't seem to talk about compulsory heterosexuality explicitly in our campaigns anymore.

Louise: I don't think that's only co-option, it's partly strategic – in campaigns like CAP the reason we are doing it is because of compulsory heterosexuality, but if we were to mention it every time we are interviewed by the media, we would be shooting ourselves in the foot. Our campaigns do open up the whole issue of sexuality, particularly male sexuality and coercive sexuality, and we can talk about it to other women in that context.

Sarah: I think it's a useful concept and it underpins the whole of my politics, but it's increasingly difficult to use now. I still do talk about it on occasion, for example in the Zero Tolerance campaign, when I was giving a talk on date rape.

Lynne: Are you optimistic about the future?

Sarah: I am optimistic – there's much that hasn't been done, but I think that radical feminism has achieved a lot in putting male violence against women on the public agenda; that is the foundation and the first step. Who would have thought at the beginning of second-wave feminism that local councils would have Zero Tolerance campaigns, that the metropolitan police would have domestic violence units? I think it's quite startling that you've got women like me training police officers, probation officers and magistrates on the politics of sexual violence and giving them the radical-feminist line about male power and control.

Louise: We are facing huge global forces against feminism. We have to measure how we are doing in a period of retrenchment where there is a massive movement to the Right and where the radical resistance to these global forces is tiny. But I think it only takes a little to shake them, because they are so unused to opposition. Given where we are starting from I think we can be optimistic.

References

Faderman, L, *Surpassing the Love of Men: Romantic Friendship and Love from the Renaissance to the Present*, The Women's Press, London, 1980.

Jeffreys, S, *Anti-climax: a Feminist Perspective on the Sexual Revolution*, The Women's Press, London, 1990.

Raymond, J, *A Passion for Friends: Towards a Philosophy of Female Affection*, The Women's Press, London, 1990.

Rich, A, *Compulsory Heterosexuality and Lesbian Existence*, Onlywomen Press, London, 1981.

Spender, D, *Women of Ideas (and what men have done to them)*, Ark Paperbacks, London, 1982.

NEITHER AN ISM NOR A CHASM:

Maintaining a Radical-Feminist Agenda in Broad-Based Coalitions

JULIE BINDEL

This article attempts to examine critically both identity politics and coalition work and will seek to suggest productive ways of organising across political and social differences that do not involve a threat to the radical–feminist agenda.

It has reasonably been argued that coalition politics is the solution to a very diversionary politics (Bunch 1988) and that a coming together of different groups to meet the same aim is somehow the opposite of and more desirable than identity politics. I would certainly agree with this but would add a note of caution. I put forward a case for working within a radical–feminist perspective in alliance with others on issues of violence against women where I assert the necessity of not allowing that perspective to be altered or diluted. To illustrate my argument I draw on the successful alliance between Justice for Women (JFW) and Southall Black Sisters (SBS) during the campaigns around battered women who kill.

In critiquing both identity politics and coalition strategies I will be concentrating in part on historical events in order to make sense of what went wrong and seek ways of finding a more united future among feminist activists.

WHAT'S WRONG WITH IDENTITY POLITICS?

By identity politics I *do not* mean fighting institutionalised oppression, such as racism and classism, but using one's identity to silence and instil fear in others, rather than fighting for change.

Identity politics takes as its starting point only the personal and experiential modes of being, and has therefore led to an inward way of looking at the world which is both retrogressive and deeply disturbing. An example of this was an article that appeared in *Spare Rib* entitled 'Ten Points for White Women to Feel Guilty About'. (quoted in *Feminist Review* 1989)

As Zimmerman has pointed out, it has also served to fragment the women's liberation movement (WLM).

> The distinction between autonomy and separatism is a delicate one ... As personal politics creates more and more specialised groups, the tendency towards fragmentation grows. (Zimmerman 1985 p 226)

There are certainly ways in which revolutionary and radical feminists have contributed to the misuse of identity politics, an example being in the way in which sado-masochism and other forms of sexual libertarianism have been opposed by radical feminists. Many radical feminist writings on sado-masochism have focused entirely on how it is offensive to black and Jewish women without even mentioning that such practices are also deeply misogynist. (see also McNeill this volume)

THE BEGINNING OF THE END – THE GENEVA LESBIAN CONFERENCE 1985

At this conference the opening plenary burst forth into accusatory comments on the 'racist, classist' manner in which the conference had been organised. By midday the poster advertising the conference had been defaced, with the words 'this [conference] is a lie and a sham, black women, disabled women and Jewish women have been oppressed and excluded from this event.' These words had been graffitied across a drawing of a black woman flying through the air.

The tragedy of this story is that these were the earlier days, not even the bitter end of the fight for oppression supremacy in the WLM of the 1980s. The slogan 'the personal is political' had become threatening. It seemed that the slogan 'organise around your own oppression' was directing energy inwards, leaving the oppressors unchallenged. This was the conference where the phrase 'speaking as a . . .' became part of the inaugural feminist discourse. The last day was charged with emotive scenarios, and included some women demanding a 'pre-plenary session for those who take oppression seriously'. This involved a group of mainly white women sitting around in a group introducing themselves, which is as far as the workshop got. 'I am a white, working–class, able–bodied, English lesbian mother', began the first participant. By the time the last woman spoke many more categories had been added, such as 'university educated', 'ill' and 'survivor of alcoholic parents'.

So why did identity politics get so much support?

TOWN BLOODY HALL

Identity politics was the perfect starting point for the development of femocracy as it enabled the equal opportunities agenda to develop and move away from a radical feminist agenda. Town Hall feminism, which developed in the early 1980s, depoliticised feminist activism and merely sought to give everyone 'what they deserved' because of their identity. It could far easier incorporate identity politics than a radical feminist agenda, because it fitted in with a municipal socialism. The site of femocracy was labour–controlled local authorities. In other words, it was a socialist–feminist politics which underpinned the takeover of identity politics within the WLM. The basis of socialist–feminist politics is that one is forced to take on every agenda, whereas radical feminism has named the oppression of women by men as the agenda. This has meant that femocrats have been able to guilt-trip radical feminists about our 'lack of concern over issues of race and class' yet at the same time blame identity politics on us.

STOP THE DEBATE, I WANT TO GET OFF: THE LONDON WLM NEWSLETTER

It has often been said that newsletters are essential in any radical movement as they act as an important source of communication, thereby serving to include those who are not involved in grass-roots work around an issue. This is particularly true for the WLM as it is not a movement comprised of signed-up members, but has a very broad base. This is what made the demise of the London WLM newsletter such a tragedy. The newsletter was a forum for some debate and discussion but it was mainly used to pass on information and publicise events and news.

In 1984, when identity politics had already emerged as an important force in the WLM, things started to go horribly wrong. There was some criticism that the newsletter was elitist and inaccessible, and new women who joined its collective met in a climate ripe for exploitation, and things began to change. One of the women who joined during that period describes her own experience of what happened.

> We had no sense of tact or diplomacy and immediately denounced the existing newsletter as an example of a racist women's movement. We evoked massive defensiveness in everyone because of the way we criticised them. We were on uncharted grounds and went overboard on our new editorial policy and in return some readers went overboard in their response. We had created a stalemate. We were not responsive to any questioning but were like rats in corners. All we could do if an outsider approached was to take a chunk out of them.
>
> Anyone who challenged our policy was dismissed and banned from contributing to the newsletter. Although the intention had been to make the newsletter more accessible, it effectively excluded anyone who was not already a seasoned politico from joining it. It was at this stage that it was decided that the collective would be closed to those women who did not have 'an oppression' – being a woman was not enough.
>
> Although we would occasionally receive letters that *should* have influenced us to rethink our position, the climate of righteousness meant that this was not going to happen.
>
> It was like being in a cult – 'we are the only ones, we are the chosen' kind of attitude. Everybody else was seen as the devil. (interview with the author, Summer 1994)

Identity politics in this example certainly gave scope for the women involved to feel powerful. It began to resemble a vanguard position similar to Maoism.

FOR (PROPER) LESBIANS ONLY

Another form of identity politics which reasserted itself in the US for the 1980s called itself *Lesbian Separatism*. I should point out here that this form of separatism is different from radical/revolutionary feminist separatism which advocates political and sexual autonomy from men as a political strategy (sometimes known as political lesbianism), and which has highlighted how women are controlled by men through the institution of heterosexuality. (Rich 1979) The British form of radical/revolutionary feminist separatism was foregrounded by the publication of the paper *Love Your Enemy* (1979, 1981) which insisted that heterosexual feminists should examine their relationships with men from the point of view of the contradictions this created for their feminism.

On the contrary, this separatism meant complete separation from heterosexual women, and denounced any woman – lesbian or heterosexual – who did not fit in to the 'pure' lesbian category. (Jeffreys this volume) The group of women advocating this politics was very small and self-contained, but unfortunately it gave the enemies of radical feminists enough ammunition to fight a third world war with. In Britain the mouthpiece for this separatist ideology was the Lesbian Information Service Newsletter (LISN).

The basis of their arguments was that men are the enemy, (fine) but that they cannot change. This contradicts the radical feminist belief that gender is not biological but is socially constructed. They decided that lesbians were also oppressed by heterosexual women because they fraternise with the enemy. They seemed less concerned with the oppression faced by all women, and more with heterosexual women's oppression of lesbians. They created a hierarchy of the most oppressed lesbian. At the top of the hierarchical tree was the butch lesbian who had never slept with men (the never-het butch), a butch lesbian who had slept with a man once came next (the once-het butch). Any lesbian who displayed an ounce of 'femininity' or who had 'taken sperm into their bodies' became a male auxiliary. (Lesbian International December/January 1989/90).

This form of neo-biological determinism led to a philosophy of hopelessness and mistrust, with most women being classed with the enemy. The concept of working even with other lesbian-feminist separatists became an impossibility unless they fitted the extremely narrow categories defined by those advocating this politics.

My reason for using this example is to suggest that this kind of separatism became a turning point for some lesbian feminists who had perhaps uncritically adopted some aspects of identity politics. This particular form of separatism enabled some of us to see the ludicrousness of its logic. We were given the opportunity to recognise that any kind of coalition work was impossible if one subscribed to such analyses.

It is perhaps the case that identity politics served to refuel some feminists who were on the edge of burn-out. It meant a shift from a feeling of powerlessness around the issues of violence against women to one of power and righteousness. There was no clear distinction between fighting oppression and identity politics, which is how it continued for so long.

> Any kind of separatism is a dead end. It is good for forging identity and gathering strength but I do feel that the strongest politics are coalition politics that cover a broad base of theories. There is no way that one oppressed group is going to topple the system by itself. Forming principled coalitions around specific issues is very important. (Smith and Smith 1981 p 12)

JUSTICE FOR WOMEN, ALL WOMEN

The formation of a British network of Justice for Women groups began around the campaign for Sara Thornton, a woman who had killed her violent husband after years of abuse. (See McNeill this volume) The injustice in the legal treatment of women who killed their violent husbands had already been highlighted by Southall Black Sisters in their campaign to free Kiranjit Ahluwalia. Her case had been featured in Gita Saghal's film 'The Provoked Wife' shown on Channel 4. (Dispatches 1991, Faction Films)

The first demonstration in Sara Thornton's name was held outside the Royal Courts of Justice in July 1991. It had been organised by an *adhoc* group of four radical and revolutionary feminists, myself included, all with a history of working within various campaigns to end violence against women.

MEN LOSE THEIR TEMPERS: WOMEN LOSE THEIR MARBLES

Malcolm Thornton was an alcoholic and during Sara's two-year relationship with him he had constantly abused her and her ten-year-old daughter. Sara suffered repeated battering and threats; she asked for help from her GP, her local church, social services, Alcoholics Anonymous and the marriage guidance council. All failed her. She called the police to her house at least five times due to his violence and he was in fact due to appear in court on a charge of assault ten days after he died.

On 14 June 1989 Malcolm Thornton was drunk and on Sara's return home he called her a 'whore' and told her to get out and take her daughter with her. Otherwise she would be 'dead meat'.[1] He threatened to kill her while she slept and taunted her with a knife. The threats of violence made Sara fear for her own and her daughter's life. She went to look for Thornton's old police truncheon but, not finding it, she took a knife. Sara pleaded with Thornton to go to bed but when the threats continued she stabbed him once and called an ambulance.

Sara pleaded guilty at the trial on the grounds of diminished responsibility, a plea which focused on her state of mind rather than the abuse she had suffered. Her defence lawyer chose to ignore completely the history of violence and provocation and Sara was not given the opportunity to contribute to her own defence. She was found guilty of murder and sentenced to life.

Her appeal in July 1991 centred around the issue of provocation. It was refused on the grounds that the sixty seconds it took to get a

---

[1] Sara Thornton's evidence at her trial in February 1990 (Birmingham Crown Court) taken from the transcript.

knife did not constitute a 'sudden and temporary loss of control'.[2] The killing was therefore classed as premeditated and provocation could not be accepted as a defence. The judge stated that Sara could have 'walked out or gone upstairs.'

Over one hundred women attended the demonstration calling for the release of Sara Thornton and all women in her situation. Slogans included 'Domestic Violence is Provocation,' 'Self Defence is No Offence' and, of course, 'Free Sara Thornton'. The organisers had made a huge effort to interest the press in this case and had spent two weeks on the telephone informing as many as possible of the event. It paid off, with an impressive array of demonstrators and press assembled outside the courts on the Strand. It was during this first demonstration that a Channel 4 news reporter became interested and was to become JFW's greatest media ally, and friend of Sara Thornton. Jennifer Nadel was driving past the Strand when she noticed the scene outside the court and stopped to find out more. She was responsible for persuading her producer to run the first national news feature about the case and went on to write the book *Sara Thornton: the story of a woman who killed*. (Nadel 1993)

SAINTS AND SINNERS

Two days after Sara's appeal was rejected, a man walked free from Birmingham Crown Court after being given a suspended sentence, having successfully used the plea of provocation. Joseph Magrail had kicked his alcoholic wife to death after allegedly suffering verbal abuse from her. The trial judge commented that he had 'every sympathy' for Magrail and that in his opinion 'the lady would have tried the patience of a saint'. (*The Guardian* July 1991) There we had it; men are saints for staying, women are sinners whatever they do. Those of us in JFW have yet to hear a judge ask a man who has killed his partner due to 'nagging' or alleged infidelity, why he didn't leave. This was not the first time a man had been given sympathy from a judge in these circumstances. (McNeill, Radford 1992) A major part of the argument JFW had focused on in highlighting the injustice of Sara Thornton's

[2] The judgment referred to the case R V Duffy (1949) 1All ER 932 CA.

case was the inequality of sentencing/judical response around spousal homicide. Suddenly, here was a perfect example of our argument and one that both the campaign and Sara Thornton were able to use in a way that illustrated what radical feminists had been saying for a long time. This contrast was a great hook for the media, especially when Sara Thornton subsequently went on hunger strike to protest the injustice.

Overnight the national media became fascinated with this openly radical-feminist campaign. At this point of media frenzy, Southall Black Sisters (SBS) contacted us to discuss joint tactics. Indeed the very first meeting at the London's Women's Centre of what was to become a coalition was filmed for News at Ten, with the commentary 'Women's groups met tonight to discuss tactics in the campaign to free Sara Thornton'.

Immediately on forming, JFW began to link up with various feminist and civil liberties groups and individuals. Our work led us into the arena of lawyers, academics and politicians, as well as feminist organisations we had not yet worked with. But it has not always been easy to involve ourselves in coalitions if the other group(s) do not have a strong sense of their own identity.

NOVEMBER WOMEN'S ACTION

Before London JFW became fully established we became heavily involved in a group which was organising a march around the International Day to End Violence Against Women. This group was made up (mostly) of radical feminists, many of whom had been involved in other feminist campaigns to end violence against women. It described itself as a coalition group working on a common issue. However, there were rarely significant political disagreements, although many of the women had not worked together before. It was decided that the event to mark the day would be a march focusing on the issue of women who kill violent men and the campaigns to free Kiranjit Ahluwalia, Sara Thornton and Amelia Rossiter.

Although the outcome of this coalition was incredibly successful, (probably because the majority of women had a similar political perspective) there were problems of ownership and ego which were present from the beginning. What we had to determine was whether it was worth the aggravation and internal wrangling to be in it. The answer was undoubtedly yes. Feminists came together from various groups to plan an extremely successful event. The women who attended the march included, in significant numbers, those who had never been on anything feminist before, let alone women-only.

Working within this coalition taught us lessons for the future.

WORKING WITH SOUTHALL BLACK SISTERS: PRECARIOUS BEGINNINGS

Southall Black Sisters (SBS) who had initiated the campaign to free Kiranjit Ahluwalia (which was subsequently successful) had attended the appeal for Sara Thornton, but did not participate in the demonstration. The group was initially suspicious of JFW and had expressed concern to one member that the agenda would be shifted from that which they had built up in order to argue Kiranjit's case.

SBS as a group define more as socialist than radical feminist. Formed in 1979, 'the group's initial emphasis was on looking at the way racism shaped Black women's lives', and in 1982 it helped to set up Southall Black Women's Centre. (Farnham 1992) They do a vast amount of campaigning work as well as giving support and advice to the thousands of women and children who have passed through their doors. SBS 'do not believe in sectarianism' (Pragna Patel, one of the founding members of SBS, in conversation with the author 1993), and have always been prepared to work alongside white feminist groups. In their civil liberties and anti-deportation work, they also work with men, both within the Southall Community and outside it. Coalition work is certainly familiar to members of SBS, and there are few women's groups in London which have not directly benefited from the experience of working with them.

Their analysis of male violence is, we would argue, a radical-feminist one. They do not blame the state, poverty or racism for it, but men. This is how it has been not only possible, but highly productive, for JFW to work in coalition with them. But the alliance was not initially without its problems. SBS were naturally concerned that the formation of JFW would mean the marginalisation of SBS by the press, and soon after Sara Thornton's appeal they contacted me to express this concern.

They often see us as just a bunch of Asian women working in Southall.' (Hannana Siddique, in conversation with the author 1991)

Thus JFW has always been aware during our work with SBS that we could end up in some way responsible for their marginalisation by the press if we did not pay constant attention to what was happening. SBS had not only initiated the campaign to free Kiranjit Ahluwalia, but had a long history of working around related issues.

Coalition is often about compromise. The two groups built up a working relationship based not only on a single issue but within that single issue, a single analysis. The sticking point/area where the two groups differed most, was around how much emphasis we put on men who killed women. The only 'loss' for JFW, if any, is that we probably would have concentrated more on men who kill than we did. Although this is a criticism of the coalition in one way, it is also the case that we need to compromise on certain matters in any alliance or coalition, however 'at one' we are politically. JFW has always been prepared to compromise if it is in the interests of our aims and objectives but we have always been careful not to relinquish control of the agenda. It is usually impossible to maintain this control, when working with men, or with those in direct conflict with radical-feminist politics, which is why working with SBS was and continues to be such a positive experience. The very fact that the two organisations were agreed on the root cause of violence against women was enough for the coalition to work.

JAMMING IT ALL TOGETHER: THE WOMEN'S INSTITUTE MEETS RADICAL FEMINISM

Perhaps one of the main ways of JFW has been different from our many radical-feminist predecessors is that we have always deliberately courted the press. As a result of the considerable media interest, we have attracted a very wide range of support from MPs of all political parties, Women's Institutes and Townswomen's guilds. Both the latter organisations have passed resolutions at their annual conferences calling for a reform in the law of provocation. A piece in the *Guardian* entitled, 'Blessed are the Jam Makers' dealt with the phenomenon of 'respectable ladies' working with radical feminists. The relationship between the two had previously been seen as less than sisterly by the press and many others and it is fair to say that it has not been an easy alliance in the past. Nor is it now, although the media like to present a much more simplistic picture. One of JFW's most hilarious moments came outside parliament as we were demonstrating in support of MP Harry Cohen's bill to redefine the law on provocation. As some JFW members were standing under our banner alongside the WI and the TWG (them complete with stiff hairdo's and coats in primary colours) another member was running up to Barbara Cartland (seen leaving parliament and making her way to her car) waving a 'Free Emma Humphries' leaflet at her, which she took. It was fortunate that the colour of the leaflet (bright purple) did not clash with her dress (fluorescent pink)!

Over the last two years we have worked closely with SBS and a number of other women's groups building on the media interest and focusing on a number of other cases of women who have killed violent men and on the campaign to reform the law on provocation. So why has JFW been so successful in working with such diverse groups?

We came up with a number of possible explanations:

- the subject matter is currently fashionable, in that it is about domestic violence (rather than pornography)
- it focuses on real women, not faceless abstract theories
- it is a dramatic subject and the media love it
- it is a civil liberties issue as well as a feminist one, therefore winning the support of some men
- it provides a stark, easy way of highlighting the contrast between the treatment of men who kill their partners and of women who kill their partners
- it is about women fighting back as well as women as 'victims'.

What have we done right? We have:

- worked with the media
- done lots of talks outside the usual internal WLM forum
- avoided an openly democratic campaign, by making the core group closed. (This has meant the group has not been open to infiltration by other groups, which has been a real problem for feminist campaigns in the past)
- not had paid workers; women do things according to their experience, skills and knowledge
- put racism high on the agenda
- lent support to loads of other campaigns
- marketed ourselves well, with leaflets and benefits
- not confused campaigning with providing a service (we believe it is impossible to do both successfully).

Another secret of our success is that in London Justice for Women, we have been prepared to bend the definition of 'collective' working (so popular with radical feminists) in order to achieve our aims and run a smooth and effective campaign. Many of us have been involved in large collectives where a quick decision is as rare as a nice man. London JFW is held together by a small, core group of women who trust each other to make decisions and do the work without having to check every fine detail with everybody involved. The following example illustrates the importance of this.

During the 'date rape' storyline in the popular television soap *Brookside*, a reporter rang the JFW line to ask for a comment on the issues raised. The conversation went like this:

'Hello, I'm from the *Daily Mirror*. I'm writing a piece on date-rape for tomorrow's edition and would like a comment from your organisation.'

'You should be asking Rape Crisis. We don't work around the issue of rape.'

'Oh, I did. She told me she couldn't give me a quote until they'd discussed it at their collective meeting next Wednesday.'

I gave the comment, but later heard on the grapevine that comments had been made about London JFW to the effect that 'they thought they knew everything and were taking over the women's movement'. The important issue for us is that *the feminist voice* was included in that piece, not about ownership of the comment.

CONCLUSION

One mistake that many radical feminists have made is to assume that there is only one way to be a feminist activist. Today, in the light of so much opposition and so little time, we have had to use our imaginations. We tend to operate in JFW along the lines of 'what is it that needs to be done and how can we do it effectively?' This can mean on occasion individuals taking decisions without consultation. We have also worked with groups who have not shared all our aims and objectives, but we have done this without relinquishing control or losing sight of our agenda, and it has worked.

Our aim for the future is to be part of a women's liberation movement which has its doors open to all women and breeds a new generation of activists.[3]

References

Bunch, C, 'Making Common Cause: Diversity and Coalitions', in C McEwan and S O'Sullivan (eds), *Out the Other Side, Contemporary Lesbian Writing*, Crossing Press, California, 1988.

Farnham, M, 'Still working Against the Grain. Interview with Southall Black Sisters', in *Trouble and Strife* No 23 Spring 1992.

Feminist Review, *The Past Before Us: Twenty Years of Feminism*, No 31 Spring 1989.

Leeds Revolutionary Feminist Group, *Love Your Enemy?*, Onlywomen Press, London, 1981.

Lesbian International, *Dykes Loving Dykes* (extract) No 25, December/January 1989/90.

Nadel, J, *Sara Thornton. The Story of a Woman Who Killed*, Gollancz, London, 1993.

Rich, A, *Compulsory Heterosexuality and Lesbian Existence*, Onlywomen Press, London, 1981.

Smith, B, and B Smith, 'Across the Kitchen Table: A Sister to Sister Dialogue' in C Moraga and G Anzaldúa (eds), *This Bridge Called My Back: Writings by Radical Women of Colour*, Kitchen Table Press, New York, 1981.

Zimmerman, B, 'The Politics of Transliteration: Lesbian Personal Narratives', in E B Freedman *et al* (eds), *The Lesbian Issue: Essays From Signs*, University of Chicago Press, Chicago, 1985.

[3] I would like to thank Sandra McNeill, Sara Maguire, Harriet Wistrich and Sara Thornton whose help made this chapter possible.

CONTRIBUTORS' NOTES

Editors

Lynne Harne researched, edited and contributed to *The Lesbian Mothers' Legal Handbook* (The Women's Press 1986). She has written articles for a number of feminist journals such as *Trouble and Strife*, *Spare Rib*, and the *Rights of Women Bulletin*. She has also contributed to *Radical Records*: B Cant and S Hemmings (eds) (1988) *68, 78, 88: From Women's Liberation to Feminism*, Amanda Sebestyen (ed) *Women's Studies: A Reader*, Stevi Jackson (ed) 1993 and *Children Living with Domestic Violence*, A Mullender and R Morley (eds) 1994.

Elaine Miller was a contributor to *Not A Passing Phase: Reclaiming Lesbians in History 1840–1985* (The Women's Press 1989). Her chapter in that book; 'Through All Changes and Through All Chances: the Relationship of Ellen Nussey and Charlotte Brontë' has been translated into both Dutch and German. She has contributed articles to journals such as *Trouble and Strife*, *The Women's History Review* and *Feminism and Psychology*. She was formerly on the collective of the London Lesbian Archive and was an active member of the Lesbian History Group from 1986 until its dissolution in 1995. She is a founder member of RADS, a London-based radical lesbian-feminist group, set up in 1995. She currently teaches English Literature and Women's Studies in further and adult education, and is a revolutionary feminist.

Contributors

Rosemary Auchmuty teaches Law and Women's Studies, including a Lesbian Studies module, at the University of Westminster. She is author of *A World Of Girls: The Appeal of the Girl's School Story* (The Women's Press 1992) and contributed two chapters to *Not A Passing Phase: Reclaiming Lesbians in History 1840–1985* (The Women's Press 1989). She has also written textbooks, articles and short stories. She is a founder member of the Lesbian History Group.

Julie Bindel has been active in the women's liberation movement since 1979, when she met members of the Leeds Revolutionary Feminist Group and never looked back! Since then, she has mainly concentrated on issues of violence against women and in 1991 co-founded the London Justice for Women Campaign in which she has been active ever since. She still believes that heterosexuality is bad for women and would like to see that debate re-opened. She does not consider Sigourney Weaver attractive in her grey vest and Godfather I is not her favourite film.

Nicola Humberstone is 47 years old. She is a part-time Women's Studies tutor and also works at Tower Hamlets Age Concern. She has an MA degree (Gender in Society).

Elaine Hutton has been a lesbian-feminist activist since the 1970s and has been involved in many campaigns and groups including Rape Crisis, Women Against Violence Against Women, Lesbians in Education and the Lesbian History Group. In her spare time, she relaxes with her feline familiars.

Sheila Jeffreys is a revolutionary-feminist historian and activist who has been involved in the women's liberation movement since 1974. She wrote the ground-breaking *The Spinster and Her Enemies: Feminism and Sexuality 1880–1939* (Pandora Press 1985); *Anticlimax: A Feminist Perspective on the Sexual Revolution* (The Women's Press 1990); and *The Lesbian Heresy: A Feminist Perspective on The Lesbian Sexual Revolution* (The Women's Press 1994). She is now a senior lecturer in the Department of Political Science at the University of Melbourne, Australia.

Celia Kitzinger is a lecturer in the Department of Social Sciences at Loughborough University. Her previous books include *The Social Construction of Lesbianism* (Sage Publications 1987); *Changing Our Minds: Lesbian Feminism and Psychology* (with Rachel Perkins: Onlywomen Press 1993); *Heterosexuality: A Feminism and Psychology Reader.* (Sage 1993); *Women and Health: Feminist Perspectives* (Taylor & Francis 1994); and *Feminism and Discourse: Psychological Perspectives* (Sage 1995). The last three publications were all co-edited with Sue Wilkinson.

Sandra McNeill is a lesbian and a revolutionary feminist. She has been part of the women's liberation movement since 1975. She has been involved mainly with issues around violence against women and women's training. In 1981 she set up East Leeds Women's Workshops – adult training workshops which prioritise: women with no qualifications; black women; single parents; women with childcare responsibilities; Irish women; and lesbians. Disabled women who can attend the courses receive absolute priority. She was one of the organisers of the Sexual Violence Against Women conference and was involved in Women Against Violence Against Women campaigns including, Free the Maw Sisters, and many others, particularly against pornography. With dusty rhodes she co-edited *Women Against Violence Against Women* (Onlywomen Press 1985). She has organised Nightlink, a women's safe-transport scheme. She is currently a member of Justice for Women and Women against Fundamentalism.

Julia Parnaby is a radical lesbian feminist who lives and works in London. She is an active radical feminist campaigner and has been a political activist for ten years.

Rachel Perkins is a consultant clinical psychologist at Springfield Hospital, London. She has a particular interest in women and lesbians with serious on-going mental health problems. She has written *Changing Our Minds: Lesbian Feminism and Psychology* (with Celia Kitzinger; Onlywomen Press 1993).

Jill Radford is co-editor (with Diana Russell) of *Femicide: The Politics of Woman Killing* (Sage Publications 1993), and has written numerous articles on male violence for various feminist journals. She has also contributed to *Women, Violence and Social Control* Hanmer *et al.* (ed) (Macmillan 1987), and *Women Policing and Male Violence* (Routledge, 1989). She is a lesbian-feminist activist, and has worked for Rights of Women. She is currently a lecturer at the University of Teeside.

Janice Raymond is Professor of Medical Ethics and Women's Studies at the University of Massachusetts in Amherst. As the Associate Director of the Institute on Women and Technology, she co-directs an organisation that evaluates technology and public policy that affect women. Dr Raymond is author of many books and articles on the subjects of feminism, medical ethics, new reproductive technologies and violence against women. Her most recent books are *RU 486: Misconceptions, Myths and Morals*, with Renate Klein and Lynette Dumble, and the recently published *Women as Wombs: Reproductive Technologies and the Battle Over Women's Bodies* (Harper Collins, USA and Spinifex, Melbourne). A long-time feminist activist, she has worked internationally against medical violence against women and is also international co-ordinator of the Coalition Against Trafficking in Women, a UN non-government organisation. She lectures internationally on violence against women, reproductive issues, feminist theory and bio-ethics, most recently in Caracas, Venezuela.

Carole Reeves has been active in the women's movement for the last fifteen years. She was employed at the London Lesbian and Gay Centre, and was instrumental in the setting up of the group Lesbians Against Sado-masochism. Currently she is owner-manager of Britain's first women-only hotel which opened in January 1988. She was an active member of the Campaign Against Pornography until early in 1995.

Sue Wilkinson is based in the Social Services Department at Loughborough University. She is the founding and current editor of *Feminism and Psychology: an International Journal* and also edits a book series entitled *Gender and Psychology: Feminist and Critical Perspectives* (both Sage Publications). Her most recent books include: *Heterosexuality: A Feminism and Psychology Reader* (Sage Publications 1993); *Women and Health: Feminist Perspectives* (Taylor & Francis 1994); and

Feminism and Discourse: Psychological Perspectives (Sage 1995) all co-edited with Celia Kitzinger.

Rachel Wingfield has been involved in the women's movement for ten years, working specifically around violence against women. She was co-ordinator of the Campaign Against Pornography until the beginning of 1995, and has published articles in *Trouble and Strife*. She is now an active member of ACCSA (Action Against Child Sexual Abuse).

FURTHER READING

Auchmuty, Rosemary, Jeffreys, Sheila and Miller, Elaine, *Lesbian History and Gay Studies: Keeping a Feminist Perspective*, Women's History Review 1/1, 1992, pp 89–108.

Barry, K. *The Prostitution of Sexuality*, New York University Press, New York, 1995.

Brodribb, Somer, *Nothing Mat(t)ers: A Feminist Critique of Post-Modernism*, Spinifex, Melbourne, 1992.

Bunch, Charlotte, 'Making Common Cause: Diversity and Coalitions', in C McEwan and S O'Sullivan (eds) *Out the Other Side: Contemporary Lesbian Writing*, Crossing Press, California, 1988.

Cant, B, and Hemmings, S, *Radical Records: Thirty Years of Lesbian and Gay History*, Routledge, London, 1988.

Cruikshank, Margaret (ed), *Lesbian Studies: Present and Future*, The Feminist Press, New York, 1982.

Daly, Mary, *Gyn/Ecology: The Metaethics of Radical Feminism*, The Women's Press, London, 1979.

—— *Pure Lust: Elemental Feminist Philosophy*, The Women's Press, London, 1984.

—— *Webster's First New Intergalactic Wickedary of the English Language*, Conjured in Cahoots with Jane Caputi, The Women's Press, London, 1988.

—— *Outercourse: The Be-Dazzling Voyage*, The Women's Press, London, 1993.

Douglas, Carol Anne, *Love and Politics: Radical Feminist and Lesbian Theories*, Ism Press, San Francisco, 1990.

Dworkin, Andrea, *Pornography, Men Possessing Women*, The Women's Press, 1981.

—— *Right-Wing Women*, The Women's Press, 1983.

—— *Intercourse*, Arrow Books, London 1988.

Evans, Mary, 'In Praise of Theory: the Case for Women's Studies', *Feminist Review*, 10, Spring 1982, p 61–74.

Everywoman, *Pornography and Sexual Violence: Evidence of the Links*, Everywoman Ltd, London, 1988.

Faderman, Lillian, *Surpassing the Love of Men: Romantic Friendship and Love Between Women from the Renaissance to the Present*, The Women's Press, London, 1985.

—— *Odd Girls and Twilight Lovers: A History of Lesbian Life in Twentieth-Century America*, Penguin Books, Harmondsworth, 1985.

Faludi, Susan, *Backlash: The Undeclared War Against Women*, Vintage, London, 1992.

Farnham, Margot, 'Still Working Against the Grain', Interview with Southall Black Sisters, in *Trouble and Strife*, No. 23, Spring 1992.

Feminist Anthology Collective, *No Turning Back: Writings from the Women's Liberation Movement*, The Women's Press, London, 1980.

Friedman, S. and Sarah, E, (eds) *On the Problems of Men: Two Feminist Conferences*, The Women's Press, London, 1982.

Frye, Marilyn, *The Politics of Reality: Essays in Feminist Theory*, Crossing Press, California, 1983.

Greenberg, Mary Lou, 'Clinics under the Gun: Blockades, Firebombs and Murder', *On the Issue*, Fall 1993, Canada.

Harne, Lynne, 'Contemporary Lesbian-Feminist History: the Politics of Lesbian Community', an unpublished paper given at the Women's Studies Network Conference, Nottingham, 1994.

Hobby, Elaine, and White, Chris, *What Lesbians Do in Books*, The Women's Press, London, 1991.

Jackson, Cath, 'School for Scandal: Tutors and Students talk to Cath Jackson about U221 – the first Open University Women's Studies course' in *Trouble and Strife* 24 1992, p 49.

Jackson, Margaret, *The Real Facts of Life: Feminism and the Politics of Sexuality 1850–1940*, Taylor and Francis, London, 1994.

Jay, Carla, and Glasgow, Joanne (eds), *Lesbian Texts and Contexts: Radical Revisions*, Onlywomen Press, London, 1992.

Jeffreys, Sheila *The Spinster and Her Enemies: Feminism and Sexuality 1880–1930*, Pandora Press, London, 1985.

—— *Anticlimax: A Feminist Perspective on the Sexual Revolution*, The Women's Press, London, 1990.

—— *The Lesbian Heresy: A Feminist Perspective on the Lesbian Sexual Revolution*, Spinifex, Melbourne, and The Women's Press, London, 1993.

—— 'The Queer Disappearance of Lesbians' in *Women's Studies International Forum* 17. (5) 1994, pp 459–72.

Kelly, Liz and Radford, Jill, 'Minimising Dominance, Maximising Difference: the inversion and denial of feminist challenges to the sexualisation of women and children', paper at the British Sociology Conference, Preston, as yet unpublished, 1994.

Kelly, Liz, McCollum, Hilary and Radford, Jill, 'Wars Against Women' in *Trouble and Strife 29*, 1994, pp 12–18.

Kelly, Liz, Radford, Jill and Scanlon, Joan, 'Feminism/Feminisms: Fighting Back for Women's Liberation', as yet unpublished, presentation at Open University, Women's Studies Summer School, 1992.

Kitzinger, Celia and Wilkinson, Sue, 'Sexual Identities/Sexual Communities' in *Gender and Society* 8 (3) 1994, pp 444–63.

Kitzinger, Celia, and Perkins, Rachel, *Changing our Minds: Lesbian Feminism and Psychology*, Onlywomen Press, London, 1993.

Lesbian History Group, *Not A Passing Phase: Reclaiming Lesbians in History 1840–1985*, The Women's Press, London, 1989.

Lorde, Audre, *Sister Outsider*, Crossing Press, California, 1984.

—— 'Age, Race, Class and Sex: Women Redefining Difference', in *Sister Outsider: Essays and Speeches*, Crossing Press, California, 1984.

MacKinnon, Catharine 'Turning Rape into Pornography: Postmodern Genocide in *Ms* magazine, Vol 4, No 1, July/August, 1993.

Millett, Kate, *Sexual Politics*, Hart-Davis, London, 1979.

Miriam, Kathy, in Reti, Irene (ed), *Unleashing Feminism: Critiquing*

Lesbian Sadomasochism in the Gay Nineties, Herbooks, Santa Cruz, 1993.

Nadel, J. *Sara Thornton: The Story of a Woman Who Killed*, Gollancz, London, 1993.

post, dianne and free-woman, olivia, *off our backs* Aug/Sept 1994, p 20.

Oram, Alison, 'Embittered, Sexless or Homosexual: Attacks on Spinster Teachers 1918–1939' in Lesbian History Group (eds) *Not a Passing Phase: Reclaiming Lesbians in History 1840–1985*, The Women's Press, London, 1989.

Radford, Jill, 'History of Women's Liberation Movements in Britain: A Reflective Personal History' in Griffin *et al* (eds) *Stirring It: Challenges for Feminism*, Taylor and Francis, London, 1994.

Raitt, Suzanne, *Volcanoes and Pearl Divers: Essays in Lesbian Feminist Studies*, Onlywomen Press, London, 1995.

Raymond, Janice, *A Passion for Friends: Towards a Philosophy of Female Affection*, The Women's Press, London, 1986.

Raymond, Janice, 'The Politics of Transgender' in *Feminism and Psychology*, 4(4): pp 628–33.

Rich, Adrienne, 'Compulsory Heterosexuality and Lesbian Existence' in *Signs*, Vol 5, No 4, Onlywomen Press, London, 1980.

Rich, Adrienne, *What Is found There*, W W Norton & Co, New York and London, 1993.

Sa'adawi, Nawal el, 'Thinking and Acting: The Challenge of Global Feminism', keynote speech, Women's Studies Network UK Annual Conference 1994, University of Portsmouth and also keynote speech at National Women's Studies Conference (USA) at Ames, Iowa, as reported by Karla Mantilla in *off our backs*, Aug/Sept 1994, pp 8–9.

Sanders, Sue, 'Why are Lesbians Invisible in Women's Studies?' unpublished paper at the 1984 Women's Studies Conference in Bradford.

—— 'Was She a Dyke?: Proposing Lesbian Studies, in *Radical and Revolutionary Feminist Newspaper*, 1985.

Taylor, Mary, *Miss Miles: A Tale of Yorkshire Life Sixty Years Ago*, Remington & Co, London, 1890, and OUP, New York and Oxford, 1990.

Spender, Dale, *Women of Ideas and What Men Have Done To Them: From Aphra Behn to Adrienne Rich*, Ark paperbacks, RKP, London, 1983.

Taking Liberties Collective, *Learning the Hard Way: Women's Oppression in Men's Education*, MacMillan, London, 1989.

Trouble and Strife: The Radical Feminist Magazine, PO Box 8 Diss, Norfolk IP22 3XG.

Wilkinson, Sue and Kitzinger, Celia, 'The Queer Backlash' in Bell, D. and Klein, R (eds) *Radically Speaking: Feminism Reclaimed* Spinifex, Melbourne, 1995.

—— *Heterosexuality: A Feminism and Psychology Reader*, Sage, London, 1993.

Zimmerman, Bonnie 'The Politics of Transliteration: Lesbian Personal Narratives' in E B Freedman *et al* (eds), *The Lesbian Issue: Essays From Signs*, University of Chicago Press, Chicago, 1985.

INDEX

Note: Page numbers followed by *n* indicate references to footnotes.